Andrew Tait Jarboe is Assistant Professor of History at Berklee College of Music, Boston. He is also a history teacher at Roxbury Preparatory High School, Boston. He holds a PhD in History from Northeastern University and is co-editor (with Richard Fogarty) of *Empires in World War I: Shifting Frontiers and Imperial Dynamics in a Global Conflict* (I.B.Tauris, 2014).

'*War News In India: The Punjabi Press During World War I* raises the veil from over one of the most heavily recruited, ravaged yet hitherto silent of the colonial home fronts: the province of Punjab, which contributed more than half of the combatants from undivided India during World War I. Andrew Tait Jarboe's marvellous selection of the translated extracts of newspapers, framed by his thoughtful prefaces, reveals the intensity and diversity with which the war was discussed, debated and manipulated in the Punjabi press: from reports of various international events to Hindu, Muslim and Sikh aspirations and anxieties around recruitment and imperial "duty", to deliberations on self-government, or a deep questioning of European civilisation. In the midst of the war's centennial commemoration, Jarboe has gifted us with a singularly rich and important archive which will be crucial to the writing of a more nuanced global history of the conflict as well as to anyone interested in the tangled lives of war, empire and the media.'

– **Santanu Das, Reader in English Literature,**
King's College, London

WAR NEWS IN INDIA

The Punjabi Press During World War I

Edited by
ANDREW TAIT JARBOE

BLOOMSBURY ACADEMIC
LONDON • NEW YORK • OXFORD • NEW DELHI • SYDNEY

BLOOMSBURY ACADEMIC
Bloomsbury Publishing Plc
50 Bedford Square, London, WC1B 3DP, UK
1385 Broadway, New York, NY 10018, USA

BLOOMSBURY, BLOOMSBURY ACADEMIC and the Diana logo
are trademarks of Bloomsbury Publishing Plc

First published 2016 by I.B. Tauris & Co. Ltd.
Paperback edition first published by Bloomsbury Academic 2020

A catalogue record for this book is available from the British Library.

A catalog record for this book is available from the Library of Congress.

ISBN: HB: 978-1-7845-3191-1
PB: 978-1-3501-5331-8
ePDF: 978-0-8577-2702-2
ePub: 978-0-8577-2906-4

Typeset by OKS Prepress Services, Chennai, India

To find out more about our authors and books visit
www.bloomsbury.com and sign up for our newsletters.

CONTENTS

ACKNOWLEDGEMENTS

I would like to thank my editor Joanna Godfrey at I.B.Tauris for her initial enthusiasm and continued belief in and support of this project. Thanks to the anonymous readers of I.B.Tauris, all of whom helped make this a better book. Additionally, I would like to extend my sincerest appreciation to the friends without whom this book would not have been possible. Rakhshan Zahid and her husband, Mark Lukmani, generously opened their home to me during my research stay in London, providing food, drink and camaraderie. Jason Zelek quite literally saved this project, rescuing the manuscript from a corrupted flash drive. Last, but certainly not least, I would like to thank my wife, Melanie, for her own special, and crucial, brand of belief in and patience with my academic pursuits. She bravely held down the fort, not to mention our especially precocious toddler, Maren, while I flitted off to London. Melanie has been my greatest champion from the very start of graduate school, in 2008, learning along the way more about India in World War I than I am sure she ever cared to know. I dedicate this book to her.

LIST OF TABLES

TIMELINE OF MAIN EVENTS OF THE WAR AS THEY RELATED TO INDIA AND PUNJAB

1914

28 June	Assassination of Archduke Franz Ferdinand at Sarajevo.
5 July	War Council at Potsdam.
23 July	Austria-Hungary sends ultimatum to Serbia.
24 July	Sir E. Grey suggests international conference.
25 July	Serbia orders mobilisation.
26 July	Admiralty countermands orders for dispersal of British Fleet.
27 July	France and Italy accept British proposals for international conference.
29 July	Belgrade bombarded by Austrians (first shots of war). Admiralty send 'Warning Telegram' to the fleet. The War Office order 'Precautionary Period' to be put into force. Germany makes proposals to secure British neutrality.
30 July	British Government reject German proposals for neutrality.
1 August	Germany declares war on Russia.

2 August	German ultimatum to Belgium.
3 August	Germany declares war on France.
4 August	Great Britain declares war on Germany. German army invades Belgium.
12 August	Great Britain and France declare war on Austria-Hungary.
16 August	Disembarkation of BEF in France completed.
23 August	Battle of Mons. Retreat from Mons begins. Battle of Tannenberg begins.
6 September	Battle of the Marne begins.
25 September	Race to the sea begins.
19 October	Battle of Ypres begins.
1 November	Great Britain and Turkey commence hostilities.
5 November	Basra operations begin.
14 November	Sultan in Constantinople declares Jihad (*Jehad*).

1915

26 January	Defence of the Suez Canal begins.
19 February	Naval attack on the Dardanelles begins.
10–13 March	Battle of Neuve Chapelle.
9 April	General Sir John Nixon assumes command of British forces in Mesopotamia.
14 April	Basra operations end.
22 April	Battle of Ypres. Gas attack.
25 April	Allied Expeditionary Force land at Gallipoli.
1 May	Spring offensive in Galicia begins. Battle of Gorlice-Tarnow begins.
23 May	Italy declares war on Austria.
31 May	Advance up Tigris begins.
27 June	Advance up Euphrates begins.
28 September	Battle of Kut.
3 October	Allied troops land at Salonika.
9 October	Belgrade taken by Austrians. Montenegro invaded by Austrians.

11 November	Advance on Baghdad begins.
19 December	General Sir Douglas Haig appointed C-in-C. British Armies in France.

1916

4 January	Attempts to relieve Kut begin.
21 February	Battle of Verdun begins.
29 April	Capitulation of Kut.
5 June	Sherif of Mecca begins revolt against Turkish rule.
13 June	Capture of Mecca.
1 July	Operations on the Somme begin.
27 August	Romania declares war on Austria-Hungary.
29 October	Sherif of Mecca proclaimed 'King of the Arabs'.
18 November	Operations on the Somme end.
13 December	Operations for capture of Kut begin.
16 December	Battle of Verdun ends.

1917

25 February	Operations for capture of Kut end. Pursuit to Baghdad begins.
2 March	Operations against Mahsuds begin.
11 March	Occupation of Baghdad.
12 March	Outbreak of revolution in Russia.
24 March	First Palestine offensive begins.
26 March	First Battle of Gaza.
6 April	United States declares war on Germany.
31 July	Battle of Ypres begins.
20 August	Secretary of State for India Edwin Montagu establishes 'Responsible Government' as the goal for India.
10 December	Armistice between Central Powers and Romania.
11 December	Occupation of Jerusalem.
17 December	Armistice concluded between Central Powers and Russia.
30 December	Defence of Jerusalem ends.

1918

3 March	Peace signed between Russia and Central Powers at Brest-Litovsk.
15 March	German offensive in Picardy begins.
8 April	German offensive in Flanders begins.
17 May	Peace signed between Romania and Central Powers.
27 May	German offensive in Champagne begins.
18 July	Allied offensive of 1918 begins.
18 August	Advance in Flanders begins.
26 August	Breaking of the Hindenburg Line begins.
29 September	Armistice between Bulgaria and the Entente Powers.
23 October	Advance on Mosul begins.
27 October	Austrian Government asks Italy for an Armistice.
30 October	Armistice between Turkey and Entente Powers signed at Mudros.
31 October	Hostilities between Entente and Turkey cease at 12 noon.
3 November	Armistice between Entente and Austria-Hungary signed.
5 November	Hostilities between Entente and Austria-Hungary cease.
11 November	Armistice concluded between Entente Powers and Germany. Hostilities cease at 11 a.m.

INDIA'S MILITARY CONTRIBUTION DURING THE WAR (JANUARY 1920)

Table 1   Strength of the army in India at the outbreak of the war

BRITISH	
British officers	4,744
British other ranks	72,209
INDIAN	
Serving	159,134
Reservists	34,767
Non-combatants	45,660
TOTALS	
British	76,953
Indian	239,561

Table 2   Total recruited in India (Indian ranks) during the
war, up to 31 December 1919

INDIAN RANKS	
Combatants	877,068
Non-combatants	563,369
TOTAL	1,440,437

Table 3   Number sent on service overseas from India, up to
31 December 1919

THEATRE	COMBATANTS			
	British officers	Other ranks	Indian officers	Other ranks
France	2,395	18,353	1,923	87,412
East Africa	928	4,681	848	33,835
Mesopotamia	18,669	166,822	9,514	317,142
Egypt	3,188	17,067	2,204	107,742
Gallipoli	42	18	90	3,041
Salonika	86	85	132	6,545
Aden	952	7,267	480	19,936
Persian Gulf	991	1,059	967	29,408

MAPS

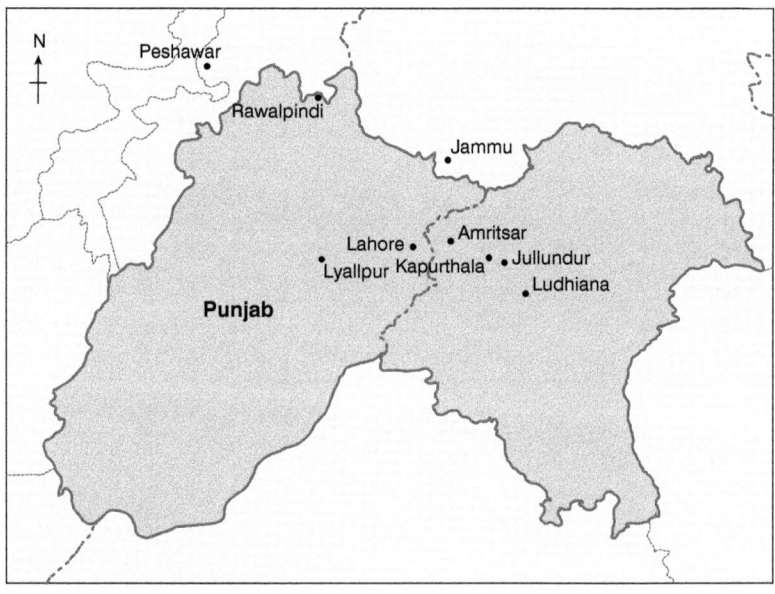

Map 1   The Punjab in World War I

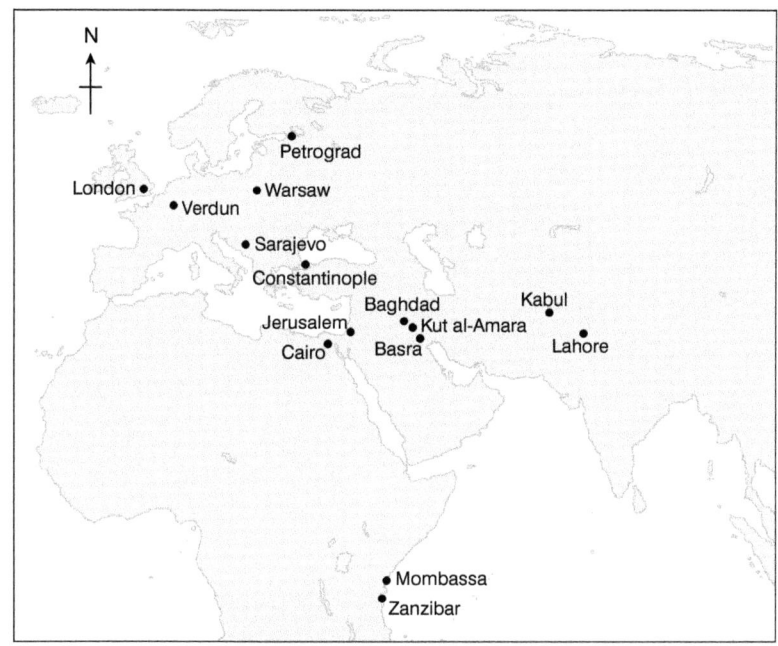

Map 2   Europe, Asia and Africa during World War I

INTRODUCTION

In the final days of July 1914, Austrian artillery opened fire on the Serbian city of Belgrade, across the Danube river. These shots signalled the start of what some statesmen still hoped might only be another Balkan war – the third in as many years. But halfway around the world, in Lahore, India, newspapermen like Zafar Ali at *Zamindar* saw the writing on the wall. The coming war, his newspaper reported to its Urdu-language readership, would not be confined to Austria and Serbia, 'but will be a universal war in which all the great empires of Europe will be involved.'

> The result of it all will be that the giant which has so far been ruining Asia will now be engaged in ruining himself; the materials of war which have so far been used to destroy Orientals will now be employed in the destruction of Europeans. In time to come the world will find that the same causes were at work as in the day when the Babylonian Empire received its death-blow and the glory of Nineveh shone no more.[1]

One hundred years after the outbreak of World War I, scholars now consider seriously the conflict's global dimensions and impacts.[2] At the time it was fought, writes Heather Jones, 'the Great War was seen as a "world" war – it was only in the post-1945 period that it came to be depicted as primarily a European conflict in comparison to the Second World War.'[3] To a significant degree, comprehending the 'globality' of World War I necessarily involves writing the colonial presence into histories of the conflict. Important works on the experiences of African and Asian combatants and non-combatants challenge dominant Eurocentric narratives; it will no longer do, for instance, to treat the protracted campaigns in Africa and Asia offhandedly as 'sideshows.'[4] Another line of work situates the experiences of colonial subjects alongside those of Europeans, enabling us to draw comparisons and tease out long-overlooked connections that were (or were not) readily apparent to the war's contemporaries.[5] Important works of this sort – by way of example, take those of Richard Fogarty, Santanu Das and Heike Liebau – allow us to better capture the pre-1918 world 'in all its integrated and multifarious complexity.'[6] Santanu Das writes, 'The global reverberations of what at the time Germany alone, among the European nations, called the "*world* war" (Weltkrieg) become apparent as we substitute people, processes and effects of the war for places and events.'[7] Battles and place names no doubt serve as one marker of the war's globality. The myriad cross-cultural and interracial encounters engendered by the wartime mobilisation of millions of human beings from almost every corner of the globe, the discursive representations of those encounters and the implications of these on peoples near and far – these encompass a second and no less important aspect of the war's global reach.[8]

This volume presents the translated extracts of newspaper articles published during World War I, intended for Indian audiences in the Punjab.[9] These newspaper articles were originally translated during the war by British officials and Indian clerks employed by the Criminal Investigation Department in Lahore. The extracts survive today in British intelligence reports on the Indian vernacular press, filed during the war years. Constituting an invaluable and heretofore largely unexamined source record, these documents offer a lens into the anxieties and aspirations of Punjabis, a population that committed treasure, foodstuffs and more than 360,000 combatants to the British war effort between 1914 and 1918 – more than any other province in British India.[10]

India and the war

Among the belligerent powers of World War I, none drew more extensively on overseas colonial resources than Great Britain, and no overseas territory contributed more to Britain's imperial war effort than India. Between 1914 and 1918, Indians supplied money, materiel and manpower: £100 million flowed outright from Indian coffers in 1914, and another £20 to £30 million each year through the end of the war. At the start of the conflict, the Indian Army constituted the only overseas professional force available to Great Britain. One of India's largest employers, the army numbered 39 regiments of cavalry and 139 battalions of infantry in August 1914, comprising in total some 160,000 Indian ranks. Up to 31 December 1919, the Indian Army recruited another 877,068 combatants and 563,369 non-combatants.[11] This constituted the single greatest contribution made by any of Britain's colonies or dominions. Between August 1914 and December 1919, India deployed 622,224 soldiers and 474,789 non-combatants overseas, to fronts in France and Belgium, Gallipoli, Egypt and Palestine, East Africa and Mesopotamia.[12] In the late autumn of 1914, soldiers employed by the Indian Army (Indian and British) made up one-third of the British Expeditionary Force then engaged on the Western Front.[13] Between October 1914 and December 1915, Indian infantry fought in the trenches of Belgium and France at Ypres, Festubert, Givenchy, Neuve Chapelle, Second Ypres and Loos. In Mesopotamia, Indian troops deployed to Basra on 6 November 1914. In January 1915, Indians held the Suez Canal against attacking Turkish forces. In 1916, Indian cavalry fought on the Somme. Infantry tried, and failed, to rescue their surrounded comrades of the 6th Division at Kut. In March 1917, Indian troops participated in the capture of Baghdad. In December, Indian soldiers marched into Jerusalem.

In Great Britain, the topic of 'India in the war' practically became an industry unto itself during the war years. Newspapers regaled audiences with the exploits of Indian troops – especially of those serving embedded within the British Expeditionary Force on the continent. Newspapers captured the imagination of their home readership with headlines like 'Indian Troops in Action,' 'Dash of the Indian Troops,' or 'Valour of the Indian Troops.'[14] Penny pamphlets declared that India was 'Heart and Soul' with Great Britain, that the war had 'swept away all hesitation, all doubt' and any misgivings about British rule.[15] 'In battle, the Indian troops were once again covered in glory with the kukri of the Gurkhas playing, as always, its terrible role,' French audiences read in the newspapers.[16] This sort of sensational reporting and propaganda – for that is what it was – was not the result of any coordinated effort of the part of the embattled governments of the Allies (not at this early point in the war, anyway). Rather, the press barons and their staff took the lead in framing the discussion about the war and its meaning.[17] The British government was happy to let them, believing plainly that the government required this kind of propaganda to sustain civilian morale.[18]

There is at long last a real push to rescue Indian perspectives and incorporate these into the larger narrative of the war. There exists now a small but productive cohort of scholars uncovering a range of Indian perspectives from the war. Important existing works and forthcoming works by David Omissi; Santanu Das; Franziska Roy, Heike Liebau and Ravi Ahuja; Gajendra Singh; and Rozina Visram come to mind.[19] A collection of sound recordings of Indian soldiers, taken between 1915 and 1916 at a German prisoner of war camp, has recently been found at Humboldt University in Berlin and is presently being digitised. At the recent conference, 'Perspectives on the "Great" War,' hosted by Queen Mary University of London to mark the centennial of the war, there was an entire strand devoted to the subject of Indian perspectives.

Still, historian Tan Tai Yong reminds us that measuring the impact of the war on Indian society is no easy task, 'given the variable impact of the demands of war on different parts of the subcontinent.' 'There could be no better place to carry out such an examination than the Punjab, without a doubt the province in India most affected by the war.'[20] Between August 1914 and the November 1918 Armistice, about 60 per cent of all combat troops raised in India were Punjabis.[21] In fact, the Indian Army recruited in the Punjab to the very near exclusion of some other provinces. By 1918, Punjabi Sikhs, who made up less than 1 per cent of the population of British India, accounted for 90,000 combatants, or one-eighth of all Indian soldiers deployed overseas during the war.[22] Bengal, with a male population of roughly 23 million, had only a single combat battalion at the front at the end of the war.[23] This policy was the product of design, not accident or oversight. Annexed by the East India Company in 1849, the Punjab (like much of India) came under Crown rule in 1858. The preceding year had witnessed a massive popular rebellion, sparked by a mutiny among Bengal infantry and cavalry stationed in Meerut. The 'Sepoy Mutiny' (as many in Britain preferred to call it at the time) very nearly drove the British from South Asia altogether. But in June 1858, the last of the rebel strongholds in Gwalior fell to the British. Grateful to the nearly 30,000 Punjabis who helped put down the rebellion, the British began immediately to replace 'disgraced' Bengal units with soldiers mustered in the Punjab. By June 1858, of the 80,000 native troops in the Bengal army, 75,000 were Punjabis, with Sikhs alone numbering 23,000.[24]

Recruitment in India remained largely haphazard for some time after that, but Russian expansion into Central Asia in the 1880s combined with the explosion of social Darwinist racial theories at the end of the nineteenth century left policy makers scrambling to find South Asia's best fighting material, the so-called 'martial races' of India.[25] Army policy narrowed the pool of potential recruits to select groups – Sikhs, Muslims, Dogras and Hindu Jats of the Punjab, Pathans from the North West Frontier, Gurkhas from Nepal.[26] This was an army, by British thinking, 'based on a systematic grouping of men by race and sept and clan, with a view to the full development of race thinking.'[27] 'It is one of the essential differences between the East and the West,' wrote one popular commentator, 'with certain exceptions, only certain clans and classes can bear arms; the others have not the physical courage necessary for the warrior.'[28] By 1914, nearly 75 per cent of the Indian army hailed from the Punjab, the North West Frontier and Nepal.[29]

The demands of war brought about profound changes in the administration of the Punjab. Starting in 1915, the state began directing all of its energies towards supporting the war effort. By 1917, 'the whole administrative structure of the province was converted into a formidable and monolithic recruiting machine, utilised mainly for the purpose of supplying military manpower for the Indian Army.'[30] In 1918, Punjabis who prior to the war otherwise had little or no contact with the Punjabi state or the Indian Army might then have dealt with both as facets of daily life. The army earmarked 75 new classes as eligible for recruitment during the war, and Sir Michael O'Dwyer, the Punjab's wartime Lieutenant Governor, toured the countryside alternatively exhorting, shaming, or threatening young men into uniform.[31] Still, much of India never experienced anything like the kind of levy *en masse* underway across much of Europe during the war. In his postwar memoirs, Lieutenant Governor O'Dwyer highlighted this very fact in order to discredit what he called those 'down-country politicians' who spoke 'eloquently of India's war achievements.' 'As a matter of fact,' he wrote, 'even including the Punjab, the only great Province which made a really serious war effort, the death-casualties for all India, with 320 millions of people, were less than those of Canada with her 8 millions, of Australia with only 5 millions, and only double those of New Zealand with little over a million of people.'[32]

Table 4   Total combatant recruits raised in India and Nepal, 1914–18[33]

	Punjab	India (including Punjab)	India (excluding Punjab)	Nepal
1914	14,000	28,000	14,000	3,000
1915	46,000	93,000	47,000	14,000
1916	50,000	104,000	54,000	5,000
1917	95,000	186,000	91,000	12,000
1918	134,000	317,000	183,000	10,000

The Punjabi press and the war

Urban centres in the Punjab boasted a variety of English, Urdu and Gurmukhi language newspapers at the outbreak of the war. Lahore was the epicentre of this industry, where readers could choose from more than 70 titles in August 1914. That same month, Amritsar housed no fewer than 28 newspapers, Rawalpindi had at least seven, and Jullundur offered three. Most newspapers had a modest circulation of fewer than 1,000 copies. Some, like the English-language *Tribune*, printed in Lahore, had a more robust daily run of 2,000 copies. Competing for an English-language Indian readership was the *Panjabee*, which circulated 2,400 copies daily. These dailies shared the streets with Bal Kishen's Urdu-language *Akhbar-i-' Am*, which printed 1,000 copies each day. The largest Lahore daily in August 1914 was the Urdu-language *Zamindar*, edited by Zafar Ali, which circulated 15,000 copies. The only other Urdu newspaper that could match the circulation of *Zamindar* at the outbreak of the war was *Hindustan*, offered to Lahore readers on a weekly basis. Meanwhile, in Lahore, the Criminal Investigation Department had been filing weekly reports on the content and tenor of hundreds of Punjabi newspapers since 1896. It continued to do so into the interwar years. In these weekly reports, the Inspector-General and his staff did not reprint the entire contents of each newspaper they reviewed. Rather, they translated, and then reproduced those articles of interest to them, allocating each to one of seven broad topical categories to which the Criminal Investigation Department believed they most aptly pertained: (i) Politics, both foreign and domestic; (ii) Afghanistan and the Trans-Frontier; (iii) Native States; (iv) Kine-Killing; (v) Native Societies and Religious Matters; (vi) Legislation; and (vii) General Administration.

Through 1916, much of the task of compiling newspaper reports fell to H.E.C. Beaver, Personal Assistant to the Deputy Inspector-General and Officer-in-Charge of the Press Branch of the Punjab Criminal Investigation Department. His 30 September 1916 report offered 45 newspaper excerpts. War news had taken something of a back seat at that time. Only two excerpts dealt chiefly with the war.

A few others dealt with issues germane to the war, like the recently formed Bengali Double Company, or frontier raids on the Afghan border. Most of the entries for his 30 September report had little or nothing to do with the war: obstruction of the Ganges near Hardwar, Sikh and Hindu relations, political arrests, free and compulsory education in India, landowners and predatory money-lenders. Some weeks, however, the Punjabi press focused on the war to the very near exclusion of everything else. At other times, they offered nothing on the war, but a great deal on reform proposals, the Punjab Muslim League, the National Congress, the Press Act, high prices, the arrest of Mrs Annie Besant (co-founder in 1916 of the All India Home Rule League) for protesting the Defence of India Act, or the plight of Indian emigrants in South Africa or Canada.

The appetite Punjabi newspapers showed for reporting war news ebbed and flowed between late 1914 and the close of 1918. The war received considerable attention in the heady opening months of the conflict. Newspapers pledged their unflinching support for the British Empire. They urged young men to enlist, expressed outrage when they learned that the Indian Army would not admit educated Indians to its ranks, and voiced their shock and disgust at the behaviour of German troops in occupied Belgium. In November 1914, Muslim newspapers lamented Turkey's decision to enter the war, but maintained that Indian Muslims did not owe any allegiance to the Sultan in Constantinople. It was manifest, newspapers proclaimed again and again, that the Turks had fallen victim to the machinations of the Kaiser. The year 1915 witnessed the Dardanelles campaign, Germany's decision to unleash submarines and flame-throwers, fighting in the Caucasus and Mesopotamia, stalemate in France and atrocities in Armenia. Also in 1915, Italy joined the war for the Allies, and Bulgaria joined the Central Powers. In 1916, the Punjabi press followed the uprisings in Ireland and the Hedjaz with rapt attention. Newspapers followed closely the developments at Verdun. The Punjabi press showed comparably little interest in battlefronts in 1917 and overwhelmingly turned its focus to the discussion surrounding Home Rule for India. But the toppling of the Tsar's government sparked some comment, as did America's decision to join the Allies. The German offensives on the Western Front in March 1918 very nearly stirred a panic in the Punjab when David Lloyd George reportedly said in a speech delivered to Parliament that if the Germans won the war in France they would turn their focus next to Asia. Again the Punjabi press called loudly for volunteers, urging men to volunteer to defend 'their country.'[34]

Unlike many European or American newspapers that had staff at the front wiring reports as events unfolded, the Punjabi press generally did not have dedicated staff providing firsthand accounts or exclusive-access reports. Newspaper staff nonetheless wanted to bring reliable war news home to their readers. Punjabi newspapers, therefore, got their news where they could. They relied heavily on Reuters and on official reports issued by the British and Indian governments. They cross-referenced these with what they culled from European, American and other Indian newspapers. It is worth bearing in mind that these were professional newspapermen and they wanted their newspapers to be taken credibly. They complained when the war news they received from official channels offered contradictory reports on rapidly unfolding events. 'It is impossible to see any consistency in the war news which is officially published throughout the country,' lamented *Jhang Sial* (Lahore) in October 1914. 'Sometimes we hear of British successes, sometimes of their reverses. The ordinary man is thrown into a state of confusion. He is at a loss to know what to believe.'[35] Other times the Punjabi press protested that the Government of India failed to provide them any information at all on what was happening on the war's various fronts. In late 1914, a group of editors formed the Punjabi War News Association, which attempted to act as a news agency like Reuters to which Punjabi newspapers could turn for reliable and vetted war news. Still, getting the story right was never easy. Similar to European newspapers, the Association had a tendency to overstate the significance of Allied victories, or the exhaustion of the enemy. Sometimes Punjabi newspapers just got the story wrong. A November 1916 edition of the *Tribune* (Lahore) lamented, 'Mr. Woodrow Wilson's defeat at the Presidential election is a blow to the cause of progress.'[36] On occasion, the press offered totally outlandish analysis. On 11 November 1916, *Panjabee* (Lahore) reported happily that Germany was considering legalising polygamy. 'This does not show that the Germans are inclined towards Islam, but it assuredly proves that the social teachings of Islam are applicable to the needs of all countries and all times.'[37]

War news and empire

It is important here to note that the wartime Punjabi press was not an entirely free press. Like newspapers in wartime Britain, newspapers in the Punjab existed (formally) only so long as the Government of India allowed them to exist. This is not to say that they had to tow the party line, reporting things only as the Government of India prescribed. Newspapers were free to criticise British or Government of India policy or the handling of the war to a degree. They made policy recommendations and voiced their disappointment when imperial authorities did not listen. But newspaper editors had to know that if they took things too far, the Punjabi state might shut them down – a power granted to the Punjabi state by the Defence of India Act, passed in March 1915. In 1916, *Panjabee* (Lahore) called attention to 'a hardening of the official attitude' of the state, 'which is the more surprising because the press all over the country has nobly responded to the call of duty and has eschewed much of the criticism in which it indulges in ordinary times.'[38] Other newspapers bristled when they felt unjustly browbeat by the seemingly arbitrary hand of wartime censorship regulations. *Zamindar* was in and out of print through 1915, its editor periodically confined to house arrest per order of Lieutenant Governor O'Dwyer.[39] In 1916, its editorial staff received word that their newspaper would no longer be permitted to publish war news. They protested in their 8 March edition:

> It may be remembered that sometime ago [*Zamindar*] was forbidden to publish translations, extracts and comments of all kinds relating to the war, except the telegrams sent by Reuters Agency and the Secretary of State. The *Zamindar* scrupulously followed the instructions until January last. In February,

however, the paper was permitted to publish translations and extracts from the English newspapers also, subject to the approval of 'the censorial department,' the order being received on the 3rd February. But ten days had scarcely elapsed when the whole thing underwent a change, and on the 13th February it received a communication directing Akhtar Ali Khan to see Mr Kettlewell at the Civil Secretariat. New instructions were given, in compliance with which the *Zamindar* stopped the publication of all war news, except Reuters and the Secretary of State's telegrams. And yet on the 26th February, Raja Ghulam Qadir Khan, printer and publisher of the *Zamindar*, received a further communication, directing him not to publish any news, articles, criticisms and memos on any subject relating, in the least, to the war. As these are strange orders, it was necessary to explain matters to the authorities and a representation was submitted on the 28th February. But no reply has been hitherto received. We have every hope that His Honour [Lieutenant Governor Michael O'Dwyer] will be pleased to withdraw at an early date the deplorable restrictions, which are likely not only to impose a restraint on the *Zamindar's* freedom but also injuriously affect its very existence.[40]

Two further points are important to note. The first of these is that these sources exist because they were collected and translated during the war by men whose job it was to anticipate and then disrupt possible threats to the security and stability of British imperial rule in South Asia. The second (interrelated) point is that Punjabi newspapers were vehicles for political agendas. The precise agenda of a given paper might be difficult to detect from just a cursory reading of one or two of its articles. By 1917, the Criminal Intelligence Department felt confident that it had examined enough of each newspaper to identify its preferred political leanings in what was a very wide field of opinion. The English-language daily *Bulletin*, then with a print-run of 2,900 copies, was classified as a 'Hindu, orthodox' newspaper. *Panjabee*, then with a circulation of 1,000 copies, was 'Hindu, advanced nationalist.' The bi-weekly *Observer* was

'Muhammadan, All-India Muslim Leaguer.' *Desh*, with 1,250 copies was 'Hindu, sectarian with Arya leanings.' *Kisan*, with a daily run of 2,000 copies was 'Muhammadan, advanced.' The *Punjab*, with 2,000 copies, was 'Muhammadan, All-India Muslim Leaguer.' The weekly Gurmukhi newspaper *Khalsa Samachar*, with 2,857 daily copies was 'Sikh, moderate.'[41] All of the newspapers were pro-British, in that they pledged again and again their support for the Empire in its war against Germany. None of the newspapers offered here supported the more radical, revolutionary pro-independence elements that also existed in the Punjab at the time.[42]

The diversity of political agendas pursued by the Punjabi press reveals that loyalty to the Empire did not preclude demands for considerably seismic shifts in how the Empire's members related to one another. Self-government and Home Rule had long been topics of consternation to British statesmen. The Punjabi press was far from one mind on the matter, however. As the war progressed, the topic of Home Rule appeared with ever-greater frequency in Punjabi newspapers, evidenced by the frequency with which it appeared as a topic in the weekly reports of the Criminal Intelligence Department. 'The news of Mr. Montagu's visit to India has given great pleasure to Indians and filled their minds with hope,' observed *Vakil* (Amritsar), in August 1917 upon the arrival of the new Secretary of State for India in South Asia.[43] The Hindu newspaper wanted Home Rule. Muslim newspapers balked at this demand. *Ar-Rai* (Lahore), a Muslim newspaper, asked in its 22 September 1917 edition, 'Home Rule or Hindu Rule?' and stated that it did not approve 'of any policy in India which threatens the existence of the weaker communities. The innumerable followers of Islam who by God's will live in the protection of England are not to be deceived by those who preach passive resistance and agitation against Government, who wish to obliterate the Urdu language; who create disturbances on the Id; who fly Home Rule flags instead of the Empire's flag.'[44] The *Vakil* (Amritsar), another Muslim newspaper, issued the following on 7 November 1917. 'Even before the advent of Mr. Montagu in India the Muhammadans have received the first installment of Home Rule. Our Hindu countrymen have again brought back the days of

Changhiz Khan, with the result that no Muhammadan can sleep in security.'[45] Hindu newspapers cried foul, offering headlines decrying 'Sikh treachery to the common cause,' or 'the Muhammadan revolt against Home Rule.' 'Certain narrow-minded workers of the Anjuman-i-Islamia have held an anti-Home Rule meeting at Gaya,' reported the Hindu-newspaper *Desh* (Lahore), on 4 November 1917. 'It is indeed painful that [a certain number] of our Indian brethren have fallen victims to a misunderstanding and have begun to oppose a movement which affects not one community but all communities.'[46]

That something had to give by the end of the war, few could doubt. Two days after, at last the guns went silent on the Western Front, the *Tribune* (Lahore) anticipated a hopeful future for India within the folds of the British Empire.

> The reward for all the pains and sufferings endured by the world through this relentless and protracted war must be commensurate to the price paid for it, and it is to be found in the establishment of the war aims of the Allied powers. These aims [. . .] are not based either on aggrandizement and greed – not on conquest and annexation of territories, but on the security of liberty and justice for all and the prevention of future wars.[47]

Between 1914 and 1918, World War I engulfed millions of people from every corner of the globe. British Pals and German *Frontschwein*, French *poilus*, ANZACS, Maoris, Sikhs and Muslims from South Asia, Moroccans, Algerians, Tunisians, West Africans, First Nation Canadians, Americans, Japanese, Irish, Scottish, Italians, Turks, Russians, Mongolians and Jamaicans butchered each other wholesale. By the time the dust finally settled, more than 10 million lives had been lost. The war unleashed new instruments of mass death and destruction. It ushered in an age in which states perpetrated genocide against their own people and alien subjects. At war's end, the empires of the Romanovs, Habsburgs and Hohenzollerns lay in ruin. That of the Ottoman sultans followed shortly thereafter. Emboldened nationalist movements prepared to take on the empires of the British and the French. Indians discovered in the course of the formal peace proceedings held in Paris in 1919 that the lofty ideas for which the Allies had ostensibly fought did not apply to them. The coming years and decades witnessed mounting discontent with British rule. In 1919, the Government of India handed down a series of laws called the Rowlatt Bills, which extended the Defence of India Act of 1915 into peacetime, permitting the detention (without trial) of those suspected of political crimes. These sparked Gandhi's first nationwide campaign of *satyagraha*, a coordinated series of non-violent protests, strikes and fasts that did not abate until 1922. At the Jallianwala Bagh in Amritsar, on 13 April, Brigadier-General Reginald Dyer, commander of the Jullunder Brigade, ordered a detachment of sepoys under his command (90 total, 50 of whom were armed) to fire into a crowd of 20,000 people, murdering 379 and wounding over 1,000. Delhi and the Punjab exploded in widespread civil unrest.

At the time of the November 1918 Armistice, these events all lay unforeseen in the future. How and to what extent World War I galvanised demands for change in India is an important subject, one to which this volume hopes to make a contribution. Each newspaper extract has something to offer. Each is better appreciated when read alongside the other sources presented within this volume's pages. Students may find especially useful the introductory comments at the start of each chapter, which help to frame for the modern reader some of the issues to which the Punjabi press could offhandedly reference to its wartime readership. It is to the sources then that we now turn.

CHAPTER 1

1914

On 28 June 1914, in Sarajevo, a young Serbian nationalist murdered the heir to the throne of the Austro-Hungarian Empire. Six months later, war raged across much of the earth's land and water surfaces. In the Balkans, the Austrians began their war against Serbia on 28 August. Germany had declared war on Russia on 1 August, and France on 3 August. On 4 August, Germany invaded neutral Belgium and Great Britain declared war on Germany. Events unfolded quickly at first. The British Expeditionary Force landed on the continent on 16 August just as German forces were smashing their way through tiny Belgium *en route* to Paris. Combined British and French forces finally checked the German army's advance on the Western Front in early September at the Battle of the Marne, an epic, weeklong struggle involving more than 2 million men. German high command ordered a general retreat to higher ground behind the Aisne river. Thereafter commenced the 'Race to the Sea,' as both sides tried to outflank the other in the vain hope of salvaging a conclusive victory. By late November, soldiers of the British, French, and German armies, after sustaining hundreds of thousands of casualties (combined) on the battlefields of Western Europe, had dug a seemingly impenetrable 475-mile-long network of trenches, barbed wire, and machine-gun nests that snaked its way from the English Channel to the border of neutral Switzerland. These men faced the bleak prospects of stalemate. In East Prussia, German forces under the command of Paul von Hindenburg and Erich Ludendorff won a stunning victory over badly outmatched Russian forces at Tannenberg in August. By December, the Russians were backpedalling through Poland. Another Russian army squared off against the Austrians in sub-zero temperatures in the Carpathians. The year 1914 witnessed operations in Togoland, Cameroon, South-West Africa and German East Africa. Imperial armies massed in Egypt and the Persian Gulf.

At the start of the war, the Indian Army constituted Britain's only overseas professional force, employing some 239,561 soldiers, British and Indian. As guns first erupted in the Balkans in late July 1914, the Government of India outlined that if called upon, the Indian Army could spare two divisions of infantry and one brigade of cavalry for overseas operations. In the war's opening months, Indian soldiers deployed to fronts in France and Belgium, Egypt, East Africa and the Persian Gulf – to every major theatre in which British forces were then involved, in fact. Some 23,000 British and 78,000 Indian troops deployed overseas, a contribution far in excess of the maximum stipulated by the Government of India.[1] By the end of 1914, India had sent abroad six expeditionary forces. The demand for Indian manpower fell most heavily on the Punjab. The Home government asked for 21,000 combat recruits from India in the last four months of 1914; recruiters secured 28,000, of whom 14,000 were Punjabis.[2] At an emergency war council meeting on 6 August, the Secretary of State for War, Lord Kitchener, and the commander of the British Expeditionary Force's I Corps, Douglas Haig, persuaded members of the council to deploy the 3rd and 7th Indian Divisions to Egypt for eventual use in Europe. Indian Expeditionary Force (IEF) A arrived in France at the end of September. Rushed to the trenches in late October, Indians participated in some of the fiercest fighting that winter. At the start of November 1914, nearly one third of all men serving in the British Expeditionary Force hailed from India. Indian troops also deployed to Egypt and the Persian Gulf where they secured British installations and spearheaded British-led campaigns against the Ottomans. On 29 October, Turkey joined the war on the side of the Germans. On 6 November, the 6th Indian Division deployed to Basra in the Persian Gulf to protect the Abadan pipe-line. At the same time, Indian forces deployed to East Africa to secure Zanzibar and the Mombasa-Nairobi railway.

Selections from the Indian newspapers published in the Punjab, 1914

CONTENTS

---

[1] *Zamindar* (Lahore), 30 July 1914

War will not be confined to Austria and Serbia but will be a universal war in which all the great empires of Europe will be involved; for having partitioned Asia and Africa, they have no hunting grounds left, and will now descend into the arena and hunt each other. The result of it all will be that the giant which has so far been ruining Asia will now be engaged in ruining himself; the materials of war which have so far been used to destroy Orientals will now be employed in the destruction of Europeans. In time to come the world will find that the same causes were at work as in the day when the Babylonian Empire received its death-blow and the glory of Nineveh shone no more.

[2] *Panjabee* (Lahore), 4 August 1914

Public opinion will, we feel sure, accord the whole weight of its moral support to Servia in the present conflict. Not only does the sympathy of the civilised man go forth to the weaker party, and especially to a party which represents the principle of nationality and may be said to be fighting for its very existence as a nation, but in the present case Austria is clearly the aggressor. Making all the allowance one can for her outraged feeling owing to the assassination of the Archduke, one cannot help feeling that Austria acted in a most high-handed manner in addressing the ultimatum she did to Servia. Would she have dared to address so severe and insulting an ultimatum, if the conspiracy had been hatched in a territory under a first-class power? The thing is unthinkable. The bullying in which Austria indulged was cowardly to a degree, because Austria knew very well that Servia had not the strength to measure swords with her singlehanded; and she probably thought that Russia might, after all, be prevented from siding with Servia by the knowledge that Germany would in such event almost certainly side with Austria. However that may be, now that the war has actually begun and the long-threatened European conflagration may be expected any moment, there is nothing for the world to do except await the issue, hoping all the while that Servia may retain her independence.

As a part of the British Empire, India will hope that Great Britain may yet find it possible, without detriment to her vital interests, to avoid being drawn into the war.

[3] *Panjabee* (Lahore), 6 August 1914

In view of the gravity of the situation that has arisen and the assurances that have been forthcoming from the Colonies, His Excellency the Viceroy has done well in cabling to His Majesty's Government that 'the people of England can count on every man and every gun of the Army of India, whether British or Indian, if the need arises, and that England may remain confident in the loyalty of the people of India to cope with any emergency that may arise.' How much more fitting would it be if this assurance could be conveyed by an Indian. The assurances from the self-governing Colonies have been conveyed by Premiers and ex-Premiers. In India no Indian holds the responsible official position from which he could speak with authority on behalf of his countrymen. The loyalty of India can, indeed, be relied upon absolutely to the end; but it is a passive, not an active loyalty; it is the loyalty of men who are inalienably attached to the British connection, but who are not to have an opportunity of doing anything – except for the handful of Indians in the army – to demonstrate their love of England and the Empire in an active manner. Everywhere else – from every other part of the Empire – offers of active help will come from individuals and communities. The people of India can make no offer of the kind, because they are not permitted to do so. When will British statesmen realise that in the valour, intelligence and the patriotism of the people of India they have a vast potential source of strength which, if it could only be actualised, would be an important asset of far greater value than almost anything else that could be thought of?

[4] *Observer* (Lahore), 8 August 1914

Our readers are perhaps aware that we had promised in our last [issue] to consider in our leader of to-day the remaining objections of Lord

Curzon to the India Council Bill, but we felt that, in the light of the knowledge that war between England and Germany has commenced and the first shot has been fired, we deem it a sacred duty to the Great Empire of which we are proud to be the subjects and which has beyond doubt given to India a new, better and a higher life, to cease discussing questions of a political hue, likely to embarrass and cause anxiety to the authorities out here, and to concentrate all our energies in giving such support and assistance as is but the adequate expression of that splendid loyalty and devotion which has ever been the proud boast of His Majesty's humble Indian subject.

. . .

It is therefore with us a sacred duty to desist from any public agitation which is likely to cause anxiety and embarrassment to our noble and loved Viceroy, Lord Hardinge, and we, therefore, appeal to all our countrymen, Hindu, Muslim, Christian and Parsi, to rise to the height of the occasion and to bid good-bye for the present to all agitation, howsoever constitutional or urgent. We entertain the most fervent hope that our appeal will be duly and cheerfully responded to and that every Indian without distinction of caste or creed will come forward to lay down his life and shed his quantum of blood in defence of the honour of Great Britain.

[5] *Panjabee* (Lahore), 8 August 1914

Apart from the exhibition of moral sympathy there is one and but one way which the citizens of an Empire can support it in a crisis like the present, and that is by taking up arms to fight for her. Will the people of India be permitted to do so if need be? We remember that some years ago when a war was about to break out between England and Russia a number of educated young men in India offered their services as volunteers. The offer was not accepted. The present crisis is much graver and India itself is now far more self-conscious and far abler to give effective help to England than she was a quarter of a century ago. Will British statesmanship rise to the height of the occasion and permit India to do her duty to the Empire?

[6] *Zamindar* (Lahore), 8 August 1914

The West in the storm of calamity

It is scarcely possible for those who lead a life of peace and comfort in India to realise the agonizing calamity which has recently overtaken Europe. Yes, it is the Europe which had made other nations war against each other while she stood aloof; which had sharpened her weapons of war by cutting the throats of Muhammadans in Persia, Morocco, Tripoli and the Balkans; and whose powder was fondly believed by the Pope to breathe annihilation to Islam. Her mighty pretensions to education led Europe to claim the power of resurrecting the dead, and putting them again to the sword. War was denounced by Europe as barbarous and opposed to the spirit of civilisation: but now we see every nation of that continent rushing headlong into it. So much for her peaceful pretensions. England alone can command any respect in the present crisis. She resolutely refused to plunge into war hastily and exercised every effort to secure an amicable settlement. England's participation is due to the unprincipled conduct of Germany.

[7] *Khalsa Akhbar* (Lyallpur), 14 August 1914

Germany may be proud of her superior land forces; but the Imperial and Indian Governments are proud of their loyal Sikh subjects. Sikhs are ready to fight and shed their blood for the King-Emperor. The gravity of the present crisis forbids our thoughts turning towards the ill-treatment of Sikhs in Canada and the unpleasant speeches made by His Honour the Lieutenant-Governor about the Sikh community.

[8] *Panjabee* (Lahore), 15 August 1914

There is no reason to believe that the present war is the last in which England will have to engage; and in any case the question is one not so much of sending the Indian volunteers, as soon as they are recruited, to the front, as of enabling the Indian community to feel that they too can have their rightful share in the defence of the

Empire, of which they are an indissoluble part. The distinction that has hitherto been made in this respect between Indians and other classes of the King's subjects is galling to the self-respect of the Indian and is a great hindrance in the way of his thinking 'imperially' and having that Imperial patriotism which he has been asked by friends and foes alike to cultivate. The distinction must be removed if Indian loyalty is to be placed on the active and satisfactory footing on which it ought to be put – both in India's interest and in that of the Empire.

[9] *Loyal Gazette* (Lahore), 16 August 1914

Sikhs must now unsheathe their swords

Enemies of Government denounce Sikhs for serving in the army on a paltry pay of Rs. 10 per month and attempt to dissuade them from doing so. Sikhs should turn a deaf ear to these scoundrels and should request Government to send them to the front. Moreover, they should desist from agitation of every description; for such action cannot but damn them as traitors to their country and Government.

[10] *Amrit* (Lahore), 18 August 1914

The rise in prices of imported goods has clearly demonstrated to India the pressing need of the Swadeshi movement. India as a whole, of course, believes in the eventual success of British arms; but there is no gainsaying the fact that there are some people who are haunted by whimsical notions, against which there is no remedy. A lesson ought to be learnt from the present situation and an attempt made to revive indigenous industries.

[11] *Zamindar* (Lahore), 18 August 1914

At this critical juncture in the affairs of the Empire, Indian Muhammadans should, as Britishers, give their whole-hearted support to Great Britain. Hindu-Muhammadan dissensions, the colour question, and the demand for rights and justice should be dropped.

[12] *Panjabee* (Lahore), 20 August 1914

The *Englishman* [says] the following in a recent issue with reference to the offer of Indians to serve as Volunteers:

> Judging from the resolutions passed at some meetings in Calcutta, those offering their service as Volunteers and asking for the privilege to carry arms seem to be under the impression that one has only to take up the rifle to become an efficient soldier. They seem to forget that it requires years of patient labour to acquire the rudiments of military knowledge, just as much as it requires years of laborious study to become a lawyer. Moreover, the value of a Volunteer depends entirely upon his efficiency as a soldier and no country can even dream of employing inefficient Volunteers. While the readiness with which Indians have in the present crisis come forward with offers to take up arms in the defence of the Empire is very praiseworthy, one cannot help feeling that those who have done so have not realised what it exactly means to be a good soldier.

If the Indian community have not realised what it exactly means to be a good soldier, the *Englishman* surely knows that it is not their fault. The Indians as a people would long ago have ceased to exist if they had always been what the *Englishman* tells its readers they are to-day. But the present is not the time for discussing the matter in a controversial spirit. The Indians' offer to serve as Volunteers should, in our opinion, be looked at from a higher point of view than that of immediate utility. Here are a whole people who feel it alike their right and their duty to take up arms in defence of their country and the Empire. To them the question is, above everything else, one of national self-respect. Are the Government to tell them that their offers cannot be accepted, because not having been trained in the use of arms they cannot become good soldiers at a moment's notice? For one thing the argument, if valid, would apply as much to a considerable minority of Anglo-Indian aspirants for military service as to the majority of Indian would-be Volunteers. But our contention is that it does not apply to either. If the war will last a good while, both will probably have time to acquire the necessary training. If it will not, they may do other things than actually engaging in war. And in any case the moral value of a national movement among Indians to serve the King and his Government as Volunteers would be incalculable.

[13] *Zamindar* (Lahore), 20 August 1914

The blessings of war: The liberty of Poland: We also expect (to receive its) kind looks

Poland has striven for her autonomy for many long years and she is now to get it. India, however, has never entertained such hopes nor is she anxious to be deprived of the protection of the British Government. However, we hope that we shall benefit by this War by such favours as the repeal of the Press Act [of 1910] and other distasteful measures.

[14] *Dipak* (Lahore), 22 August 1914

Germany's mean move: Efforts to create unrest in British possessions

The Vienna correspondent of the *Standard* states that Germany has sent agents to Egypt, India, Central Asia, Algeria and Morocco to stir up the inhabitants of those countries. To our mind this action is disgraceful and we feel convinced that in India, at any rate, Germany's nefarious attempts to create unrest will be totally unsuccessful.

[15] *Tribune* (Lahore), 25 August 1914

Columns of 'war news' are published daily in the papers, but there is little that is stirring coming from the seat of the most terrible war now being waged. We only receive such news as refer[s] to small skirmishes and there is a monotonous ring about the results. The reports are favourable to the French and the Belgians, the Germans being held to be of no account. There is considerable mistrust of the war news now sent and the strict censorship has led to the starting of sensational rumours by the imaginative.

[16] *Tribune* (Lahore), 26 August 1914

The decision of the Government of India not to accept the numerous offers made by educated Indians volunteering their services in the war can only be regretted. In the Punjab it will be more regretted because the people feel more keenly on the subject. Throughout India people have expressed their steadfast loyalty to the Government and we do not think that anybody can doubt the people's sincere and heartfelt expressions. Popular loyalty to Government at present has nothing to do with popular contentment or discontent with several administrative measures. Just as in England the suffragists, the Ulster volunteers, the Home Rulers, the Labourites have all joined together and forgotten their discontent and party strife for the time being, so the people of India have, in the presence of a common danger and in a political crisis, ignored their differences. There is nothing unusual or artificial about this attitude. On the question of loyalty to the British Government all people are united, and we are sure no sensible man can doubt it. Under these circumstances people also expect the Government to trust the people to a greater extent than before and acknowledge their loyalty and their desire for active service in a more practicable manner.

[17] *Prabhat* (Lahore), 29 August 1914

It must be remembered that Indians are divided into two distinct classes – the educated and the illiterate. To pit the latter against German soldiers who are fighting with a spirit of patriotism is ridiculous. What Government should do is to enlist the services of educated Indians. Such men have a conception of the meaning of patriotism and would thus be fit to meet Germans in the battlefield.

[18] *Zamindar* (Lahore), 30 August 1914

A meeting was recently held in the house of the Hon'ble Mr. Ghaznavi to consider the question of the possibility of Turkey joining hands with Germany in the present war, and the consequent attitude of Indian Muhammadans. It is surely abundantly clear that the Muhammadans of India must stand by Great Britain. The European war is not a religious one and hence Muhammadans are under no religious obligations to Turkey. To talk of the possibility of Turkey being ranged against Great Britain in this war is absurd. Moreover it is unwise, as Muhammadans in this country are liable to get the erroneous idea that Turkey is really on the verge of war with Great Britain. To foster such an idea (as such meetings as the above certainly tend to do) is impolitic in the extreme.

[19] *Akhbar-i-' Am* (Lahore), 30 August 1914

In the first place true news can with difficulty be received from the seat of war and secondly whatever news is received is pruned by the official Press censor. Under these circumstances, it cannot be said with certainty that the news of victory or defeat is true. 'Our' enemies are not degenerated powers like Turkey, Persia &c., but are mighty empires backed up by mighty and warlike armies. Is it becoming, then, that some papers should, while dwelling on the reverses of the enemy, write in a confident vein as if the German Power is about to cease to exist and Austria about to be swept off the face of the earth? It is surely opposed to civilization and humanity to abuse others from a distance. Of course, 'we' should always be ready to pray for the success of British arms.

[20] *Jhang Sial* (Lahore), 1 September 1914

In the present war all colour distinctions have been removed. Three Divisions of 'our' Indian army have been sent to France where they will fight side by side with the French and English soldiers against Germany. We have not yet, however, completely realised our wish. We desire every Indian to play his part in the present crisis. Volunteers should be raised who could be sent abroad for service if the occasion arose.

[21] *Tribune* (Lahore), 1 September 1914

There is no doubt that Lord Crewe [Secretary of State for India, 1911–15] has spoken what is exactly true and the decision of the

Government to employ the Indian troops against Germans has been a wise one. We do not know whether the flower of the Indian army have been despatched. But in any case Indian soldiers are sure to stand side by side with English and French soldiers and fight with valour becoming the noble sons of India against the enemies of the Empire. Sir Ian Hamilton has recorded his carefully formed opinion of the Indian fighting men that 'they will shake the artificial society of Europe to its foundations.' What the Indians, in military or civil employment, want is opportunity, equal and fair. We are sure that the German soldiers will find more than their match in the Indian. And as for the safety of India, we must acknowledge the appreciative terms in which Lord Crewe has spoken of Indian loyalty. There will certainly be no internal trouble in India and we can safely guarantee that. May we in this connection repeat our suggestion that an Indian Volunteer Corps should be formed and the willing young men trained for any emergency whether internal or external? There can be no good reason why the willing services of Indians should not be used and we hope that Lord Crewe will grant his approval to a scheme of raising an Indian Volunteer Corps in all provinces.

[22] *Panjabee* (Lahore), 1 September 1914

Speaking of the withdrawal of these troops and its possible consequences, Lord Crewe said he believed 'the Indian frontier would be adequately secured and that the enthusiasm pervading in all classes and races in India would render internal trouble absolutely impossible.' Lord Crewe's belief in this regard will be shared by all who know anything about India. Indeed if it had not been for the disability under which the people of India labour in respect of the bearing of arms and for the virtual absence of representative institutions Indian leaders could have assured England, just as Mr. Redmond assured her, that she might remove every individual soldier from India, European or Indian, and depend upon Indian Volunteers to protect India alike from external aggression and internal trouble.

[23] *Vakil* (Amritsar), 2 September 1914

Although Turkey shows a certain amount of activity in her military preparations yet it is scarcely justifiable to say that she intends throwing her lot into the war. She should refrain from doing so, as she now has an opportunity to recoup her strength. To advise Turkey to join hands with Great Britain (and consequently with France and Russia) is unwise. The Allies are sufficiently strong enough to cope with Germany, and moreover Russia is still hungering for Constantinople. Were Turkey to join Germany we feel sure that Indian Muhammadans would remain loyal to Great Britain, although they would be loath to snap their spiritual connections with Turkey.

[24] *Tribune* (Lahore), 3 September 1914

Nor is this the first time that the analogy of Algeria has been urged upon the attention of Government. Students of Indian history will recollect that over a half century ago the great soldier statesman Henry Lawrence prominently brought this question forward in a letter to Lord Stanley. He then wrote: 'France has its Arab Generals and Russia has many Asiatic Generals, but Liberal England restricts its best native officers to posts subordinate to that of sergeant-major, obtainable too only by some thirty to fifty years' service [...]' The lot of Indian soldiers has been bettered since then in some respects, but we are still a long way off the ideal held out to us by Henry Lawrence. No one, however, complains of it at present. On the contrary every one rejoices that Indian soldiers have at last been given an opportunity to prove the steadfastness of their loyalty and the depth of their devotion to the British Crown. We renew our grateful acknowledgement to Lord Hardinge and Lord Crewe for bringing in the Algerian analogy.

[25] *Akhbar-i-' Am* (Lahore), 4 September 1914

Both Persia and China have tasted Russian oppression. Russia has forcibly deprived China of Mongolia. There is, therefore, quite a possibility of these two oppressed nations rising up against Russia if the latter suffers any serious reverse in the present European struggle.

[26] *Vakil* (Amritsar), 5 September 1914

France has spared no efforts to annihilate Islam, as was seen in the case of Morocco. And yet we see her employing Algerian Arabs in commercial and industrial enterprises. These Asiatics are tolerated in Europe so long as they are contented with their status of slavery; but no sooner do they show a desire to earn a livelihood on the same footing as the European workmen than they are immediately evicted from Europe. Again the French possessions in India send a representative to the National Assembly in France. But England, which is the professed champion of freedom, does not permit even one representative from India to sit in the British Parliament. We even see the rejection of the India Council Bill. While the *London Times* questions the loyalty of India in its article called 'The Indian Peril' we find the English newspapers here eulogizing the loyalty of India in the present crisis. Such are a few of the anomalies of modern civilisation.

[27] *Panjabee* (Lahore), 5 September 1914

Sir John Hewett says, in a letter to the *Times*, that the employment of Indian troops side by side with the best troops in the world will do more to make British rule in India popular than any other step the Government could take. While there is no doubt the decision of Government in this matter is as gratifying to the people of India as a contrary decision would have been disappointing, we think it a pity that officials and ex-officials should look at the matter merely from the point of view of its effect upon the popularity of British rule. There are higher and more important things even to officials – for they, too, are above everything else men – than the popularity of the Government which employs them. One of these things is the self-respect of the people whose affairs they administer. The employment of Indian troops in the present war is to be commended principally for the reason that it is a step towards the eventual obliteration of existing racial prejudice, so essential to India's self-fulfillment as a nation and an integral part of the Empire. It is also an act of much-needed justice both to Indian capacity and Indian aspirations.

[28] *Zamindar* (Lahore), 6 September 1914

Turkey and Egypt

The *Express* understands that the Turkish mobilisation is not directed against any of the Balkan States but has Egypt as its objective. The advance is to be through Syria, and use will be made of the various recently constructed railways. The railway to Mecca will especially aid in a rapid transport of Turkish troops towards the Egyptian frontier, while the various forces in Arabia will be transported to the north. The Khedive is now in Constantinople and is not over[ly]-friendly to Great Britain. Enver Pasha, the Turkish War Minister, is a pro-German. He has whipped up the remnants of the Turkish Army into a respectable fighting force. There are now something like 200,000 Turkish troops available for any enterprise which this ambitious young man – egged on by Germany – may care to undertake. A large proportion of these troops are already in Asia Minor.

[29] *Paisa Akhbar* (Lahore), 9 September 1914

The war and the price of hides

The European war has demonstrated the necessity of a revival of the Swadeshi movement in India. The hide trade is temporarily paralysed owing to the war, and in consequence Muhammadan dealers are suffering throughout India. Had we been able to tan and make leather ourselves we would not have been hit so hard. To relieve the slump therefore in the hide trade we would suggest that Government compel mahajans to buy hides from Muhammadan butchers.

[30] *Akhbar-i-' Am* (Lahore), 12 September 1914

The effect of the war on India

Grain dealers are utilising the war for their own selfish ends. They have raised the price of wheat and the poorer classes are suffering greatly in consequence of their action. Some people are led to believe that all the grain produced in the country is being sent to the seat of war. This is an erroneous idea. Government should take strong measures against these grain dealers, who are prospering at the expense of the poor people.

[31] *Khalsa Sowar* (Amritsar), 14 September 1914

What is the best Government for India?

The recent appearance of a German cruiser in the Bay of Bengal has created an impression here of the possibility of an invasion of India. Such a contingency is secretly welcomed by certain Indians. But surely these people do not really desire German rule in this country! Surely they have learnt to abhor Germans, whose barbarous cruelty has been seen in their treatment of their colonists and of the French and Belgians in the war. Indians are not yet fitted for self-government and the British alone are capable of giving them peace and education. Let Indians assist Government during the present crisis, and then we feel sure that Government will feel more disposed to grant self-government to India in the future.

[32] *Panjabee* (Lahore), 15 September 1914

At a time when the rest of the Empire, notably the United Kingdom, is loud in its appreciation of the offers of assistance made by all sections of the Indian community, when the Viceroy's message has made a tremendous sensation in the Houses of Parliament, in the British Press as well as in the Colonies, when every part of the Empire is expecting great things from Indian troops, when even such a man as Lord Curzon, so notoriously unfriendly to Indian aspirations, is looking forward to Bengal Lancers making their appearance in the streets of Berlin and Gurkhas taking their ease in the gardens of Potsdam – at such a time it was reserved for an Anglo-Indian journal to repay the debt it owes to this country by making a stupid and senseless attack upon His Majesty's Indian troops. In a leading article in its issue of Saturday it writes – 'It is no disparagement to Indian troops to say that even when trained and led by British officers, a very small portion of them come up to the British standard. If they did the

British would not be in India.' It is for the great British nation to ask itself if it is a compliment to it to be told that it is in India merely because British soldiers are better than Indian soldiers. It is *our* right and *our* duty to ask that the insult which the *Pioneer* hurls at the vast majority of His Majesty's Indian troops should not go unnoticed. The *Pioneer* should be asked to substantiate its allegation, to cite concrete instances, in which Indian troops have during the last half century failed to come up to the standard, and, if it fails to do so, should be compelled to withdraw its statement. The statement, which would have been unfortunate and untrue at all times, is specially impolitic and mischievous at a moment like this, when the whole of India is pulsating with feelings of loyalty and devotion to the British Throne and when so much depends upon the encouragement which the Indian troops both here and at the front receive.

[33] *Dipak* (Lahore), 15 September 1914

How can false rumours about the war be suppressed?

Needless to say that every attempt should be made to suppress false rumours in regard to the war. Government should issue a vernacular Gazette containing all war news issued by the Press Bureau. This Gazette should be distributed in order that the parents and relations of soldiers at the front may become acquainted with authenticated news.

[34] *Zamindar* (Lahore), 16 September 1914

All alike [His Majesty the King Emperor, His Excellency the Viceroy and various other high Ministers of State] express high appreciation of the expressions of loyalty displayed by India. It is a misfortune, then, that Indians have been unable to prove their loyalty in a practical manner. We feel confident that, had Indians been put in the field at the very outset of the war, Germany would have been crushed by this time. The blame, however, lies mainly on our shoulders. We should improve ourselves by strenuous physical exercise; we should train ourselves in the use of arms and we should make boy scouts of our children. In this way our martial capacities would soon become apparent to the world.

[35] *Observer* (Lahore), 19 September 1914

The exhaustion of both sides must be terrible, but reports say the Allies [... still have] strength to follow up. The German's heaviest bolt is shot. They have not taken Paris and now they will never take it. For every week that passes brings on the inevitable time, when the demand for reinforcements from the East must become too urgent to be resisted.

[36] *Vakil* (Amritsar), 19 September 1914

The new theatre of war: A sudden change

It is commonly believed that the reverse on the Marne has demoralised the Germans. In our opinion there are no reasonable grounds for believing that such is the case. All the recent movements of the German army seem to be prompted by some important strategical consideration. They have failed to take Paris, but we should not be surprised if they now divert their attention towards Petrograd. The Germans have great powers of endurance and we believe that the recent reverses have not affected the 'morale' of their army in the slightest degree.

[37] *Shanti* (Rawalpindi), 19 September 1914

Will Turkey also participate in the war?

Although Turkey has assured the European Powers of her neutrality, yet the mobilisation of her army tends to show that she is anxious to participate in the war. That this is true will appear from the fact that she has recently purchased two warships.

[38] *Paisa Akhbar* (Lahore), 20 September 1914

[Rumour purports that] the Germans have cut off the heads of some Gurkha and Sikh soldiers and have sent them to the Powers with the complaint that the English are sending Indian soldiers to the front. The English have never attempted to conceal the fact that they intended sending Indian soldiers to the war and hence we cannot help thinking that the rumour is absurdly untrue.

[39] *Jhang Sial* (Lahore), 21 September 1914

The circle of the publication of true reports should be widened

It is absurd to attempt to conceal true war news – whether it be of victory or defeat. We are glad to see that England and France do not act in this manner. Then why should Russia keep a guarded silence about German and Austrian moves in Poland? Russia, too, should publish a full and true account of the progress of the war on her frontiers.

[40] *Hindu* (Lahore), 22 September 1914

May God save us from such civilisation

Europe claims to be the champion of civilisation; she claims to bring peace and good will among men. And yet we see this very Europe engaged in the most bloody war ever known in the world's history. If this be the civilisation of which Europe boasts, may it never be our lot to have such civilisation.

[41] *Jhang Sial* (Lahore), 22 September 1914

There is a rumour current in the bazar that the Germans, when faced by a British and Indian regiment, refused to fight against the latter, though they did so against the former, on the plea that the Indians were friends of Germany. Of course we do not consider this rumour worthy of credence. Surely the Germans do not consider Indians their friends when they are fully aware that Indians are ranged against them in the war.

[42] *Dipak* (Lahore), 22 September 1914

Unfounded rumours about the war in Multan

Many unfounded rumours are afloat in Multan. Some illiterate people say that the Germans have reached Karachi and will in a few days attack Multan; while others declare that school boys are being drilled in order to fight in the war. There is also a rumour to the effect that a German airship has been seen over Multan and has taken photographs of the place. People should be warned of these unfounded rumours in order that they may not be deceived.

[43] *Hindu* (Lahore), 25 September 1914

Some mischief monger lets loose big firework balloons in the sky every night, thus creating false rumours about German aeroplanes amongst the ignorant masses.

[44] *Khalsa Advocate* (Amritsar), 26 September 1914

Now in order to make it clear [. . .] who the fittest are, we beg to draw the attention of the Government towards the old Sikh soldiers who have been serving the British Government for years and years together [. . .] The Sikhs are a fighting nation and the first duty that is inculcated among them is the duty of sacrifice. They are hardy, robust, bold and courageous. For instance, a Sikh when asked by somebody whether he would fight, replied that he knew nothing else. To fight for those under whose protection they live is the sole business of the Sikhs, and really they know nothing else.

[45] *Vakil* (Amritsar), 26 September 1914

There was a general belief that the battle of the Marne would be the turning point in the war; but this belief has been falsified. That battle was of no particular significance and its effect on the ultimate result of the war was inconsiderable. Many Indians picture, with the utmost consternation, the fate of India in the event of Germany's ultimate success. But their fears are groundless. Great Britain's mighty resources almost make German success an impossibility; and, moreover, if we anticipate the worst and presume that Germany will emerge victorious, surely there is no reason why India should be affected thereby to any appreciable extent.

[46] *Prabhat* (Lahore), 26 September 1914

Government should obviate [the spreading of false rumours about the war] by announcing true war news in the villages and towns. For instance we see certain editors publishing German casualties in a particular case as 5,000 when the true figures are really only 500. This is a poor way of attempting to curry favour with the Government. These editors should be severely punished for such publication of false news.

[47] *Paisa Akhbar* (Lahore), 30 September 1914

The bombardment of the magnificent and historical cathedral of Rheims by the Germans has caused universal grief throughout Europe. But Russia also bombarded Mashhad and destroyed its sacred building – an act which shocked the Muhammadan world. No doubt Europe did not realise the sacrilege of this act of Russian barbarism.

[48] *Naurattan* (Amritsar), 1 October 1914

We have recently heard a rumour that 12 thousand Sikh soldiers have been made prisoners by the Germans who have shaved their heads. This news is utterly false and appears to owe its origins to certain Aryas.

[49] *Akhbar-i-' Am* (Lahore), 2 October 1914

Unfounded rumours about the war

We are not a little surprised at the large number of unfounded rumours that are prevalent in the country. For instance it is generally rumoured in the villages that the Germans have reached Paris; that they have defeated the Russian and the French armies and that they have reached London. There is also another rumour that while the German soldiers fought with the British soldiers, they refused to fight against the Indians, on the plea that the latter were their friends.

[50] *Vakil* (Amritsar), 3 October 1914

Reality of rumours

The following rumours are afloat in the country:

1. That the standard of rebellion has been raised in Egypt against the English.
2. That the Indian Army in Egypt has been destroyed.
3. That a sanguinary war is raging between the English and the Turks.
4. That Turkey has given an ultimatum to Russia.
5. That the Turks are fighting against the Allies disguised as Germans.
6. That the *Emden* is really a Turkish cruiser; that its real name is the *Muhammadan* and that it has come towards India to spread terror on behalf of Germany.
7. That a very large Turkish army is being mobilised and collected in Basra.

These rumours are supported by certain English newspapers. Needless to say there is no truth in them, and they should gain no credence in this country. Even Turkish newspapers make no mention of these fantastic rumours.

[51] *Zamindar* (Lahore), 3 October 1914

The Afghan peril

It is absurd to suppose [. . .] that, if in the event of England and Russia being forced to unsheathe the sword against Turkey, the Afghans, whose natural sympathies are with Turkey and who possess a large and powerful army, are offered territorial concessions in the region of Nasratabad as the price of their maintenance of neutrality, they will be ready to accept such terms. They will never be ready to see the Turks wiped out of existence on such terms, as it would be tantamount to digging their own graves.

If it is true that any such proposal is being entertained, England must lose all title to be considered the protector of the weak, whereas in the present war England has joined for the defence of noble principles and is shedding the blood of thousands of her sons in the cause of justice.

Moreover, Afghanistan will never accept Nasratabad as the price of a neutrality, which will involve the shedding of the blood of her own co-religionists, the Turks. In any case this is all mere speculation, as we are convinced that Turkey will never take the offensive and no opportunity for showing her sympathy with the Turks will arise in the case of Afghanistan.

Afghanistan is a rising and ambitious country. It used to be called the Bulgaria of Asia, but the Amir's ambition is to see it transformed into the Japan of Central Asia. We hope that she will prove a tower of strength to England in Central Asia as Japan has done in the Far East. Japan has received compensation in Korea and Port Arthur; Afghanistan too must get something in return for her friendship.

If Russia, who is now the Ally of the British, comes out [of] the war victorious, she will turn her thoughts to India and then Afghanistan alone will stand in her way. If, on the other hand, Russia is exhausted by the war the regions of Russian Turkistan, Askabad and Murghab, of which the Russians took possession by acts of brigandage, ought to be ceded to Afghanistan. Such an act on the part of the British Government will win the approval of all Muhammadans and will constitute a great political victory for England.

[52] *Chakrawarti* (Lahore), 4 October 1914

An appeal to the British Government to help the brave men of the Indian Expeditionary Force

We feel confident that Government will appreciate, in a full measure, the services of its Indian troops in the war. As a fit reward for these services we would suggest that grants of land be given to the families of those sepoys who are killed at the front.

[53] *Zamindar* (Lahore), 8 October 1914

The Indian Army in Europe: We invite the attention of the Commander-in-Chief

After being apprised of the landing of the Indian contingent in France we have heard nothing further in this connection. We admit that it would be inadvisable to publish the movements of the Indian troops. But surely we are entitled to hear of their doings. Surely the relatives of the Indian soldiers on service should be made acquainted with the latter's welfare or otherwise. Some means should be adopted whereby such news could be given.

[54] *Jhang Sial* (Lahore), 9 October 1914

War and war news

It is impossible to see any consistency in the war news which is officially published throughout the country. Sometimes we hear of British successes, sometimes of their reverses. The ordinary man is thrown into a state of confusion. He is at a loss to know what to believe. In spite of this, however, we are anxious for the success of the British arms.

[55] *Lyall Akhbar* (Lyallpur), 9 October 1914

[*Zamindar*] is publishing war news from the German point of view, which is quite opposed to officially published war news and which is likely to create unrest in the country and to discredit other newspaper reports. It is essential, therefore, that the *Zamindar* should, when publishing false pro-German news, simultaneously contradict the same and keep the public informed of the real situation.

[56] *Zamindar* (Lahore), 12 October 1914

A rumour about compulsion

We recently heard that Government proposed sending about 20 blacksmiths and carpenters of Gujranwala to the war and that peons and chaprasis were ordered to summon these people. On hearing this the blacksmiths and carpenters fled and concealed themselves. They were eventually brought before the Sialkot Cantonment Magistrate, who, on finding that they were unwilling to go to the war, gave them their liberty. Such compulsion, if this rumour be true, is contrary to the spirit of the British administration. We are glad that the Cantonment Magistrate realised this fact, and we trust that all British officers will act with similar justice.

[57] *Zamindar* (Lahore), 13 October 1914

German spies in Lahore

We have often heard of the activity of German spies in London and England generally. But the existence of such spies in Lahore comes as a great surprise to the ordinary man. And yet it is none the less nonetheless true. These spies are at work in Government offices. They are straining every nerve to widen the gulf between rulers and ruled. The attainment of such an object would obviously be to the detriment of Government. And some of these spies are members of our own community!

[58] *Desh* (Lahore), 13 October 1914

As the Muhammadans live in different parts of the world they can, when forced by necessity, take up arms against Great Britain. As a matter of fact Muhammadan soldiers, though comparatively small in number, are fighting against Great Britain and France on behalf of Austria and Germany. On the other hand, the Sikhs, the Rajputs and the Gurkhas are sacrificing their lives for preserving the honour of Great Britain. It is impossible for any Hindu to take up arms against the latter on behalf of Germany. The reason for this is that the interests of the Hindus, for good or for evil, are bound up with Great Britain. The Muhammadans on the other hand are spread over different parts of the world thus rendering it difficult to reconcile the interests of all of them with those of Great Britain.

[59] *Zamindar* (Lahore), 16 October 1914

The war has its advantages and disadvantages. Its disadvantages consist in the terrible loss of life and the consequent suffering which inevitably ensues. Its advantages will be seen in the benefits which it will bring to India. We are convinced that self-government will be granted to this country – even if it be compensation for the services of Indians during the war. Our sepoys who have gone to the front will see Europe with their own eyes. They will see European institutions and will see that there is no difference – except in colour – between Indians and Europeans. Their ideas will broaden and this will naturally have some effect on their fellow countrymen. We hail with joy the approaching day of our liberty and we feel that it is not far distant.

[60] *Khalsa Akhbar* (Lahore), 23 October 1914

Pension[s] to the widows of Indian soldiers

We applaud the beneficence of Government in starting a fund for the relief of the families of Indian soldiers who are killed in the war. We would suggest, however, that the present rates of pensions granted to the widows of soldiers killed in action be raised. A pension of Rs. 2-12-0 and in several cases less than this amount is scarcely sufficient.

[61] *Prabhat* (Lahore), 24 October 1914

Will Turkey take part in the war?

Turkey's participation in the war will undoubtedly be followed by trouble in Egypt and Tripoli. The war spirit will eventually spread throughout the Muslim World. Persia will lose no time in shaking off the yoke of Russia and England. Frontier Pathans will immediately fall on India. And then we shall have to see whether Indian Muhammadans will pray in their mosques for the victory of the Union Jack! The wave of Pan-Islamism in Asia is more powerful than the Pan-Slavism of Europe. Turkey's entry into the war will be the signal for a general upheaval of the Islamic world.

[62] *Akhbar-i-' Am* (Lahore), 25 October 1914

It is now unmistakably clear that Germany alone is responsible for this war. However, we cannot but admire the unflinching courage of the Kaiser's soldiers. As long as German soldiers are prepared to meet death in this manner for their Kaiser, it will be difficult indeed to overcome them.

[63] *Paisa Akhbar* (Lahore), 28 October 1914

India and England (from its London correspondent)

The British nation is truly proud of the magnificent response made by India at the present crisis. The Kaiser had hoped to sever the British connection with India; but instead, we see the bond of friendship growing stronger. British policy, in allowing India to play her part in the European war, has proved its wisdom. This action, more than anything else, will help eradicate the canker known as 'Indian unrest' and we have British statesmanship to thank for this.

[64] *Paisa Akhbar* (Lahore), 30 October 1914

Japan's object in lending assistance to England against the Germans is obviously to gain some material advantages. Chief among these is the right of Japanese emigration to the British colonies, and, in particular, to Australia. This is quite justifiable, and we see no reason why Japan should not succeed in gaining her object. Surely, then, Indians deserve some substantial compensation for their services in the war, and in our opinion they too can be adequately rewarded by being granted the full rights of citizenship in the British colonies.

[65] *Zamindar* (Lahore), 30 October 1914

The ignorance and illiteracy of the general public affords a fertile soil for the dissemination of [false rumours about the war]. However, we are pleased to note the praiseworthy attitude adopted by the Vernacular Press in refusing to give credence to these reports. In our opinion the only solution to the difficulty in question is for the Government to encourage public lectures and by this means inform the people of the true progress of the war.

[66] *Akhbar-i-'Am* (Lahore), 31 October 1914

On having been shown a cold shoulder by Italy, Germany made friends with poor inoffensive Turkey. If poor innocent Turkey refuses to be amicably disposed towards Germany, she is made to recall the Balkan War and, if she sides with Germany, the *Triple Entente* is sure to place her in danger. Thus poor unfortunate Turkey is forced to make a move. She mobilised her forces, purchased the *Goeben* and the *Breslau*, assured the *Triple Entente* of her neutrality and, in short, she did what she could possibly do under existing circumstances. It is a sin to doubt the loyalty of the Indian Musalmans to the British Government. It is immaterial if Turkey becomes our enemy.

[67] *Jhang Siyal* (Lahore), 4 November 1914

God alone knows what the consequences of the mistake of Turkey will be. But the present is the hour of the Indian Musalmans' trial and we pray sincerely that they may successfully emerge out of the ordeal. No doubt, Turkey is a Muhammadan Power and Muhammadans sympathise with her, but the present war, into which Turkey has deliberately chosen to plunge, is a political war, and there is no reason why Musalmans as such should have any sympathy with her. It is to be hoped that Indian Muslims will persevere in their loyalty to the British Government and save the honour of India.

[68] *Hindu* (Lahore), 4 November 1914

The blasts of war are gradually working their way towards the East. This new, although perhaps not unexpected, development of the war will cause consternation in India.

[69] *Observer* (Lahore), 4 November 1914

The one big contingency, which the Muslims of India had long been dreading and to avert which they had been praying with all the sincerity of their convictions, has at last happened. Turkey, despite the entreaties of the whole Muslim world to stand aloof and against her own best interests, has succumbed to the chauvinistic influences which were ruling her and has decided to plunge her people into a bloody war, which must spell for them utter pain and spoliation. The tactics of the Wilhelmstrasse, be it admitted, have wonderfully succeeded and the blandishments that were being so freely lavished upon the Committee of Union and Progress have achieved their desired end. Turkey's gratuitous intervention at the present moment is all of her own seeking and she must reap the full consequences of her mad act. So far as we, the Muslims of India, who have always displayed a profound interest in the welfare of a people, who are our co-religionists and also the guardians of the Holy Places of Islam, are concerned, we have discharged our duty in time and in the clearest language possible [...] That duty having been discharged, Turkey's future fate ceases to have any concern for us. We are the loyal subjects of His British Majesty, and his flag is the only one under which we mean to live and prosper.

[70] *Sher-i-Punjab* (Lahore), 4 November 1914

Turkey has shown herself a mere puppet in the hands of the Germans. Germany is endeavouring to stir up the Muslim world against Great Britain, and, to achieve this end, she has inveigled Turkey into the war. German calculations will not succeed in Egypt. We cannot speak of the chances of success in Morocco, Algeria and

Tripoli. As for India we feel confident that Muhammadans here will remain loyal to Great Britain. Turkey is not fighting for her rights; she has entered the war at the instigation of Germany. Hence Turkey must expect no sympathy from India.

[71] *Bilji* (Lahore), 5 November 1914

It is obvious that Turkey has fallen a victim to German intrigue. She has disregarded the prayers of Indian Muhammadans who begged her to maintain neutrality. In view of this we feel sure that no Muhammadan in this country will sympathise with Turkey in her approaching troubles. Muhammadans will remain loyal to the British Government.

[72] *Hindu* (Lahore), 6 November 1914

The Germans have begun to circulate false rumours about India. For instance, when the Indian Army landed in France, the Berlin authorities announced that the Indian Army has been brought to Europe simply for show. In the beginning of October another non-official newspaper remarked that the Amir of Kabul had sent four lakhs [400,000] of soldiers to the frontier under the command of his brother Nasrullah Khan with a view to taking possession of Peshawar, the 'key to India' and that he sent three lakhs of Afghans to the frontier of Russia. The paper says that according to German news agents seven lakhs of Afghan soldiers are invading Russia and India but we all know that the relations between Afghanistan and Great Britain are friendly.

[73] *Paisa Akhbar* (Lahore), 7 November 1914

On the face of it [the rumour now prevalent among Muhammadans that the Kaiser intends to embrace Islam] is absurd. The Kaiser has never shown himself a friend of Muhammadans. On the contrary, he has always been, if anything, anti-Muslim. And this fact is nowhere more clearly demonstrated than in the cunning way in which he has inveigled Turkey into a war, which must mean her ruin.

[74] *Dipak* (Lahore), 8 November 1914

Maintenance of the wives of soldiers who have gone to the front

In England the wife of an ordinary soldier, who goes to the war, is allowed a monthly allowance of Rs. 40. Indeed, the wives and children of those, who offer their lives for the protection of their country, deserve the sympathy and help of the nation. A similarly generous treatment should be given to the wives and families of Indian soldiers, who have gone to the war. Government might issue a *communiqué* specifying the maintenance allowance, which it intends granting in such cases.

[75] *Parkesh* (Lahore), 8 November 1914

Turkey's entry into the war will undoubtedly tend to prolong the struggle. Germany's motive in drawing the Ottoman Empire into the war is obviously to stir up Muhammadan feeling throughout the world, but we trust that her sinister designs will be frustrated. The present war is not a religious one; it is not a war between Muhammadans and Christians; hence it is the duty of all Muhammadans in this country to refuse help to Turkey.

[76] *Dipak* (Lahore), 12 November 1914

Indians, tended-hearted as they are, have been greatly moved by German atrocities in Belgium and they shrink from setting eyes on the German demons [. . .] a wicked *sowar* so frightened the people gathered at a fair which was held on the 2nd November at a temple in Mohan Lal Ganj Tahsil, Lucknow District, by reporting that the Germans had come, that all the villagers ran [a]way in great haste, and the women were so overcome by fear that they ran away leaving behind them their children, their ornaments and a good deal of other property.

[77] *Paisa Akhbar* (Lahore), 13 November 1914

There can be no doubt but that our soldiers, by their undaunted bravery, have won for themselves and for India an imperishable fame.

Their casualties may be heavy; but the reward is rich. Sir James Wilcocks [commander of the Indian Corps in France, 1914–15] has written to His Excellency the Viceroy and pointed out the invaluable services rendered by Indian soldiers during the Boxer Rising in China. Such deeds as these will win for India the honour she deserves among the nations of the world.

[78] *Bir* (Lahore), 20 November 1914

[German papers] assert that the Afghans have invaded India; that the Amir's son has crossed the frontier; and that there is a general spirit of discontent and mutiny pervading all classes in India. The situation in Africa is also said to be hopeless for the English. We cannot but wonder at the marvelous ingenuity displayed by the Germans in fabricating such grotesquely false rumours.

[79] *Parkash* (Lahore), 22 November 1914

[Referring to the warning given by the Deputy Commissioners of Lahore and Jullundur to the local journalists against publishing sensational war news] [...] In ordinary circumstances the application of the Press Act was painfully regular, but now, with the outbreak of war, the evil has increased tenfold. Why does not Government take steps to root out the real cause of such sensational news? To accomplish this end it would be necessary to prevent the entry into India of all English and American newspapers.

[80] *Siraj-ul-Akhbar* (Jhelum), 7 December 1914

The public [...] hold that the voice of the people is the voice of God and that a rumour often turns out to be correct. It is difficult to stop rumours. Moreover, we fail to understand from what source, excepting the newspapers [correct reports can be obtained]. The Muhammadan public is now-a-days anxious to hear Turkish news. It will be quite proper to make special arrangements for supplying authentic news about Turkey. If the real facts are concealed, ignorant Muhammadans will assuredly continue to indulge in all sorts of absurd rumours.

[81] *Sher-i-Panjab* (Lahore), 19 December 1914

The strength and courage of one are proportionate to the troubles and affliction to which one is subjected. For example, the Punjabis, who have borne the brunt of the invasions of India from the north-west, as a people, are harder and more courageous than the population of other parts of this country. And it is owing to this that the Austrians do not lose courage, although they may suffer defeat after defeat. The Russians and the Servians defeated them on several occasions; and yet the Austrians are still fighting, as is illustrated by their stand in the Carpathians.

[82] *Bir* (Lahore), 21 December 1914

A press communique issued from Berlin states that a part of the German fleet invaded the eastern coast of England and fired at the well-fortified ports of Scarborough and Hartlepool.

[83] *Zamindar* (Lahore), 25 December 1914

The European war has proved that not only the sons of Adam but the daughters of Eve also can fight bravely. European women, who till the other day, were adepts in the art of coquetry, who danced naked to win affection, who were the ornaments of the coffee-houses and who, in churches, were a living proof of the adage 'I shall worship God by placing the idol before me,' are now-a-days fighting with arms and ammunition [...] Innumerable men and women in Irak are enrolling themselves as volunteers in the Turkish army.

[84] *Kapurthala Akhbar* (Kapurthala), 26 December 1914

Germany must be rejoicing over her victory at Lodz. The world at large does not attach any weight to the reasons assigned by Russia for evacuating Lodz, inasmuch as it is clear that Germany captured the city after sacrificing as many as a lakh of her soldiers.

[85] *Akhbar-i-' Am* (Lahore), 27 December 1914

The Cairo correspondent of the *Daily Telegraph* has sent a report, supplied to him by an Englishman. According to this report, the German Bureau asserts that the English, along with the remaining Allied Powers, have sustained serious reverses, both on land and sea. A telegram from Berlin announces that the Turks intend to construct a military railway line from Maian to the Suez Canal.

[86] *Sher-i-Punjab* (Lahore), 30 December 1914

[A telegram] was sent by the Emperor of Germany to his heir-apparent, and states that the Shaikh-ul-Islam of Turkey has issued a *fatwa*, declaring that it is the religious duty of every Muhammadan to fight to the last breath against the English, the French and the Russians, who are the enemies of Islam. The *fatwa* is being distributed all over the world. Herein the Kaiser has resorted to a deep policy. But he has failed to gain the end in view. The Muhammadans are not so foolish as to act upon such a *fatwa*, compiled as it has been under the muzzles of German guns. Indeed, the Persians have refused to act upon it; the peoples of India, Afghanistan and Baluchistan treat it with contempt; and everybody knows that the Shaikh-ul-Islam was forced to issue the *fatwa*, because he knew that if he did not do so the friends of the Germans in Turkey would either kill him or dispense with his services.

[87] *Dipak* (Lahore), 31 December 1914

It is impossible for Italy to keep neutral much longer. She will have no other alternative but to join in the war against Austria and Turkey. Indeed, the Italian Ambassador in Constantinople has already asked the Porte to clear its position and state whether its armies are going to invade Tripoli. Such incidents lead one to conclude that Italy will take up arms against Turkey.

CHAPTER 2

1915

The war expanded dramatically in scale and ferocity in 1915, claiming the lives of soldiers and civilians. In January, German Zeppelins bombed London. On 4 February, Germany began unrestricted submarine warfare. The waters around Great Britain became a war zone, and through the end of August, German U-boats preyed on Allied and neutral shipping indiscriminately, ending the policy only under threat that continued use of unrestricted submarine warfare might bring the Americans into the war. Fighting between the Russians and Ottomans engulfed the entire Caucasus region. Italy declared war on Austria-Hungary on 23 May, having been promised Habsburg land by the Allies in exchange for its allegiance. Through the end of the year, the Italians launched a series of attacks on the Austrians along the Isonzo river, seizing little in the way of strategic ground at a cost of 230,000 dead and wounded. Bulgaria joined the Central Powers on 6 September. The year 1915 witnessed the twentieth century's first genocide. In April, Turkish forces began forcibly deporting the country's Armenian population. These actions lead directly to the deaths of some 1.5 million Armenians. On the Western Front, beleaguered British and French forces attempted repeatedly without success to break through the German lines in Champagne and Flanders. In a bid to break the stalemate, armies experimented with new weapons, like poison gas and flamethrowers. Stymied there, British and French command looked to Turkey for a knockout blow. Combined British and French forces launched an ill-conceived and even more poorly executed offensive on the Dardanelles. The 259-day campaign quickly bogged down in stalemate, gained the Allies nothing and cost the British and French more than 250,000 casualties (not to mention Churchill his spot at the Admiralty). Armies on the Eastern Front experienced much greater mobility. Warsaw fell to combined German and Austrian forces in August. By the end of September, the Russian armies had been driven from Poland and Galicia. Russian losses for the year 1915, one marked by defeat after defeat, topped 2 million.

In 1915, Indian soldiers fought in France and Mesopotamia, the Sinai, East Africa and Gallipoli. Indian Expeditionary Force D numbered only 4,700 troops when it occupied Basra in the Persian Gulf in late 1914. This force had grown to about 20,000 strong by March 1915, enough to repulse a large Ottoman counterattack at Shaiba, near Basra, in mid-April. In May, the Indian 6th Division overran Ottoman forces at Qurna and began the slow advance up the Tigris, despite inadequate water transport and medical supplies. During the summer, the Indian 6th Division had over 4,200 hospital admissions of which 1,300 were due to malaria.[1] Things in the Middle East might have offered the Allies a bright spot in an otherwise disappointing year. In late September, British and Indian forces captured Kut and began an ambitious drive on Baghdad. Owing principally to poor logistical planning, however, the operation floundered. By December, British and Indian troops found themselves back in Kut, cut off, and forced to withstand a Turkish siege. On the Western Front, the Indian Corps fought at Neuve Chapelle, Second Ypres and Loos. After 14 months in the trenches, the beleaguered corps had suffered some 34,252 casualties – British and Indian. In December, the two Indian infantry divisions in France were redeployed to the Middle East to assist in IEF D's drive on Baghdad. Of the approximately 3,000 Indian soldiers deployed to Gallipoli, 1,591 were dead by the end of the campaign.[2] In the Punjab, Lieutenant Governor O'Dwyer noted that news of the annihilation of the 14th Sikhs at Gallipoli on 4 June 'was one of the most powerful factors in securing the loyalty' of the Sikh community. 'After that the rush to the colours in the Sikh districts was extraordinary.'[3] The year 1915 witnessed a flurry of revolutionary activity in the Punjab. Founded in California in 1913, Ghadar was a loose confederation of activists committed to the violent overthrow of British rule in India. In March 1915, O'Dwyer requested and received the Defence of India Act, which permitted him to detain suspected Ghadarites indefinitely without trial. O'Dwyer made it clear to Punjabis that failure to flock to the imperial standard would cost them British patronage. In March 1915, he met with Sikh notables and told them '[Ghadar] was bringing the Sikhs as a whole into discredit, and their interests as well as their honour were involved.'[4] By midyear, Sikh collaboration had effectively neutralized any significant Ghadar threat to British rule.

Selections from the Indian newspapers published in the Punjab, 1915

CONTENTS

Turkish soldiers	182, 190
Western Front	117, 132, 137, 138, 185
Zeppelin raids	102

[88] *Az-zia* (Lahore), 1 January 1915

The following war news appeared in the *Shams-ul-Akhbar* (Madras), 24 December 1915:

Sometime ago a rumour was set afloat that the English wanted to bring their soldiers to Akaba a second time; but the *gendarmerie* and Bedouins attacked the English army, with the result that one British officer was killed and the rest fled, leaving behind their war materials. The *Shams-ul-Akhbar* thought the news was false and observed that it was similar to the story published by the Wolfe Company a short while ago, *viz.*, that the Egyptian and English armies had fallen out with each other, that blood was flowing in the streets of Cairo and that no sooner did the inhabitants of Egypt hear of the arrival of the Turks in their country than they turned the English out of it. The *Shams-ul-Akhbar* thinks that it is the Turkish officers who are spreading rumours like the above and trying to make the people believe them.

[89] *Az-zia* (Lahore), 1 January 1915

Muhammadan prisoners, who were fighting on the side of France, have been sent to Constantinople.

[90] *Akhbar-i-' Am* (Lahore), 3 January 1915

A few new-fashioned Indian Muhammadans may say that they have no connection with the Turks; but if the latter are swept out of existence, Islam, from the political standpoint, will deplore the misfortune. Indian Muhammadans consider their very existence dependent upon the mercy of the British Government and they are inactive and listless. But, instead of offering prayers and endeavouring to bring about a reconciliation between Turkey and

England, it is opposed to religious civilisation to use unbecoming language against Turkey in discussing the knotty and complicated question of the Caliphate. The late Sir Syed Ahmad Khan regarded the imitation of the Turks by Indian Muhammadans as an effective means of securing the progress of the latter. Now that the Turks have committed a political mistake in taking up arms against England, it is not proper for educated Muhammadans to call a Muslim kind silly and foolish; nor should they entirely forget the past.

[91] *Akhbar-i-' Am* (Lahore), 6 January 1915

[A fictitious correspondence between the Angel of Death and the German Kaiser, wherein the former charges the latter with massacring mankind.] In reply, the German Kaiser says that what he is doing is only a prelude to what is to follow, that he knows innumerable devices for the destruction of the world and that he can fight as long as he lives. If the whole of Poland, adds the German Kaiser, is recognised as a province, and the greater part of it is given to Austria, and if the question of letting Germany keep her fleets in the Baltic and the North Sea is solved, there is some likelihood of peace being concluded.

[92] *Bir* (Lahore), 7 January 1915

A rising against foreigners is about to take place in China. There is a movement to pay off old scores against Japan and efforts are being made to restore the deposed Manchu dynasty to the throne of China. Manchu soldiers have also revolted. It is said the revolt has taken place at the instance of the Germans, who have many spies in China. Germany is exerting herself strenuously to induce China to declare war on Japan.

[93] *Az-Zia* (Lahore), 8 January 1915
Turkish official news claims an Ottoman victory over the English and the Russians, who have been pushed beyond the Caucasian frontier, Russia suffering heavy losses in the neighbourhood of Lewan and being compelled to retreat up to the river Jaro Chak. The

mountainous tribes of Persia have also risen and are inflicting serious injury on the 'enemy' by penetrating into Russian territory.

[94] *Sirajul-Akhbar* (Jhelum), 11 January 1915

Government should allow people of all castes to work together. So far, the members of certain castes have been allowed to join the army, and it is rather curious that low caste people have been also taken in the army on their professing to belong to the higher castes. These caste distinctions should be removed at the present time, to enable a sufficiently large army to be recruited.

[95] *Jhang Sial* (Lahore), 12 January 1915

Though Persia has proclaimed her neutrality, Russia and Turkey do not allow her to live in peace. In spite of Persia's request, the Russians and the Turks do not withdraw their forces from Azerbaijan, but made it a centre of fighting. The Kurds, who tried to drive the Russians out of Urumiah, are beginning to think that Russia is fighting against Germany because the latter has embraced Islam, and that Russia herself is suffering reverses. The Kurds also wish to fight against Russia to help Germany. One of their Sheikhs, who was formerly an enemy of the Turks, is now ready to help them. The Kurds possess three German guns, and several *fidais*, under the leadership of Said-ul-Mulk, are inciting them to rise against the Russians in Azerbaijan.

[96] *Paisa Akhbar* (Lahore), 13 January 1915

Hitherto Europeans have been very proud of their descent and white skin. The fact of a man being of European descent was conclusive evidence of his being a civilised person; but if he was an Asiatic, it was taken as proving that he was an uncivilised individual. Can Asiatic nations, however, be more hard-hearted and barbarous than the Germans? Now that Indian soldiers have given proof of their civilised methods of warfare, the West will realise that European descent does not alone constitute proof of a man's being civilised and that the people of Asia also can be civilised.

[97] *Amrit* (Lahore), 15 January 1915

There was a time when the mere utterance of the word *Jehad* was sufficient to raise Musalmans against non-Muslims; and it was with the help of this talisman that the Prophet successfully fought so many battles and shed so much blood. But the progress of civilization has mitigated its effect. The Turks, at the instance of the Germans, tried the talisman in the present war by declaring that it was a holy crusade, but they have met with little success. It will be better if the question is allowed to die a natural death.

[98] *Jhang Sial* (Lahore), 23 January 1915

The conflagration of war has gradually spread over the whole of Europe and extended to Asia. When invading Kiaochau, Japan declared she would restore it to China, but Japan now refuses to do so. The Turks have resorted to a similar dodge. They have invaded Persia and declared that they have no mind to annex Azerbaijan to Turkey, but will leave it as soon as Russia withdraws her forces and the Crown Prince of Persia reaches Tabriz. Some people are satisfied with the explanation and think that the Turks violated the neutrality of Persia under circumstances similar to those in which Great Britain proceeded to help Belgium on the violation of the latter's neutrality by Germany. But they forget that the Turks are under German influence and no reliance can be placed on their word.

[99] *Zamindar* (Lahore), 24 January 1915

Although America has proclaimed her neutrality, still it appears from the recent correspondence between America and England that the relations between the two countries are not of the happiest [...] President Wilson abstains from making any mention in his speeches of the violation of Belgian neutrality by Germany [...] the President is anxious to escape from the responsibility of interfering in the matter, an anxiety that may be due to the American army and navy being so weak that America dare not throw in her lot with any of the belligerents.

[100] *Akhbar-i-' Am* (Lahore), 31 January 1915

The existing temporary union of the Powers, which have ever been rivals in politics, is not to be trusted, seeing that they are likely to change their attitude whenever it is expedient to do so. For instance, how can union between England and Russia remain steadfast? Russia has frequently defeated British foreign policy and has always conducted herself as the rival of England, both in Europe and Asia. By lending money and selling two German men-of-war to Turkey, the Germans caught the Turks in the trap of gold and iron. The Turks wanted money and battleships and not empty correspondence. Germany supplied their needs. The Allies have won over the Turks to their side by giving them 5 or 10 crores of rupees. Even the return of the two Turkish ships would have probably sufficed to secure the good will of the Turks. But British statesmen perhaps think it humiliating to pay heed to such commonplace matters.

[101] *Vakil* (Amritsar), 3 February 1915

If England comes out victorious in the war [against Turkey], her greatness will be multiplied four-fold and all distinctions of caste, creed and race will disappear from the British Empire [. . .] The greater the danger in which Turkey is involved, the larger the measure of sympathy which she will excite in the Islamic world. The Turks may have committed several mistakes, but their co-religionists must sympathise with them so long as the Turks profess Islam, and the Muslim population cannot view the destruction of the solitary independent Islamic kingdom of Turkey with complacency. At the same time, it is quite obvious that so long as the flames of war are prevented from touching the skirt of religion and the religious problems of Muhammadans, the question of the Caliphate being an instance in point, are not interfered with, Muhammadans will, in conformity with their religion, remain loyal to the Power under which they have lived in peace and comfort and will be prepared to shed their blood by fighting under its flag. All the same, English newspapers and politicians, especially those like Mr. Lloyd George who is not accustomed to weigh his words before uttering them, should never forget that the brotherly sympathy, which Muhammadans have for each other, is a living power and they should abstain from attacking Islamic feeling and inciting Muslims to hostility.

[102] *Dipak* (Lahore), 5 February 1915

The German Kaiser has not yet given up building castles in the air. He is making preparations to invade England in January 1916. New Zeppelins are being built, each of which will carry 50 bombs, which will prove effective like the shells of 15 or 16 inch guns. One thousand Germans are employed in building these Zeppelins, each of which is completed in about three weeks. The Germans think that some 18 or 19 machines of this kind will suffice for invading England. All these Zeppelins bear the inscription 'For London.'

[103] *Municipal Gazette* (Lahore), 5 February 1915

We have neither any sympathy with Russia, nor do we care for her, but we do not like the idea of the war spreading to the Indian frontiers. If the British Government does not declare war against the Persian Government or the Persian tribes, hostilities will remain confined between Russia and Persia. Great Britain has no enemies, except Germany; while from Sweden to China all are hostile to Russia. How long will our Government fight against the enemies of Russia? At the outbreak of the war, although Austria had been fighting against Russia and Servia for ten days, England did not declare war against Austria, so long as Austria did not despatch her forces to the western frontier to fight against the Allies. Similarly, it is suggested that England need not now declare war against Persia.

[104] *Prabhat* (Lahore), 6 February 1915

However barbarous and tyrannical the Germans may be, they have some regard for Indians, whom they do not desire to harass or displease. This is so because they wish that Indians should rise in revolt against the English and that Muhammadans should consider the declaration of war by Turkey as the call for *jehad* and join Turkey. The Germans do not treat Indian soldiers harshly and German officers speak a few words of Hindi with them. Recently the Germans threw from their Zeppelins printed sheets, urging Indians to revolt against the English.

[105] *Paigham-i-Sulah* (Lahore), 9 February 1915

While Reuters agency has been giving us news of the severe defeat of the Turks at Sari-Kamysh, the engagement was represented in Constantinople as a great victory and the event was celebrated with great rejoicings. The Turkish ministry was informed by two Ottoman Deputies with the army that they had taken possession of Ardahan. On this [news] flags were hoisted in Constantinople and the papers published enthusiastic articles. Count Reventolo stated at a public meeting that the whole of Germany was much pleased at the splendid victory of the Turks in the Caucasus, which assured them that the Turks would achieve a similar victory in Egypt also.

[106] *Civil and Military News* (Ludhiana), 15 February 1915

The arrival of four more German army corps in East Prussia has changed the situation. The German army has gained ground against the Russian army, which has retired to the Russian frontier. A severe engagement was probably fought on the frontier, wherein the Germans secured a victory. Russia has, therefore, announced that it is necessary to keep war news secret, and very brief details of war operations in this part of Europe will be published hereafter.

[107] *Vakil* (Amritsar), 17 February 1915

The attitude of the tribes in Azerbaijan has placed the Persian Government in a fix, and undesirable occurrences in Azerbaijan may succeed in inciting the national feeling, which the Persian Government may not be able to suppress. In view of this, and especially if Persian neutrality is not respected by the belligerents and Persia is not able to maintain her neutrality, the flames of war may spread to Afghanistan, Turkistan and Baluchistan, and finally reach the walls of India, whereby the long-cherished desire of the enemy of peace – Germany – will be realised. British statesmen should warn their ally, Russia, not to interfere with Persian neutrality. If Russian forces leave Azerbaijan, the Turks will [...] themselves depart from the province.

[108] *Desh* (Lahore), 17 February 1915

The only person who can give an approximate [...] answer to the question [of when the war will end] is the German Emperor, who commenced the war and who knows how long he can stay in the field. We should not give much credence to sensational reports. For instance, it has been reported that German military strength has been weakened, that famine is raging in Germany and that great economy is being exercised in the consumption of wheat. Such things cannot put an end to the war. The war will terminate only when the forces of the Allies gain further successes. It is premature to say more.

[109] *Paisa Akhbat* (Lahore), 18 February 1915

French statesmen desire that Japanese troops should be brought to Europe over the Siberian railway to fight against Germany. But it remains to be seen for what consideration Japan agrees to make such a heavy sacrifice. One conjecture is to the effect that after the victory of the Allies Japan will secure a portion of German territory and thus become a European power. But the idea is not feasible. No European nation, even though belonging to a third class race like the nations of the Balkan states, will tolerate the rule of an Asiatic Power. Indeed, on this very pretext, European Powers have gradually freed the Balkan states from Turkish rule. Christian Europe and the Allied Powers will find it difficult to overcome the prejudice of recognising an Asiatic sovereign as a European ruler. Moreover – and this is the most important point – the Japanese too may not care to secure any territory in Europe, for in that case they will not be as safe as they are now in their own waters. If the Japanese at all demand any territory in return for military assistance, it will probably be in close proximity to Japan and a land that will enable their superfluous population to settle there.

[110] *Zamindar* (Lahore), 24 February 1915

The greatest aspiration of Indians

During the last 57 years India has greatly changed. She has now new hopes and new aspirations. If her aspirations are legitimate, they assuredly deserve help and sympathy. The present war has still more deeply stirred up population aspirations. India now desires that her children should receive commissions in the army and command Indian armies, in the same way as Europeans do. Indians long to take part in the defence of their country side by side with their British comrades. But can the British Government trust its Indian officers? This question has been solved by the loyalty of the Indian States and the devotion and sacrifice of the Indian soldiers in the present war. A question has thus arisen in the military circles of England, as to the scions of respectable families in India being granted direct commissions. There is, however, a section of the Anglo-Indian community which ridicules Indian aspirations in this respect. But its ridicule is injuring the real interests of the Empire and Anglo-Indian editors are largely responsible for the ill-feeling which at present exists between the rulers and the ruled.

[111] *Desh* (Lahore), 26 February 1915

Refugees who have arrived at Alexandria from Baghdad claim to have read, in the course of their journey, telegrams about the war published by the Turkish officers for the information of their countrymen. Some of these telegrams announce the destruction of the British navy, the German occupation of the whole of France, the Turkish conquest of Egypt &c. If the statements of the refugees [. . . are] correct – and there is no reason to doubt their correctness – the Turkish government is keeping its subjects in the dark and has surpassed even Germany in the publication of false news.

[112] *Paisa Akhbar* (Lahore), 28 February 1915

The Turkish forts of the Dardanelles have turned out to be very strong. For the last two or three months, the Allied fleet of France

and England has been heavily bombarding the forts of the
Dardanelles, with a view to avenge the Turkish attack on the Suez
Canal. But the mouth of the Dardanelles is hardly two miles in
width; and if any man-of-war enters it without the permission of
the Turks, the latter can destroy it easily by firing from their
forts. Because of their strength, the Dardanelles forts have faced the
Allied fleet well.

[113] *Zamindar* (Lahore), 1 March 1915

The financial and economic resources of Germany have not been
exhausted. In face of this reliable information, we should not say, as is
alleged by some newspapers, that Germany has been reduced to a
state of starvation. Her financial condition is not bad, though she
cannot import grain from foreign countries. Nevertheless, the cost of
living in Germany is 10 per cent higher than in London. German
resources have not, however, reached a point that might cause anxiety
to the Germans.

[114] *Tribune* (Lahore), 9 March 1915

If difference of culture exacerbates the racial prejudice of white men
against others, surely the war will have dealt a shattering blow to
such prejudices. For if there is one fact more than another which
emerges from the war, it is that a large portion of the German
nation – white people, *par excellence* – live on an ethical level with
the Huns and possess the moral evils of the Zulus and the Masai.
That is the plain English of the doctrine of 'frightfulness.' The
inhuman atrocities in Belgium and France proclaim to all the
world the downfall of all theories of inherent moral pre-eminence of
the white man.

[115] *Zamindar* (Lahore), 10 March 1915

Every German, whether rich or poor, regards the word of the Kaiser as
the word of God. This is the reason why the Germans are gaining
victory after victory. In the eastern theatre of war [... the Germans
are also] gaining several victories.

[116] *Sher-i-Punjab* (Lahore), 11 March 1915

Although the services which the Sikhs have so far rendered have been rendered, not in the hope of compensation, but simply to discharge the duty which loyalty imposes on them, still, in view of the way in which the *Pioneer* has presented the subject [of reserving German East Africa for Indian emigrants] and also the fact that the Sikhs and the Punjabis do stand in great need of a colony where they may settle without let or hindrance, there is no reason why we should not fully support the proposal. For if the Sikhs are told that they will be allowed to settle in a certain colony after it has been conquered, they will fight all the more enthusiastically and complete the work of months in weeks.

[117] *Akhbar-i-' Am* (Lahore), 13 March 1915

The French armies are fighting with great bravery and courage in Champagne and are gradually advancing. There is no change in Flanders, and although the German armies are themselves suffering by invading this country, yet the disciples of the Kaiser do not refrain from committing mischief and are constantly making attacks. Although the Allied armies are holding their positions, yet they cannot keep the German hordes in check. But it has been reported that the British armies are guarding the English Channel, while the armies of the British Colonies and Dependencies are fighting in the battlefield. With the lapse of time, the number of British troops is increasing in the British Channel.

[118] *Siraj-ul-Akhbar* (Jhelum), 15 March 1915

Illiterate villagers are, to some extent, the originators of absurd war rumours; but in these days the wounded, who come to the hospitals of our country, narrate before the common people or their relatives' strange stories of what they have witnessed with their own eyes, which conflict with the contents of official newspapers. They should be prohibited from telling anything about the war, as such rumours especially raise obstacles in the way of recruiting new men for the army.

[119] *Mister Gazette* (Lahore), 15 March 1915

It is hoped that all the forts of the Dardanelles will be shortly reduced, when an attack will be delivered on Constantinople itself, which on conquest will be made over to Russia. We, however, fear that Russia, which is our friend to-day, may trouble us after her occupation of Turkish territory and may threaten us more than the Turks by strengthening the Dardanelles.

[120] *Al-Fazal* (Kadian), 16 March 1915

Political changes [...] are beginning to take place in the world as a result of the war. One of the consequences will be the destruction and dismemberment of the Ottoman Empire. We, however, wish that if the brave Ottomans be ever forced to give up the custody of the sacred mosque of St. Sophia, the honoured mausoleum of Ayub Ansari, and other Islamic ancient monuments, the duty of protecting the same may fall on the shoulders of the sons of Great Britain, who love liberty and truth.

[121] *Tribune* (Lahore), 17 March 1915

'Scrutator' in *Truth* comments in his own characteristic style on the anti-Indian criticism, which for some time past has been appearing in the Tory press. 'During the last few weeks,' he observes, 'it has become quite defamatory and the other day people were going about London with information that the whole Indian force was shortly to be withdrawn from the front.' Of course, no such thought could have crossed the minds of the great British statesmen, who, at [... this] psychological moment had discovered what source of strength India's millions could always be for the Empire.

[122] *Tribune* (Lahore), 24 March 1915

The new 'angle of vision' from which British statesmen propose to look at India after the war has already given us some indications. No doubt as the war progresses and the 'angle' grows wider, we shall have more. In the meantime, we must not ignore the attitude of Australians towards Indians. In a recent speech delivered by Sir Henry Galway, the Governor of South Australia, he proposed that the policy of 'white Australia' should be changed as the northern territory could not be developed by the white labour. He ventured to say that 'looking at the splendid services being rendered to the Empire by our Indian troops and by our Japanese allies,' he was one of those who thought the feelings of Australians on the colour question would undergo a change when the war was over. But this seems to have given no small offence to the white Australian party, and the Prime Minister of the Commonwealth indignantly remarked to a press representative that Sir Henry Galway's words 'constitute a grave official indiscretion which cannot be allowed to pass without notice, nor without protest.' Thereupon the latter expressed his regret for having laid the new ideal.

[123] *Punjab Samachar* (Lahore), 3 April 1915

The present war and the doomsday for Islam

The followers of Islam have been heard remarking that when Constantinople will go out of the hands of Muhammadans or the Sultan of Turkey will cease to hold the office of *Khalifar-ul-Islam* or holy places like Mecca and Medina will pass out of the hands of Muhammadan Powers, the Resurrection Day will come [...] The Turks now in authority are in reality neither believers in God, nor Muhammadans. They are, in fact, the enemies of Islam and the destroyers of the Kaaba. The Turks have looted the sacred shrine of Karbala. We emphatically assert that the Turkish party now in power is not a party of Muhammadans, but is composed of persons who bring disgrace upon Islam. This party has already shed the blood of Islam. The holy places of Muhammadans like Mecca and Medina are in the possession of Turkey in name only. Consequently, if Islamic traditions are true, the Resurrection Day has already approached.

[124] *Akhbar-i-' Am* (Lahore), 7 April 1915

Germany is losing ground everywhere. She is running short of soldiers, war material, food provisions and money; and in all these respects, the Allies are getting stronger. The scale of England and her Allies is very heavy, while that of Germany and her friends is very light. The former will, therefore, be victorious in the end.

[125] *Akhbar-i-' Am* (Lahore), 11 April 1915

The Cairo correspondent of the *Times of India* writes that, according to Arabic newspapers, nine German officers have embraced Islam. One of these is a General in the Turkish army. They have publicly become Muhammadans at Damascus and have now started to undertake the administration of Mecca and the command of the forces of that place.

[126] *Bulletin* (Lahore), 15 April 1915

A recruiting poster recently shown in London represents an angry lion surrounded by his cubs and bears the following legend: 'The Empire needs men. Australia, Canada, India, New Zealand, all answer the call. Helped by the Young Lions, the Old Lion defied his foes. Enlist now!' Unfortunately, as *India* rightly points out, nine out of every ten Indians are not permitted to do this [. . .] It is to be hoped the present war, which has been the solvent of many illusions, will open the eyes of the responsible authorities to the unwisdom of this policy of exclusion in the army recruitment for India.

[127] *Tribune* (Lahore), 29 April 1915

In the present war on the continent both Moslem and Hindu soldiers have won the much-coveted Victoria Cross and have inspired wholesome dread in German hearts, and it would seem a fitting reward if such Indian officers, as are considered well qualified, were given commission ranks in Indian regiments in France and Flanders [. . .] This would be a most appropriate recognition of the merits of Indian soldiers. The suggestion possesses the additional merit of rendering future operations more efficient than they have been.

[128] *Dipak* (Lahore), 30 April 1915

It appears from the *Siraj-ul-Akhbar* (Kabul), that 19 Muhammadan soldiers of the British Army have deserted and reached Kandahar, where they have been arrested and sent to Kabul.

[129] *Zamindar* (Lahore), 1 May 1915

The naval and military conditions of the Ottoman Empire

The German naval and military officers, who had gone to the Dardanelles, recently returned to Constantinople. They assert that the straits have been greatly strengthened and fortified with new guns. It is now quite impossible for the Allied fleet of Great Britain and France to conquer the straits [...] Thirty five thousand soldiers are at present available in the forts lying on both sides of it. These soldiers are firing from time to time on the combined fleets of the enemies [...] The Turks are enlisting in the army in large numbers. Their condition at the present moment is the same as it was in the time of Sultan Murad when he led his army even to the walls of Vienna, the capital of Austria.

[130] *Akhbar-i-ʿ Am* (Lahore), 3 May 1915

Has the Kaiser of Germany actually embraced Islam?

The Germans are still as good Christians as they formerly were. It is true that the wily Kaiser made an attempt some time ago to gain fame in the world and that it was accordingly rumoured [...] that he had embraced Islam and was about to receive help from Turkey, but this turned out in the end to be as preposterous as the one emanating from the *Bhangar Khana* of Delhi which resulted in the general massacre of Delhi by Nadir Shah.

[131] *Akhbar-i-ʿ Am* (Lahore), 10 May 1915

The special correspondent of the London *Express*, who has recently returned from Germany, says that he was surprised to find that the inhabitants of Germany had great confidence in their submarines and were convinced that they would defeat the Allies' fleet with them. It is on this account that submarines are being made now in all the naval yards of Germany. The writer proceeds to review the agricultural condition of Germany and says that the Germans have still sufficient food. While travelling in the German territory, he observed that the Germans were not in the least sad and sorrowful. From this he concludes that either the Germans have been prohibited to weep by high officials, or the death of their relatives who are fighting in the war is not communicated to them.

[132] *Desh* (Lahore), 16 May 1915

With the advent of warmer weather the war in the western theatre has, as was foretold, assumed a new aspect, and hostilities have been renewed with great energy. So far the Allies, especially the British forces, have gained the upper hand over the Germans. They first won the battle of Neuve Chapelle and subsequently that of Hill 60. The French army also defeated the Germans in several minor engagements. This must not be taken to mean that any conspicuous change has taken place in the position of the parties engaged. Nevertheless there is no cause for despair; time is on the side of the Allies. The opinion has recently been expressed by Mr. Lloyd George, as well as by General Joffre, that two or three months will see a great change in the appearance of affairs, and that change will be altogether in the Allies' favour. The army which the Allies have available in France at present is six times as large as that of the Germans, and this army is steadily increasing, while the German numbers are as steadily decreasing.

[133] *Tribune* (Lahore), 18 May 1915

A prejudiced and perverted but happily small section of Englishmen, presumably a coterie of retired Anglo-Indians, are pursuing the unpleasurable pastime of belittling the doings of Indian soldiers at the front. We have noticed many of these instances in these columns and the latest of the kind is the insinuation that the Indian officer 'in a fight which requires leading does not count.' It is astonishing how these calumniators of Indian soldiers persist in ignoring the praises showered by Field Marshal Sir John French on the heroism, tact and resourcefulness shown by Indians on countless occasions under circumstances adverse to the display of such great qualities.

[134] *Hindustan* (Lahore), 19 May 1915

[From a letter written by an Indian officer at the front] I was surprised to read to-day a passage in the *Daily Telegraph*, dated the 15th April, stating that rumours are spreading in the Punjab and other provinces that the Indian soldiers serving in the war are not well treated. I should like to contradict these false rumours and say that no distinction is made here between the English and the Indian soldier. Every possible care is shown for the Indian soldier. There is no other Government in the world that could provide for a large army in the way the British Government does. To tell the truth, the Indian soldiers are not fed as well in their own homes as they are here both in the field and in the military hospitals.

[135] *Desh* (Lahore), 20 May 1915

The English public are now being informed of the various preparations that are being made for the war. It would be very beneficial if Indians were supplied with similar information; for a knowledge of the true state of affairs would doubtless lead them to make still further sacrifices.

[136] *Desh* (Lahore), 22 May 1915

[The annexation of Mesopotamia and] its inclusion in the Empire will be of the very greatest benefit to India, as not only will it provide an outlet for the surplus population of India, but it will furnish Indian traders with a new market at not too great a distance. The question for decision is what share India is to have in colonising the new country, and what reward Indians will get for their efforts. It will be better if these questions are settled before the annexation is finally determined upon, as in the past Indians have not received rewards proportionate to the energies they devoted in colonising certain British colonies. This resulted in difficulties both in India and at home, and in order to avoid any repetition of such trouble it would be better to have the question decided at the very outset.

[137] *Dipak* (Lahore), 24 May 1915

Telegrams received from the front during the last two or three days are very encouraging. They show that while in the eastern theatre the Russians have captured three thousand Germans and several guns, in the western theatre the Allies have repulsed the Germans near Ypres. Considering that at the present moment the Allies are short of both men and munitions this state of affairs cannot but make us think that the war will not be long protracted. For it must be borne in mind that neither France nor England has yet her full strength in the field. This is apparent from Lord Kitchener's announcement that a million British troops will be dispatched to France and Belgium by the end of this month, and that a reserve of another million will be kept in England [...] England and France have been forced to use, in imitation of the Germans, asphyxiating gases [...] they have been driven, against their will, to this resource by the insensate craving for conquest of the Germans, who can only be brought to their senses by retaliatory measures. The time is fast approaching when Germany will repent her inhuman conduct in the war.

[138] *Civil and Military News* (Ludhiana), 24 May 1915

The ups and downs of the war

In the western theatre the French forces are steadily advancing northwards from Arras. They now seem to be fully equipped with munitions, and the Allies' artillery has established as ascendancy over the German gunners, while the English army near Ypres is giving a crushing defeat to the Germans. In the eastern theatre of war the Russians, although they have been compelled to retreat in the west of Galicia, continue to be successful all along the rest of the front. All this goes to show that Germany will soon be wiped out. The time is

now fast approaching when the Allies will take the offensive and force
the enemy to retire into his own territory.

[139] *Hindustan* (Lahore), 26 May 1915

A letter written by Sardar Thakar Singh, Subedar-Major of the 47th
Sikhs, to his relatives at Chak Ganda Singh, Montgomery District
[...] says that the enemy is suffering heavy losses and is retreating.
It is interesting to note, he adds, that 'the German prisoners are tired
of imprisonment and are offering themselves for arrest. When we
approach them, they throw down their rifles, and run towards us. The
enemy seems to have grown very weak, and to have given up his old
dreams of victory' [...] This letter, received directly from the field,
should do a great deal towards removing the suspicions of those
people who are frightened of the power of Germany. It will show
them that the Allies have now become so strong that they will crush
the Germans.

[140] *Dipak* (Lahore), 27 May 1915

Italy's decision will materially increase the military strength of the
Allies. The Austrian army will now be compelled to devote all its
energies towards repelling the attacks of the Italians, and large
German reinforcements will be necessary to enable them to make an
effective stand on this front. This will render the task of the Russians
very much easier. Further the German armies will not be able to be
employed in Galicia and on the western front with the same freedom
as before. Germany will now be fighting three strong powers.
We have already remarked that England alone will be able to put a
million new trained troops in the field, and France has still a very
strong reserve. These powerful additions to the Allied army, together
with the forces that Italy will be able to bring to bear, will go far
towards breaking the power of Germany and so ending the war.

[141] *Chandr* (Lahore), 28 May 1915

In spite of the very heavy losses that Germany has suffered it must not
be thought that she will die of starvation. She had been making

military preparation for a very long time, while as regards [to] her food supplies she had made complete arrangements as far back as 1911. Her alliance with Austria-Hungary also helps her food supply. Germany herself grows mustard, barley and potatoes, and she maintains thirty ships at Rotterdam, a neutral port, to bring wheat from America. She has at the present moment six million tons of meat, so that she can easily supply her armies with meat, which her savage soldiers never tire of. This shows that lack of supplies will not bring about Germany's defeat. But victory does not depend on food alone, and now that Italy has joined England, it should not be long before Germany is brought to her knees.

[142] *Intikhab-i-Lajawab* (Lahore), 28 May 1915

The weakness of the Ottoman Government and the rivalry between the various Christian governments in Europe has afforded an opportunity to the Serbs to gain independence. They are now not merely free, but have even taken possession of a large portion of the territory belonging to the Ottoman Empire. Their ambition is to get possession of that portion of Austrian territory which is inhabited by people of Servian blood; and it is this desire which has led to the present war in Europe.

[143] *Nirbal Sewak* (Lahore), 29 May 1915

The lack of correct war news is being felt in this country, and public interest has greatly decreased.

[144] *Vakil* (Amritsar), 29 May 1915

At the commencement of this great European war no one expected that Italy would, in a few months, be in a position to take up arms against her former allies. The Tripolitan war had emptied her treasury and exhausted her supply of war material to such an extent that the supply of munitions even in the forts on the Austrian frontier had been depleted. Another reason which was holding Italy back was that her encroachment on Tripoli had displeased Muhammadans generally, and she feared that if she joined in the war the Saracens of

Tripoli would give trouble. But it seems that Italy has now overcome these difficulties. Her treasury is full, she has procured an adequate supply of war material, and she has apparently no longer any cause for anxiety regarding Tripoli. Italy will be able to render valuable services to the Allies in the Mediterranean and the Dardanelles, and do immense harm to Turkey. It goes without saying, however, that the war between Austria and Italy will be fought out mainly on land [...] The result of Italy's participation in the war will be that Austria will have to loosen her grip on Galicia and turn her attention to the Italian frontier, thus liberating the Russian armies.

[145] *Desh* (Lahore), 30 May 1915

The trading vessel *Nabraskan* was carrying a large American flag when she was torpedoed by the Germans. The fact that the vessel was sunk in twilight shows that the act was not due to any mistake, but that the plot had been prepared beforehand. The whole affair gives credence to the idea that the Germans are prepared to fight America. It now remains to be seen what action America takes in connection with the destruction of her vessel.

[146] *Zamindar* (Lahore), 1 June 1915

The situation [in Gallipoli] is extremely difficult; for although our troops can maintain themselves easily as long as they remain entrenched, any advance is rendered difficult by the enemy's sharp-shooters, who pick off any man who ventures to come out of the trenches.

[147] *Tribune* (Lahore), 8 June 1915

Wounded Indian soldiers have returned home by the thousand. The enthusiastic and grateful terms in which they speak of the treatment given to Indian soldiers have been forgotten, while parlour stories of one or other of the several cantonments whispered into the ears of some correspondent are freely published for the world by the yellow press in England. It is a libel on Indians to say that they entertain any but the most grateful feelings towards the military authorities at home for their kindly attentions to our soldiers. The Government of India might give a little thought to the necessity of controlling the less responsible section of the correspondents in India who write or telegraph to the British press. These would be doing great disservice to this country if they continued to give prominence in the manner noticed to reports which even if current anywhere no one believes.

[148] *Tribune* (Lahore), 9 June 1915

We have it from such sympathetic Englishmen as Lord Hardinge, Mr. Montagu and Mr. Roberts that India after the war will be treated handsomely. We hope that the new spirit of imperial unity will be real and strong enough to secure to India the full measure of equality and status to which every other part is entitled. After the signal proof of loyalty and devotion which India has given, there should be no hesitation felt and no offending doubts cast upon India by British statesmen. Men of the type of Lord Curzon and certain class of Anglo-Indians prejudiced against Indians may wish to perpetuate the inequalities of the present and the follies of the past. But they would be making a tremendous mistake if they thought that Indians who have suffered patiently so far would continue to suffer in future also. There are great changes coming over the understanding and temper of the people. They have made up their minds that their destinies are firmly linked with those of the British nation and of this they are prepared to give any proof. But along with the new imperial responsibilities, they have also recognised certain rights, certain status and privileges which they will no longer treat with indifference.

[149] *Tribune* (Lahore), 11 June 1915

People in India who have read the accounts of warfare in the Hindu period such as the Mahabharata and the Ramayana campaigns, will find that the atrocities practised in Belgium by a nation claiming to be civilised have no parallel in the history of the civilised world – ancient or modern. Of course, semi-civilised and barbarous nations have during the dark ages in every country practised oppression and cruelties of the worst order. But in their case, it must be stated that they were neither civilised nor had developed their arts and ethics to any high standard. But mankind claims to be highly refined at the present day, having acquired considerable mental acuteness and mechanical perfections which have enabled them to assert a powerful and 'superior' position. Germanism has, therefore, staggered mankind in the falsity of such claims, and we in India know well enough how moral superiority to be genuine should be tested in times of national danger and adversity. The Germans, finding themselves thwarted in their ambition, did not hesitate to resort to barbaric methods of warfare, because evidently their civilisation is not based on the highest principles of humanity but on those of material wealth and intellectual skill.

[150] *Nirbal Sewak* (Lahore), 11 June 1915

Although the co-operation of Italy will undoubtedly be a very great asset to the Allies, it must not be expected that Italy will be able to put more than a million men in the field. It is true that Italy has done her utmost to strengthen her military forces and to make up the deficiency which was the natural result of the Tripolitan War. But she has recently been engaged in a continuous series of wars, and however complete her preparations may be she will inevitably be hampered by financial difficulties, and will find it hard to continue the war into the winter.

[151] *Panjabee* (Lahore), 22 June 1915

The question of the treatment of Indian war prisoners in Germany is one of considerable interest to our people. Lord Curzon earned our undying gratitude by raising this question in his usual pointed manner in the House of Lords. It is unfortunately the case that official reports on the subject in England have had nothing specific to say about this class of prisoners. No one can for a moment believe that His Majesty's Government have been less anxious to secure proper and humane treatment in the case of Indian prisoners than they have been in regard to English prisoners, but the silence of the official reports was obviously liable to be misunderstood. The question raised by Lord Curzon will have the wholesome effect of leading His Majesty's Government to take steps with a view to the removal of such misunderstanding. At present all that we know is from unofficial sources.

[152] *Vakil* (Amritsar), 23 June 1915

The fact that Germany is fighting in this war simply to gain her own military ends robs her of any claim to credit or sympathy; but there is one quality possessed by the Germans which must be not only appreciated but imitated. This is their intense patriotism. Every German is determined to serve his country; it is immaterial whether he considers she is fighting in a just or an unjust cause.

[153] *Paisa Akhbar* (Lahore), 23 June 1915

The American Government has threatened to break diplomatic relations with Germany in the event of any American ship being sunk or any American passenger travelling in a neutral vessel being killed. This incident raises the question whether America is really ready for war, and what injuries she could inflict on Germany if she decided to go to war. She could help England and France with all her fleet, and after destroying the coast defences of Germany could land the Allied armies on Germany's own soil, thus putting Germany in an impossible position [...] America's intervention would prove an overwhelming factor: Germany will be making a glaring mistake if she fails to put a proper estimate on the power of America before engaging in a deadly conflict with her.

[154] *Tribune* (Lahore), 25 June 1915

Even in India the effect of the war is acutely felt by the rich and the poor alike. Trade has fallen off, industries and manufactures have collapsed, and prices have risen all round. Credit having fallen practically to zero point, normal activity has been generally suspended. These are but a few directions in which the effect of the war has been felt in this country. We need not say anything of administrative and political changes that were found necessary. But it appears the grim reality of the war was not impressed on the average Australian until the return of wounded soldiers [. . .] Australians, especially the rural folk, who by the way are not ignorant and untaught, must be a singularly unimaginative people not to feel how terribly real this devastating war has been. We in the Punjab are perhaps getting a larger number of wounded soldiers than other parts of the overseas dominions and dependencies. But it can be truthfully stated that the classes in India corresponding to the Australians mentioned above realised war very much earlier.

[155] *Panjabee* (Lahore), 3 July 1915

It is perfectly clear that the temporary reverses recently sustained by Russia have in no way dampened her enthusiasm. This is as it should be. In a war like the present, temporary reverses must be regarded as things of course. A nation which has now for many years been employing all the resources of civilisation to perfect its machinery for killing fellowmen is not a nation that can be crushed at one blow. The process of crushing it must take its own time, and in the interval the operations must be attended with varying fortunes. Only the end is certain. And it is the certainty of the end from which the Allies must derive their strength and inspiration as well as from the conviction that the cause for which they have been fighting is nothing less than the scared cause of the world's liberty.

[156] *Jhang Sial* (Lahore), 7 July 1915

When the present war broke out and Indians showed their loyalty to the Empire in its hour of need, it was hoped that the old invidious distinctions between Indians and Europeans would be abolished. These hopes have not been realised. On the outbreak of war great efforts were made in Great Britain to obtain young officers from the great universities and to give them military training. Indian students at Oxford and Cambridge thereupon offered their services. The offer was refused, and the decision very naturally caused great disappointment among the students. In England as well as in India the same distinction is shown, and it is not merely a distinction of colour, but a distinction of religion. Hindus and Muhammadans are debarred from enlisting as volunteers. If they adopt Christianity they are accepted without hesitation. Such a distinction is altogether opposed to the principles of British rule.

[157] *Nirbal Sewak* (Lahore), 9 July 1915

The defeat of Turkey is imminent. There can be no doubt that the series of defeats which Russia has suffered and is suffering encouraged Turkey in her defence of Constantinople and the Bosporus. But the British attack on the Dardanelles is proceeding towards a successful issue and is a source of great danger to Turkey. Italy is also likely to join in this attack; but it will be well to remember that Italy will be heavily engaged with Austria, and will not be able to use any very great force in the direction of the Dardanelles.

[158] *Tribune* (Lahore), 10 July 1915

In marked contrast to inhuman and galling treatment as often meted out to British prisoners of war by the agents of the several enemy countries, stands out the marked clemency shown by the General Officer commanding the British forces in Mesopotamia to twenty-eight prisoners of war captured during the Qurnah-Amara operations. They were enemies taken during fighting and were lawful prisoners and, by the terms of international law, they could be interned during the continuance of the war, and their release at this juncture is a consideration which they were not entitled to claim as of right. These prisoners included two Imams, Turkish military divines and several religious volunteers connected with Karbala and other Muhammadan Holy Places, and the British General not only did a graceful act in letting off these men of religion as an act of humanity, but also evidenced a sympathetic attitude towards Islam, which should be highly appreciated by all Moslem subjects of the King-Emperor in particular. A public ceremony was held on the occasion, attention of the populace being drawn to the mark of clemency and the kindly attitude of the British Government. Ever since the outbreak of the war which has been forced upon her against her will, England has done her utmost to safeguard the interests of Islam in connection with the Holy Places and in other respects, in spite of the attitude of Turkey herself, and this latest act is but one more indication of the same solicitude.

[159] *Panjabee* (Lahore), 13 July 1915

It is necessary in the interests of all concerned to bring the war to a speedy end; and there is no more effective way of bringing it to a speedy end than by raising citizen armies in India. In his speech Lord Kitchener paid a tribute to the Dominions and India for their splendid efforts. We do not know if the Colonies have done their best. Speaking of our own country we may say that she has not been permitted to do her best.

[160] *Panjabee* (Lahore), 14 July 1915

When precisely the settlement will be, no man at least in India knows. We can only ask our people not to be too sanguine. The great British race is at heart just and generous, and there are evident indications of a change in the angle of vision even of those who are more directly concerned in the Government of India. But the change may not be quite adequate, and justice and generosity may fail to assert themselves either through ignorance or for other reasons. For one thing we have powerful opponents both in India and England, the representatives of vested interests, who may be depended upon to do their best or their worst to prevent England from doing the right thing, even if she were inclined to do it.

[161] *Vakil* (Amritsar), 17 July 1915

The British casualties [...] are of course far lighter than those of either France or Russia, but the British army being an army of picked men, it is the very finest of England's manhood that is being lost. It is the regular thing that the autocracy tends to be swept out of existence in war. The fighting families reach their zenith and are then swept away. This phenomenon was very marked in the Wars of the Roses.

[162] *Desh* (Lahore), 23 July 1915

Reports have been received that the German Ambassador has left Constantinople with his staff; that the Turks are anxious to come to terms with the Allies; and that their representatives have reached Bulgaria on their way to Switzerland to treat for peace. In spite of the great natural and artificial strength of the defensive positions held by the Turks in Gallipoli, it is clear that the final forcing of the straits and the capture of the capital will not be long delayed; and the difficulties which Germany is feeling with regard to her supply of war munitions go to show that she will not be able to hold out for any great length of time. Probably these are the reasons that have led to Turkey's efforts for peace. She feels that she may get better terms at the present moment than she is likely to do later.

[163] *Akhbar-i-' Am* (Lahore), 25 July 1915

The Russians have been compelled to retreat before the heavy German artillery, but it would be quite a mistake to infer from this that the Russian soldier is inferior to the German. Even if Warsaw falls and the Russians are obliged to evacuate Poland no decisive result will have been attained. The Russians will be fighting nearer their base and Germany will be in a worse position than before. The Germans evidently have no desire to keep their armies permanently engaged on this front; their idea is to force a Russian retreat and then transfer a large part of their forces to the western theatre. Germany may gain temporary or partial successes, but the general situation is in favour of the Allies.

[164] *Tribune* (Lahore), 25 July 1915

Another fact which is likely to add considerably to the delicacy of this question [regarding Indians and military commissions] is that Indian soldiers who are to-day fighting shoulder to shoulder with their British and colonial comrades, facing common dangers, enduring common hardships and sharing common glory will return to this country with a broader outlook, wider experience, greater knowledge and higher aspirations. Their services have admittedly been of the utmost value to the Empire in this hour of England's greatest need. Slow as they are they cannot fail to perceive with perfect clearness that their risks being equal, their prospects should also be equal. The invidious distinction was sufficiently galling already; it will become twice as galling after their return from Europe. Their intercourse with the citizens of European countries, their exchange of ideas with them under conditions of war which have the wonderful effect of levelling distinctions, their contact with the free institutions of Great Britain and other European countries, and the manner in which they have been received by foreigners and treated by their own officers cannot fail to instil into them a spirit which will resent the badge of inferiority which has hitherto been placed on them.

[165] *Dipak* (Lahore), 26 July 1915

The Russians [...] are bound ultimately to prove successful in Galicia. The enemy's offensive may effect a few rapid successes in Poland, but eventually it must lose its force. Russia, on the other hand, though temporarily unsuccessful will certainly come out victorious in the end. The successes which Germany has gained in the western theatre are not of any importance, and the success of the British war loans is bound to have a disheartening effect on Germany. If the war is long protracted, both Austria and Germany will be reduced to a condition of insolvency.

[166] *Urdu Bulletin* (Lahore), 29 July 1915

The loyalty and bravery displayed by the Indian soldiers in the present war has again revived the question of awarding them commissions in the Army [...] The enthusiasm, bravery and loyalty which Indian armies are displaying in Europe, Asia and Africa have no parallel. Surely these services should be rewarded by granting Indian officers their real rights and by raising them to commissioned rank. We have every hope that one of the reforms which will be effected in the administration of India on the termination of the war will be the grant of equal treatment to military officers without distinction of nationality.

[167] *Desh* (Lahore), 1 August 1915

A year of war

None of the belligerents have so far gained their object; but the situation is altogether in the Allies' favour. They are convinced of the certainty of ultimate victory and will fight on till Germany is finally crushed. The last few months have shown that the war is certain to be protracted. It is true that the Allies have not yet begun to attack in France and Belgium; that the Dardanelles are not yet forced; that Germany is pushing on towards Warsaw. But none of these things need discourage the Allies. The Russian armies are daily increasing in strength, and Germany can gain no permanent success against her. The very vastness of the field of operations and the difficulties of terrain are in Russia's favour. The attack on the Dardanelles is proceeding successfully; while on the western front the Allies are strongly entrenched, and will be able to repulse the tired armies which the enemy may bring up from the eastern theatre. The Italian campaign against Austria is going on satisfactorily. The Germans may hold most of Belgium and a part of France and may have penetrated into Russian Poland; but the events of the year show that they have gained no conspicuous success, and they have failed entirely to crush Russia or to dishearten the Allied armies in France. Meantime Germany's fleet has been shut up in the Kiel Canal, her trade has ceased to exist, and all her colonies except one or two have been taken from her. Her losses will be enormous if the war is prolonged and she must eventually yield to the Allies.

[168] *Tribune* (Lahore), 6 August 1915

The 4th of August has come and gone. It is the day on which a year ago England threw herself into the war to repel an unrighteous invasion and to maintain the integrity of small and helpless states against the aggression and rapacity of an enemy which knows no law and respects no treaties. The last twelve months have brought home to humanity the grim fact that in the pursuit of her nefarious

designs Germany has as little regard for the instincts of humanity as
for the principles of warfare. It was in the fitness of things that the
anniversary of that day, so long as the war continues, should be
observed as a solemn day throughout the world-wide British
Empire, and wherever subjects of King George may be found. It is a
day of stern and inflexible resolve – a determination to carry the war
through at all cost – men, money and material must be found
ungrudgingly, unhesitatingly and with a fervour born of the
righteousness of the cause – to lay at the altar of country, Empire
and humanity. It is a day of prayer and supplication to invoke the
intervention of the Almighty on behalf of the cause of Great Britain
and her Allies. It is a day of thanksgiving that we are on the side of
right and truth.

[169] *Tribune* (Lahore), 10 August 1915

The long expected news of the evacuation of Warsaw has at last been
received, but there is no reason to be down-hearted. It is only a
strategic move, and it has been carefully planned and dexterously
carried out. The Germans may retain temporarily occupation of the
historic city, but the Russians are sure to make good their promise to
grant autonomy for Poland. We may be sure that Poland will
meanwhile show her loyal adherence to the ideal of autonomy under
the Russian Crown. What is worthy of notice in the evacuation is the
methodical manner in which it has been effected by the Grand Duke
without wasting men and material.

[170] *Shahid* (Lahore), 11 August 1915

A new weapon which the Germans are using for close fighting [. . .]
consists of a syringe, carried on the soldier's back and filled half with
air and half with oil. When this is pressed it discharges a current of
fire, which causes death with great agony.

[171] *Desh* (Lahore), 11 August 1915

At the beginning of the war the Russians took the offensive and
invaded Germany; but they were subsequently compelled to take up

a defensive position on their own frontier. The task which the enemy then set himself was so to weaken the military strength of Russia as to render her incapable of advancing into Galicia when the Germans took the offensive in France. The Germans hoped thus to be able to bring their full force to bear against the British and the French armies. But though they have succeeded in forcing the Russians back and compelling them to evacuate Warsaw, still they have failed to weaken the military strength of their enemy. The Russians will be able to carry out their original object and take the offensive when the great attack in the west is delivered. Germany will then have to fight France and England on one side, Russia on another and Servia and Montenegro on a third.

[172] *Desh* (Lahore), 13 August 1915

In spite of the fact that the Russian Prime Minister on the occasion of the anniversary of the war admitted that the British Government had rendered the most conspicuous services to the Allies in the war, Germany is nevertheless sedulously endeavouring to create general misapprehension by declaring that Great Britain has done nothing in the war. But no one can deny the brilliant achievements of Great Britain in the war. It is no exaggeration to say that it was the British army alone which effectually checked the rapid advance of the German forces towards Paris. Besides, the British sea power is bound to have a great effect on the ultimate issue. The blockade of Germany especially and the bottling up of the German navy in the Kiel Canal, which have effectually arrested the development and progress of German trade, arts and industries, will largely contribute towards ending the war in the Allies' favour [...] Great Britain has organised an army of three million men, the greater part of which is already in the field [...] she has collected apart from taxation twenty-five million pounds in various funds. All these facts show that Great Britain has taken a very great part in the present war. Her achievements have no parallel in history, and must prove of the very greatest assistance to the Allies in enabling them successfully to prosecute the war.

[173] *Watan* (Lahore), 19 August 1915

It is stated by a Russian general that the Germans have now adopted new tactics. General Mackensen was observed employing these for the first time at Lodz. They select a point on which they make a concentrated attack with their entire strength. General Mackensen makes very great use of artillery. He divides his artillery into three or four rows. The first row consists of field guns. The second is formed of guns of medium size. Behind them are guns of 6 and 8 inches, 122 calibre and behind them again 9 and 12 inch guns. Such a combination can only be effectively countered by the use of artillery of an equal quantity and quality. The range of the Russian field-guns, however, is so limited that its shells cannot touch the enemy. Had it been otherwise, the enemy would have been crushed by 12 inch guns.

[174] *Desh* (Lahore), 21 August 1915

When the war is over Indian expectations will be realised and all Indian difficulties will be put straight. Rulers and ruled will be reconciled and Hindus and Muhammadans will cease to quarrel. All the aspirations for which prayers have been offered for years will be realised. England will issue orders for the grant of autonomy to India as a reward for her sacrifices. Free compulsory education will be introduced and schools will be stated in every village. The Arms Act will be repealed and the people of India will be allowed to carry daggers and lances. The authorities will stop no newspapers, nor demand security from presses. All the world will be open to us, and we shall not be condemned in foreign countries.

[175] *Akhbar-i-' Am* (Lahore), 25 August 1915

Germany has suffered heavily. Her army has been totally destroyed, and her connections with the outer world have been severed. At least 141,660 German families are living on the charity of the Berlin municipality. In the first month of the war 62,980 German families were starving. In June a quarter of a million was spent on the relief of starving persons, and fifty thousand pounds were given to the needy families of Germany by way of charity to enable them to pay up their house-rents and other expenses. But in spite of all this, the German army has partially succeeded in its objects. The German fleet, however, is so cowed that it never ventures to come out of the Kiel Canal. Italy is greatly harassing Austria, the ally of Germany. Russia has appreciated the deeds which the brave Allies are accomplishing on land and sea in the Dardanelles and Gallipoli. She has thanked the Allies in emphatic terms, and has stated that the retreat of the Russian army is not unconnected with strategic reasons, and that she is watching an opportunity completely to overpower the enemy.

[176] *Siraj-ul-Akhbar* (Jhelum), 30 August 1915

In the present war the sword and the rifle play a very small part indeed, and all the fighting is being carried on by means of machinery. Among other instances of the use of machinery [...] Germany adopted petroleum for use in the trench warfare, and her example was followed by the French. It is due to this that the Germans have not been able to advance a step further on French soil since their original invasion. Motor-guns, aeroplanes, Zeppelins and cruisers are all worked by machinery. Fighting now-a-days does not consist of a display of physical strength and skill in swordsmanship. This is a war of machinery, carried on with the help of science and ingenuity.

[177] *Akhbar-i-'Am* (Lahore), 4 September 1915

Germany has, in the pride of her strength, always supposed that she could single-handed[ly] withstand half of Europe and overawe the other half. She has believed that in consequence of her handling of the Russian army in Galicia and her invasion of the Baltic Provinces, the neutral powers would be overawed and join her. But the constant reverses of the Russian army were really due to the shortage of ammunition, which also accounted for the slow progress of the English and French armies. The Kaiser is well aware that the life and death of his nation depend on victory and defeat in the present war, and that is the reason why the German campaign is now showing signs of unusual activity. He thinks that if Germany is to gain a victory at all, she should gain it soon. The Germans assert that when they declared war, the German force stood at eight million and three hundred thousand men. If we deduct from this figure four millions as the number of troops fighting in both the eastern and western theatres of the war, three-quarters of a million as the troops who are under training, together with two millions as the number employed in different works, the balance is a little over a million and a half, which must be the number of troops killed in the war. If so, the standing army of Germany is not capable of withstanding the innumerable horde of the Allies. The Kaiser realises this and apprehends that he will have to make peace in the end and yield to the terms of the Allied Powers.

[178] *Desh* (Lahore), 8 September 1915

A perusal of the speech of the Russian Foreign Minister in the Duma shows that the Germans are vigorously carrying on their machinations in Persia. They are distributing money to the Persians to induce them to create disturbances and are organising armed societies, supplying arms, machine guns and ammunition to the people. Russia took measures for the suppression of German intrigues, but could not succeed, owing to the existence of permanent causes of disturbance in the country. Great Britain is also helping Persia in suppressing German machinations, and it is hoped that quiet will be soon restored.

[179] *Akhbar-i-' Am* (Lahore), 9 September 1915

German spies have created a disturbance in Persia, with the result that rebellions have broken out and a strong tide of feeling against Great Britain and Russia is passing over Persia. The Tsar of Russia has, therefore, felt the need of sending a powerful army to the country to check the tide. A Russian newspaper learns that the German agents are going about in Persia and purchasing articles of copper. They have also given out that they will purchase old brass and copper guns from the Teheran arsenal. This shows that the number of guns and rifles is daily decreasing in the German army.

[180] *Desh* (Lahore), 11 September 1915

Before the outbreak of war the total area of the British Empire was 11,445,862 square miles. To this area the war has added 3,236,000 square miles, that is, about a third as much again. Of the newly acquired territory, an area of about a hundred thousand square miles has fallen to Australia and about 1,050 square miles to New Zealand. This total, however, does not include Mesopotamia, which has been conquered by the Indian troops. It seems likely that the administration of Mesopotamia will be handed over to India. This is as it should be. Mesopotamia is not only near India in [. . . terms] of distance, but resembles it in many ways. It is very suitable for Indian colonisation and it will be encouraging if the country is placed under the Indian administration. The increase in the area of the British Empire on account of the war will still further add to the power of the British Government; and it is the prayer of the Indian people that the Government may always continue to rise and that its enemies and ill-wishers may be brought low.

[181] *Desh* (Lahore), 12 September 1915

At the beginning of the war when Lord Hardinge's message telling of India's loyalty and her readiness to help Great Britain was read in Parliament, not only the members of Parliament themselves but the whole British public and the whole British press were loud in their praise of India. The view was repeatedly expressed that India had a great future before her and that she would be granted self-government under the British Government. These views were still heard when the year 1914 came to an end. In the subsequent year the Indians remained as steadfast in their loyalty as ever and continued to give practical proof of their devotion to the British Government on the battlefield. It is hard to see why all the enthusiasm and ardour evoked in the minds of the British people has subsided [. . .] The India of 1915 is the same as she was in 1914. The change, therefore, which has taken place in the attitude of the majority of British statesmen towards her must naturally cause her some anxiety. But probably the reason for this change is that the British statesmen and

Ministers are devoting their entire attention to the war. We should rest assured that when at the end of the war the time for the settlement arrives, India will not be forgotten and her desires will be realised. The India of to-day is not the India of Lord Landsdowne or Lord Curzon.

[182] *Kashmiri Magazine* (Lahore), 21 September 1915

An instance of Turkish nobility

People who are acquainted with the Turks realise that the Turks are not like the Germans, but they are perfect soldiers whose bravery and gallantry are undeniable [. . .] At one point in the Caucasus the Turkish and the Russian trenches ran close to one [an]other, and in the intervening space lay a wounded Russian soldier. But owing to the fire of the Turkish artillery the Russians could not venture into the open to carry away the wounded soldier. The Russian soldiers were waiting for the dark to get out of the trenches. Meanwhile a Russian lady, who was with the Russian Army as a nurse, at once got out of the trench and bravely made for the wounded soldier. The Russians were paralysed with fear, thinking as they all did that she could not possibly return alive and that the Turks would make her a target for their fire. But not a shot did the Turks fire. They watched the lady till she reached the wounded soldier, who slowly walked towards the Russian trenches with her support. Then the Turkish officer called out loudly from the trenches praising the gallantry of her action.

[183] *Khalsa Akhbar* (Lahore), 1 October 1915

Russia has done a great deal towards helping the cause of freedom. She announced freedom for Poland on the very outbreak of the war and is now thinking of extending a similar concession to Finland. The Russian proposal strengthens the demand of freedom for India under the aegis of the British Crown. When a Government like the Russian [one] is helping the cause of freedom, it may confidently be hoped that the British Government will grant freedom to India on the conclusion of the war.

[184] *Desh* (Lahore), 6 October 1915

It is clear that the situation in Bulgaria is critical. Germany is using all her powers to force Bulgaria to fight with her neighbours, and those who hold the reins of power in the Balkan States are willing to submit to Germany's persuasions.

[185] *Desh* (Lahore), 7 October 1915

The recent successes of the Allies on the western frontier are the prelude to the great advance which has been planned for months past, and in driving out the enemy from strongly fortified trenches they have achieved signal success. If the driving power of the Allies is as great as we have reason to believe it is, the Germans will not be able to make a stand. The question of the supply of munitions has been solved. Great Britain is quite ready to land new forces in France and the recent attack on the Germans will be the beginning of the end. The Allies will now succeed in forcing back the Germans in this area.

[186] *Paisa Akhbar* (Lahore), 8 October 1915

Russia's strong action in sending an ultimatum to Bulgaria [...] will smash the network of German intrigue. But if Bulgaria still persists in joining Germany in the war, it may be safely concluded that her future will not remain unaffected and her dreams of re-gaining her lost possessions and rising to the position of a great Power will receive a rude knock on the head. Although Russia may not at present be able to carry on a campaign against Bulgaria, via the Black Sea or through Rumania, still if Bulgaria pays no heed to the Tsar's ultimatum Russia will cut off her friendly relations with Bulgaria and remain on the look-out for an opportunity to punish her properly.

[187] *Desh* (Lahore), 9 October 1915

Germany [...] has reached a stage where she can never dream of victory, and will be soon suing for peace; because she is aware that a peace made on the settlement of final issues will not be so advantageous to her as a peace concluded before the final settlement.

[188] *Bulletin* (Lahore), 10 October 1915

The unscrupulous machinations of the wily Hun and the Magyar have carried Bulgaria to such a dangerously delicate position that it becomes extremely hazardous, with the present information before us, to venture any guess as regards Bulgarian policy and even the future Balkan combination. But one cannot help expressing regret and surprise how the Bulgars, with the Turkish lesson before them, allowed themselves to be gulled by the Central Powers, and went to the extent of permitting German and Austrian officers inundating their country and actually importing them with a view to actively directing the Bulgarian army.

[189] *Paisa Akhbar* (Lahore), 10 October 1915

If properly trained the Persian army might become the best of armies. It is, however, a pity that Persian statesmen are sleeping and have not learnt a lesson from their past mistakes. Russia has always been anxious to invade Persia and has recently succeeded in capturing Azerbaijan and Tabriz. Even this has not succeeded in opening the eyes of the Persians. Indeed but for the British influence in southern Persia the country would have become Russian territory long ago.

[190] *Paisa Akhbar* (Lahore), 23 October 1915

The British soldiers [. . .] are remarkably unanimous in their opinions on the fighting qualities of the Turks. They like the clear and straightforward way in which the Turks carry on the war. They admit that the Turks are first-rate soldiers, and tell many stories to show this. On one occasion a party went out to bury their dead comrades. By accident the Turks came out to the same spot. The two parties had a long friendly conversation, in the course of which the Turks declared that they had no idea at all why they were fighting against the British, whom they always regarded as their best friends, and that in fighting with them they were merely obeying the commands of the authorities. All these incidents go to strengthen the belief of those who hold that the Turks are by nature of a gentlemanly character, but

that at the present moment they are mere puppets in the hands of a
few scheming politicians.

[191] *Desh* (Lahore), 28 October 1915

During the past few months the Russians have not merely checked the
progress of the Germans, but have actually defeated them in several
places. The German generals [. . .] have altogether failed to achieve the
object which they hoped to gain by their offensive in the eastern
theatre. They have failed to envelop or destroy the Russian field
armies. Their plan to endanger Petrograd by capturing Riga has
come to nothing. Twice the German fleet has been defeated and
compelled to retire. The Germans also failed to capture Riga at the
end of September when they attacked the place from land with long
range guns. Their dream that the capture of Poland would force
Russia to make peace also remained unrealised. Germany put a great
temptation before Russia when she offered to make peace and
promised to allot her territory in Galicia. But even this effort proved
a failure. As for Russia herself, it should be remembered that factories
have been now started in the country where abundant ammunition is
being prepared; and recent events show that the Russians will soon
inflict a crushing defeat on the Germans. Russia has undoubtedly lost
several hundred thousand men in the war, but she is preparing a
further two million to put in the field at the end of the winter.
According to Russian experts the enemy has lost half of his troops
since he came to Poland; the total number of his troops being three
and a half million. It appears from the statements made by the
German and Austrian prisoners that neither Germany nor Austria
have any further reserve of troops and are now sending old men of
fifty to the front. These facts show how serious the exhaustion of the
German resources is.

[192] *Panjab Samachar* (Lahore), 30 October 1915

So far Berlin has been enjoying every advantage in the game. But Servia
is fighting with great gallantry and will be regularly helped by the
Allies. A glance, however, at the present military situation shows that

the end of the war is still far off, and that England has not yet brought into the field all the troops that will be required from her. As matters stand it will not be surprising if some system of conscription is introduced in England, especially as without conscription the wishes of Lord Kitchener do not appear to be realised. As for the continual stories that there is a dearth of foodstuffs in Germany, and that the public and the police are at loggerheads in the streets of Berlin, it should be remembered that these rumours are only rumours. It is also reported that there is a famine of copper in Germany. All these rumours were set afloat by the Germans themselves in order to impress it on America that owing to the British maritime blockade the people of Germany were dying of starvation. The outbreak of war in the Balkans has brought a new element into the situation. We should, however, neither feel bewildered nor unduly elated whatever may happen, but should rather patiently watch the progress of events.

[193] *Desh* (Lahore), 10 November 1915

Lord Kitchener has stated that the Germans are now in a state of exhaustion and that the utmost they can now hope for is to spend the winter in the trenches. Whatever the cause of this may be, the Russians will gain breathing time to train their armies and to manufacture munitions; and they will be able to bring men, guns and ammunition against the Germans in the spring. The Germans, on the other hand, will by that time be very short of men and ammunition. The Allies have already the superiority in actual numbers, and these numbers will go on continually increasing, while the enemy's numbers will continue diminishing unless they succeed in winning over the neutral powers to their side, and thus secure a direct line of communication with Turkey; and this, if there is any truth in the news at present coming from the seat of war, is not probably. Germany and Austria cannot long go on raising additional troops, but the Allies can secure new armies for an unlimited period. The utmost that the enemy can do is to bring back troops from Russia to reinforce their fronts in Belgium and France. The Germans have received a distinct check in Russia and have signally failed to achieve the object which they had in view when they invaded that country. As a matter of fact the Germans hold a large but useless area in Russia. They were able neither to destroy the armies of Russia, not to break the resolute spirit of her people. The losses which Germany has suffered during the summer campaign have permanently crippled her military power, and have brought the end of the war perceptibly nearer.

[194] *Panjab Samachar* (Lahore), 27 November 1915

Lord Brassey declared [before representatives of the Australian press] that he had not met a single naval or military officer who did not hold that the expedition [on the Dardanelles] was a gross blunder. Mr. Churchill was a bold administrator, but he failed entirely to realise the difficulties involved in such a campaign. Lord Brassey gave a detailed account of the history of the campaign, and declared that the Government should have [. . .] realised the futility of all its efforts to bring the endeavour to a successful conclusion, and should have saved the army so much unnecessary loss in men and material.

[195] *Desh* (Lahore), 4 December 1915

England and France [. . .] are straining every nerve to augment their field forces, and the British Colonies and Dependencies are similarly rendering every form of assistance to the mother country. This state of affairs naturally gives rise to the question why India has not contributed her full share in men, and why practical measures have been officially adopted to recruit a large army from this country. It is true that recruiting does continue in India; but the number of recruits secured so far is very small when the vast population of India and the enthusiastic loyalty which the war has evoked in the country are compared. There can be no doubt that if adequate arrangements were made an army of twenty million could be raised in India. The enthusiasm with which the Indians have welcomed the opportunity of active service and the bravery and self-restraint shown by them on every occasion since the war began have once and for all removed the wrong impression which obsessed the minds of certain people that

Indian soldiers are not equal to European soldiers. It is true that Government will have to face various difficulties in raising a large Indian army, but when more troops are admittedly required in order to crush the enemy, and when good soldiers can be procured in sufficient numbers from India, it is essential that Indians should be recruited in large numbers.

[196] *Paisa Akhbar* (Lahore), 10 December 1915

Such news as the report that the Austrian soldiers are not enthusiastic for the war must be accepted with caution, as it cannot be wholly true. It is obvious that Austria must be grateful to Germany for engaging in a campaign against the Servians whom she herself had failed to conquer, and for co-operating with her in bringing about the present universal war owing to the murder of an Austrian prince. It is difficult to see how Austria has dissociated herself from the Kaiser's schemes of world domination. She cannot do other than throw in her lot with the Kaiser in his war of deception and fraud, although there are moments when she may very well fell the impropriety of an alliance with Germany and sigh for peace.

[197] *Desh* (Lahore), 10 December 1915

The present war [. . .] has not only weakened the foundations of Europe, but has also infused a new life into Asia. It is indeed actually the war which has awakened Asia and infused a longing for progress. This awakening is far more active than that which Europe felt in the eighteenth century [. . .] A great change will take place in the station of India and her value and position will increase in the estimation of the civilised and progressive nations [. . .] There can be no denying the fact that India can make satisfactory progress only if she is granted self-government, that is, self-government under British rule. Without it the position of India in the world can never be raised.

[198] *Chandr* (Lahore), 17 December 1915

Lord David stated [in the House of Lords] that the losses incurred by the British army in the recent fighting round Loos were due to the inexperience of the Staff Officers, who were in the habit of playing Bridge with women throughout the night.

[199] *Desh* (Lahore), 22 December 1915

[From a communicated article written for the Punjab War News Association] The Germans have beaten a retreat from Russia [. . .] the Russian armies are in high spirits, so much so that they are fully confident of victory [. . .] the Russians are in no way inferior to the Germans in guns and munitions. It is quite apparent from the events which took place in the first fortnight of December that the Germans have actually decided to withdraw their forces from the Russian front. During the past three months the Allies' aeroplanes have done splendid work in bombarding several German magazines, and have caused the enemy considerable loss [. . .] Bulgaria has joined Germany and Austria, and [. . .] it was for this very object that Germany extended the war to the Balkans. The Bulgarian army has now reached Gallipoli to reinforce the Turkish army. Meanwhile the German submarines have sunk a number of merchant vessels in the Mediterranean Sea. But if anything disquieting has taken place during the last three weeks, it is the defeat and destruction of Servia. But the war will not come to an end in the Balkans, but rather on the fields of Russia, where the Germans are suffering defeat after defeat, and are in such straits as to be driven to put forward proposals of peace.

[200] *Panjabee* (Lahore), 22 December 1915

The Armenian atrocities

What punishment is to be reserved for [Turkey's] German masters? Not only does the ultimate responsibility for all that the Turks are alleged to have done rest with Germany, but there is evidence to show that Germany could have actually stopped all this brutality if she had so desired. From May to October 1915, when the vast tragedy was being perpetrated, there were German Consuls all-powerful at every town. Not only did they do nothing of their own accord, but they refused all demands made to them by the Armenian Consul to appeal for stoppage or amelioration of the horrors. The inaction of the Consuls is explicable only on one hypothesis. They knew that their own Government had done similar, if slightly less atrocious, things in Belgium and that they were in complete sympathy with what was being done by the Turks [. . .] Christian Germany is certainly every bit as bad as the non-Christian perpetrators of the Armenian atrocities, and history will treat both in the same manner, without holding the religion professed by each in any way responsible for their misdeeds.

[201] *Desh* (Lahore), 24 December 1915

Among the various statements made by Lord Kitchener on the subject of the war during the time he was staying in Salonika and Athens which appeared in the Greek newspapers, one was that when war was declared the Allies were not prepared and that so far as England is concerned she will commence the war in real earnest in March next, when she will be able to put four million troops in the field, and when her munition factories will be in a position to manufacture all kinds of war material and to equip the six million troops which are being raised by Russia with modern weapons. Those people who imagine that the war will soon be at an end are mistaken; but nevertheless the Allies are certainly ultimately to emerge victorious.

[202] *Panjab Samachar* (Lahore), 25 December 1915

Efforts are being made to inflame the passions of the Indian Muhammadans by distributing sheets among them containing the proclamation of *jehad* against the Allies written the Arabic language and signed by the Sultan of Turkey, the Heir-Apparent of Turkey, the Sheikh-ul-Islam and Enver Pasha. These sheets are sent to India via Shanghai.

[203] *Bulletin* (Lahore), 29 December 1915

Owing to the Allies' attack on the Dardanelles [. . .] all the Turkish plans have been brought to nothing. It was [. . .] a result of this very attack that the Indian troops were able to push back the Turks in

November 1914 so far as Baghdad, and [...] conquer a very fertile territory. The Dardanelles operations, therefore, so far from being the outcome of a short-sighted policy, have led to many beneficial results. It is undeniable that the Allies have suffered considerable losses in the expedition, but these losses are small when compared with the advantages which have been derived from this attack on the very centre of the Ottoman Empire.

CHAPTER 3

1916

In December 1915, senior members representing the French, British, Russian, Italian and Serbian governments and armies met at Chantilly to coordinate their operations for the upcoming year. The thinking was that simultaneous offensives launched on multiple fronts would overwhelm the German army, forcing a breakthrough. The first of these offensives came in late March, where the Italians launched their fifth assault on the Isonzo. Hoping to break the stalemate there, the Austrians struck out in May on the Asiago plain where they quickly overran the Italian First Army. In June, Russian forces under the command of Alexei Brusilov began their planned offensive in the Carpathians. The Russians quickly punched a massive hole in the Austrian line and captured 200,000 Austrian soldiers. The attack petered out in October after the Austrians and Russians had lost some 2.5 million men. On the Western Front, the British, now under the command of General Douglas Haig, began their planned attack on the Somme on 1 July. This offensive represented a first test for Britain's all-volunteer New Armies. On the first day of the battle, the British Army sustained 57,470 casualties. By November, British losses totalled more than 419,000. French losses topped 200,000. German casualties likely hit 600,000. The French hoped for the opportunity to wait until the summer for their planned operations, but on 21 February 1916, the Germans attacked the French fortresses at Verdun. Nicknamed Operation *Gericht*

(Judgment) by German command, the attack represented the heaviest concentration of artillery to date. On the first day at Verdun, the Germans deployed some 1,600 pieces of artillery that loosed 100,000 shells per hour along a narrow eight-mile front. The German plan, however, was not to achieve so much as a breakthrough, but to, in the words of the German commander, General Erich von Falkenhayn, 'bleed France white.' By the end of June, however, both the French and the Germans had nearly bled to death outside the ancient fortress city. The French suffered 275,000 casualties. The Germans lost 240,000 of their own.

The Punjabi press followed these developments, among others. The short-lived Easter Rebellion in Dublin in April and the Arab Revolt against Ottoman rule, which began in June and would last through 1918, also garnered considerable attention. Two topics dominated headlines, however. These were the war in Mesopotamia, and the increasingly burdensome demand for manpower. Between December 1915 and March 1916, the strength of IEF D grew by 139,000 soldiers. The top priority in Mesopotamia that spring was to break through the Ottoman lines surrounding the Indian 6th Division in Kut. After repeated failed breakthroughs, General Townshend and 10,000 British and Indian soldiers surrendered to the Turks on 29 April. Four thousand of those died in captivity. British and Indian forces did not retake Kut until the end of the year. By November, the strength of IEF D reached 64,800 British and 156,350 Indians. In the span of 1916, India enrolled a further 104,000 combatant soldiers. Fifty thousand of these came from the Punjab. 'By the end of 1916,' Lieutenant Governor O'Dwyer boasted, 'the Punjab, which had started the War with 100,000 men in the army, had supplied 110,000 out of the 192,000 fighting men *raised in India*.' The rest of India, with eleven-twelfths of the population, had supplied only 68,000. 'Thus, while the Punjab was redeeming its pledge, other Provinces, and especially those who were loudest in their claims for political concessions as a reward for India's (?) war services, were taking matters very lightly.'[1]

Selections from the Indian newspapers published in the Punjab, 1916

CONTENTS

[204] *Arorbans Gazette* (Amritsar), 1 January 1916

The year 1915 was the greatest enemy of peace, for it saw the greatest bloodshed ever witnessed by the world. The conflagration of war is daily approaching nearer us. We have full confidence in the loyalty of the Amir of Kabul, but the area of the war is widening. The great conflagration which in August 1914 was confined to the French and German frontiers, in December of the same year reached as far as Constantinople. In the beginning of 1915 the conflagration reached Irak and some of its sparks touched the Arabian coast. Now at the close of the year we find that the condition of Persia is unsatisfactory. The Government of that country is undoubtedly with us, but the people's minds have been so inflamed by Turkish and German intrigues that they are anxious to have done with peace.

[205] *Panjabee* (Lahore), 5 January 1916

What will strike most dispassionate observers in connection with the scheme of compulsion in England is the contrast between the state of things in England and in India. In England, even the ready response voluntarily made by so large a section of the people to the call of duty is regarded as inadequate, and steps are being taken to compel even those who are unwilling to serve the country in the supreme hour of need. In India, no steps have been taken to enlist even those who have been burning with the desire to serve their King and country. Undoubtedly, the work of recruitment is going on, but it is recruitment to the regular army and is, therefore, necessarily restricted in its scope. In any case it does not affect the vast majority of the people. Why [. . .] this contrast? We cannot help thinking that if the Government had withdrawn the restriction on volunteering in India, it might not have been necessary for them to resort to compulsion in England. A Voluntary army raised from among a population of nearly three hundred millions would be much larger than an army raised by conscription from among the population of the British Isles.

[206] *Panjab Samachar* (Lahore), 15 January 1916

A party of the enemy which approached the Suez Canal was dispersed by an Indian Brigade. This might lead the casual reader to infer that the Turks have begun to stir again. This is not the case. After the last winter campaign the Turks maintained themselves round Sinai. Their army at first consisted of Turkish troops, but these were subsequently replaced by the frontier Bedouins, who were fitted out with regular arms and ammunition. During the whole of the hot weather this army occupied itself in ravaging the desert of Sinai. Our aircraft, however, kept a watch over their movements; and although they approached the Suez Canal, we did not disturb them until the 22nd November, when our troops encountered them. No change has occurred in the situation on the eastern frontier. It must not be inferred from these reports that the Turks have again commenced offensive operations. But it is undeniable that movements will soon take place in Sinai. The Suez Canal zone is at present calm, but an attack on it is anticipated from the enemy as soon as the winter is over. Precautionary measures are, therefore, being adopted beforehand, and it is believed that we shall be as successful in repulsing the enemy this time as we were last February.

[207] *Shanti* (Rawalpindi), 22 January 1916

Another rumour states that an invasion of India by four hundred thousand Turks reinforced by a hundred thousand Germans under the command of von Der Goltz Pasha will take place in the coming spring. It does not seem probable that the Germans, after the severe handling they have received from Indian troops in France and elsewhere, will venture thus to throw themselves on Indian bayonets. After all, this is one of the many rumours that we have continually heard ever since the outbreak of war.

[208] *Desh* (Lahore), 27 January 1916

At the close of 1915 [. . .] the Russians remained firm and refused to yield although reduced to a condition in which no warlike nation could escape from being conquered. Two-thirds of the Russian army was without guns, and yet they bravely faced the storm of the German offensive and retired in good order. Now they are receiving guns and ammunition from England, Japan, the United States of America and South Africa, which indicates that so far as the supply of munitions is concerned their condition is satisfactory. Their position will be still more improved by next spring, when the vigour of their attack will inevitably discourage the enemy.

[209] *Desh* (Lahore), 29 January 1916

The withdrawal of the British and French troops from the Dardanelles will have a greater and a more speedy effect on the Russians than on the other Allies; for it is an admitted fact that the major portion of the Turkish troops which were engaged in the Dardanelles will now be used against the Russians in the Caucasus. It is only reasonable to suppose that half a dozen Turkish Divisions will now be concentrated against them. There are no signs of any immediate Turkish attack on Egypt, and it may therefore be surmised that the major portion of the Turkish troops stationed in Gallipoli will be despatched to the Caucasus. Russia, however, is in a position to face the new situation. Indeed, the latest reports received from this theatre go to show that the Russians have actually adopted the offensive, while the Turks are acting on the defensive [. . .] Unless Great Britain reinforces her troops in Mesopotamia and prepares to deliver a vigorous attack on the Turks, the Russians will be obliged to bring up very large reinforcements in the Caucasus. Whatever happens there can be no doubt that the fighting in the Caucasus region and in the Ottoman Empire is likely to become very hot.

[210] *Zamindar* (Lahore), 30 January 1916

Turkish and German intrigues in Persia

In order to create unrest in Persia the enemy is giving currency to the rumour that the Turks and the Germans are planning an advance towards India via Baghdad and Persia. The Turkish and German agents made an attempt under cover of night to paste up leaflets urging the people to practice tyranny in the name of *jehad* on the English and the Russians; but the people found pasting these leaflets were promptly arrested on the spot. Further, the telegraphic communications in Persia are in the hands of the enemy, who has destroyed them as far as southern Persia is concerned. The British population of Shiraz is still imprisoned in the mountains; and nothing is known about the British population of Nairo (?); telegraphic communication with the latter place having been cut off.

[211] *Desh* (Lahore), 6 February 1916

Why did the war break out in western Egypt?

The greatest portion of Tripoli [. . .] is in the possession of Italy, who has joined the Allies and is fighting in co-operation with them in the battle-field. Sheikh Sennousi, on the other hand, who commands great influence over the Arabian tribes of Tripoli and the neighbouring *ilakas* of western Egypt, is on friendly terms with the Egyptian Government. Besides, a large British army is at present located in Egypt. In view of these circumstances the question naturally arises why war broke out on the frontier of [. . .] western Egypt. The reply is this. England had every hope that Italy would be able to keep the Berbers under control, but she failed to do this, with the result that the latter naturally raised an insurrection. Some Arabian tribes also, which escaped the influence of Sheikh Sennousi and came under the influence of the Turks and which were inciting (the Berbers) in the capacity of German agents, rose into insurrection. This is the reason why war broke out on the frontier of [. . .] western Egypt [. . .] These insurrections cannot prove unfavourable to the Allies, seeing that neither the Berbers, nor the Arabs can inflict any loss on the Egyptian Government or the British army in Egypt, especially as the Arabs have suffered the heaviest injury in the fighting which has so far taken place. It is true that the Arabs and the Berbers are fond of committing depredations and that they attack others only when they feel confident that they are not likely to suffer any loss and are sure to obtain booty. But in the fighting which took place in western Egypt the Arabs and the Berbers not only failed to get booty but suffered a severe loss both in men and money. They will, therefore, now abstain from raising insurrections.

[212] *Panjabee* (Lahore), 15 February 1916

It was a remarkable speech which His Majesty the King Emperor made in reply to a loyal address presented to him by 27 convalescent Indian officers. The speech, which will be found in another column, breathes the same genuine love of the people of India, the same sympathy with their aspirations, of which His Majesty gave so many and such striking proofs during his Indian tour. The occasion was an ordinary one, and the King, if he had so chosen, might have confined himself to merely thanking the officers for their loyal address. But the officers, in presenting their address, had spoken not merely for themselves but for the whole of the King's Indian Army and had thus afforded the King an opportunity of covering a wider field in his reply – an opportunity of which His Majesty readily availed himself. 'I welcome your presence,' he said, 'as a symbol of the unity of the Empire and as setting a seal on the heroic efforts and sacrifices in which my Indian soldiers – yourselves amongst them – have borne a common part with all my forces from overseas and from the Mother-country.' The officers had naturally spoken in terms of generous appreciation of the kindliness and brotherly feeling which they had met with at the hands of their fellow-subjects in Great Britain. This kindliness and this brotherly feeling was thus explained by His Majesty: 'They are conscious, as I am, that the loyal devotion of India to the common heritage for which we are fighting – a devotion to which we have never looked in vain – has been consecrated afresh by the blood of India's sons, shed far from their homes, and in a quarrel, which, whilst the might of the Empire protects India's shores, does not come near to the lives and fortunes of their kith and kin.' If His Majesty has correctly interpreted the feeling of the people of Great Britain generally, as he has doubtless correctly interpreted the feeling of the better mind of England, the blood which India's sons have so freely shed will not only have cemented the bonds of Empire, but will have gone far to win for India a larger share of the common heritage for which she has been fighting.

It is gratifying to observe His Majesty, at any rate, is under no delusion. This is perfectly clear from his declaration that 'the liberties of the Empire were put into the scale, and with them the liberties which India has enjoyed under our rule, and which, please God, she will enjoy in an increasing measure as she advances in the path of social improvement and political experience.' The declaration is in striking contrast with the view of those who would have us believe that India, while fighting to secure to Belgium her birthright, is indifferent to her own liberties. It means nothing less than that in the opinion of His Majesty India is fighting for the liberties of the Empire, liberties which she already partially enjoys and which she shall enjoy in a fuller measure in the coming years. Thus understood, the declaration of His Majesty is a re-affirmation of one of the most sacred pledges given to India by the late Queen Victoria. There will certainly be a difference of opinion as to the extent to which the pledge has been redeemed, the adequacy or otherwise of the measure of liberties which India already enjoys as well as the test of social improvement and political experience that is to determine what India shall have in the immediate future; but His Majesty, as befits his position, is only laying down a general proposition, and as a general proposition his declaration will be accepted by all his loyal and law-abiding subjects in India. The task of properly interpreting this declaration and giving effect to it under the British Constitution left to the King's ministers and to the House of Parliament, and it is to the latter that we must look for the fulfillment of the royal pledge.

[213] *Vakil* (Amritsar), 16 February 1916

The Allies are willing to conclude peace on certain conditions. One of these conditions is that Austria and Germany should admit that the Allies enjoy the right of disposing of the Turkish dominions, the Balkan States and (certain) countries in Asia in any manner they like and that they will decide about these matters themselves.

The Allies will force Bulgaria to evacuate Servia and will direct King Ferdinand to abdicate the throne. They will disarm every opposition that Turkey can offer and will make over Constantinople to Russia. France will take possession of Syria and Great Britain will take possession of Iraq-i-Arab, the holy land and Arabia. Russia will annex the rest of Armenia. These are, however, mere conjectures, because the main and the foremost object of the Allies is to crush the military power of Germany.

[214] *Panjabee* (Lahore), 17 February 1916

One of the many unexpected and unwelcome surprises of the present war is the unprecedented outburst of savagery with which it has been attended. It is not Germany alone that has acted like a highway robber rushing upon her unprepared and peaceful neighbours; Austria and Turkey have also, as our readers are aware, followed her diabolical methods [. . .] Such barbarity must defeat its own ends whatever they are. If this is the outcome of the vaunted civilisation of Germany and her allies, it stands self-condemned. Such gratuitous infliction of suffering as has been caused by them must have dire consequences for them when they return to civil life.

[215] *Desh* (Lahore), 17 February 1916

Events [. . .] have not come up to our expectations in France and Belgium. It is true that the Belgians have done splendid work in the war; but notwithstanding their success we failed to make any advance during the last winter. The most important event which occurred at the commencement of the cold weather was that after the vigorous attack of Loos we made some advance with our army. But our advance could not make up the loss which we sustained in the attack. Moreover, we were short of ammunition and hence we could not effect a breach in the German line in the way we hoped to do. But sufficient ammunition has now arrived, with the result that we are now ready. Our army is now elated and full of hope. As for the Dardanelles, we must confess that we met with a failure there [...] On the Russian battlefield, the Germans put a heavy pressure on the Russians; but the entrance of the Italians in the list has gone a great way in lightening the pressure. Notwithstanding this, however, the Germans took possession, in the month of June of Lemburg and Przemysl and in July they broke the Russian lines and repulsed the Russians and forced them back to take their stand on the defensive line of Riga and Bukhovina. But although a considerable part of the country fell to the hands of [the] Germans, still the German losses in men and money were more heavy than their gain. The Russians for the present have taken up a strong position on the defensive line of Riga and Bukhovina. Nay, they are also advancing. They have several million soldiers to serve in their army and are provided with a sufficient quantity of shells and gunpowder. As soon as the spring appears the Russians will attack the Germans with redoubled vigour and energy. If, however, the Germans and the Turks invade Egypt, it will be still more advantageous for the Allies. The wider they spread, the more they will lose their power in Poland, France and Belgium. It is a piece of wise stratagem to induce the Germans to make an attempt to invade Egypt. As for financial condition, it should be borne in mind that, instead of being weakened, the financial prospect of England and France is brighter than before. Germany, on the other hand, in spite of her vigorous efforts, has totally failed to improve her financial condition. She has greatly lost her credit in foreign countries. The trade of Germany and Austria has also been totally ruined.

[216] *Desh* (Lahore), 20 February 1916

It appears from news that has reached India from Constantinople that the defeat inflicted on the Turks at Erzerum has created consternation in Constantinople. The Turkish army in Constantinople refuses to fight, because of the scarcity of provisions. It has been acknowledged in Constantinople that the pressure which the Russian army has brought to bear on Turkey has destroyed every possibility of an invasion being made on the Suez Canal.

[217] *Nazzara* (Lahore), March Edition 1916

The new Royal Proclamation

The present dreadful and disastrous war has, to some extent, proved useful to Indians, because it has offered them an opportunity to fight on European soil side by side with the English and show their loyalty and bravery by sacrificing their lives in the cause of their King. This has made a deep impression on the English nation – from the men in the street to the greatest statesmen and right up to the King-Emperor [. . .] It behoves all English officers, high and low, who hold the reins of administration in this country, to give practical proof of the just and sympathetic spirit expressed in the recent proclamation [delivered by the King-Emperor to wounded Indian soldiers on 11 February], so that the wishes of the King-Emperor may be duly complied with.

[218] *Paisa Akhbar* (Lahore), 5 March 1916

German expectations [at Verdun] have been falsified and German activities have ended in dismal failure. It appears from the distracted attacks of the enemy that his condition is growing weak and he is making his final effort. The Allies can now prepare themselves for their offensive. It is also time for the German fleet to come out of its hiding place and participate in the mad German move, so that Germany may realise that her game is up.

[219] *Zamindar* (Lahore), 8 March 1916

It may be remembered that sometime ago [*Zamindar*] was forbidden to publish translations, extracts and comments of all kinds relating to the war, except the telegrams sent by Reuters Agency and the Secretary of State. The *Zamindar* scrupulously followed the instructions until January last. In February, however, the paper was permitted to publish translations and extracts from the English newspapers also, subject to the approval of 'the censorial department,' the order being received on the 3rd February. But ten days had scarcely elapsed when the whole thing underwent a change, and on the 13th February it received a communication directing Akhtar Ali Khan to see Mr. Kettlewell at the Civil Secretariat. New instructions were given, in compliance with which the *Zamindar* stopped the publication of all war news, except Reuters and the Secretary of State's telegrams. And yet on the 26th February, Raja Ghulam Qadir Khan, printer and publisher of the *Zamindar*, received a further communication, directing him not to publish any news, articles, criticisms and memos on any subject relating, in the least, to the war. As these are strange orders, it was necessary to explain matters to the authorities and a representation was submitted on the 28th February. But no reply has been hitherto received. We have every hope that His Honour [Lieutenant Governor Michael O'Dwyer] will be pleased to withdraw at an early date the deplorable restrictions, which are likely not only to impose a restraint on the *Zamindar's* freedom but also injuriously affect its very existence.

[220] *Aftab-i-Hind* (Jullundur), 8 March 1916

Muhammadans nearly all over the world are favourably inclined towards the Allies and are shedding their blood under England's flag. Even Turkey has not willingly entered the lists and become the cat's paw in the hands of German friends. The latter are said to have no love for their religion and, acting under the belief that Germany would emerge successful out of the war, they thought this country would stand to gain by joining her. But their expectation have been falsified and they feel repentant, being convinced of the deception practiced by Germany. All the same, they have tried to misguide the Muhammadans of other countries by impressing on their minds that the present war is a religious conflict.

[221] *Vakil* (Amritsar), 11 March 1916

Far from gaining anything, Germany is losing her colonies. The Allies have conquered most German colonies, which they will divide among themselves, after the war is over. Russia, however, does not stand in need of any colonies, as she already possesses a vast territory, which it will take her long to colonise and cultivate. It is, therefore, almost certain that Russia will get none of the German colonies and the larger portion of these will go to England and France to compensate the latter for her losses. Belgium may also receive some of the German colonies in Africa.

[222] *Civil and Military News* (Ludhiana), 13 March 1916

Sir William Vincent and General Bingley have sailed for Basra to inquire into the difficulties experienced in Mesopotamia in the transport of sick and wounded. The fact is that in the course of their progress some men belonging to General Aylmer's army were wounded and some others fell ill, while the light vessels and boats, which were sent to bring them back to the Tigris, became unfit for use and the doctors, under whose treatment they were placed, were totally exhausted by fatigue. The transport ships also failed to bear the strain of carrying them back, with the result that the removal of the sick and the wounded to Basra was greatly delayed. There is also another reason for the delay, and that is that the troops fell sick and were wounded in larger numbers than was originally estimated. So that transport arrangements were not equal to the strain and the wounded could not be satisfactorily treated till they reach Basra. There can, however, be no doubt that the experience gained in the present instance will prove advantageous in future.

[223] *Paisa Akhbar* (Lahore), 16 March 1916

The French Government, in appealing to its Indian subjects for volunteers, has set up a standard which the British Government would do well to adopt. Thus thousands of recruits would be obtained to replenish the Empire's depleted ranks. A far more important point is that it would mean the final abandonment of all differences between the ruled and the rulers. The proved loyalty of Indian troops justifies the demand for such a step.

[224] *Khalsa Akhbar* (Lahore), 17 March 1916

In the fighting in [Mesopotamia] the [British] Expeditionary Force has suffered only one reverse. Otherwise, since the 7th November

1914 to the 26th November 1915, the British forces have continually gained victories. [At the battle at Ctesiphon] [. . .] the British lost 3,000 men but inflicted a defeat on the Turks. The arrival of large Turkish reinforcements forced General Townshend to fall back on Kut-ul-Amara, at a distance of 80 miles from Ctesiphon, and General Townshend has entrenched his forces there. Further reinforcements have been sent from India. They were at first under the command of General Aylmer, but now Sir Percy Lake has taken over the command. In several minor actions against the Turkish regulars and the Arab freebooters, the British have always been successful. The victory of the Russians at Erzerum and the Russian occupation of Kermanshah must produce a deep impression on the Turkish position in Mesopotamia.

[225] *Desh* (Lahore), 18 March 1916

The present military strength of Great Britain is more than sufficient for all purposes and exceeds that of her enemies. Large British armies are operating in Europe, Africa and Asia and a new army is being trained in Great Britain and her colonies. The Germans stigmatised the British army as contemptible; but it has been daily increasing since the outbreak of the war and has reached the large figure of several millions. This military strength is supported by another and still more powerful force, the force of the consciousness that England is fighting in the cause of liberty, truth and justice. Sir Robert Borden remarked that the British army would display its full vigour next summer and take a year more to achieve complete victory over the Germans – a victory which would restore peace for several years, if not forever.

[226] *Lamaat* (Lahore), 20 March 1916

Our forces are experiencing difficulties in their advance in Mesopotamia. It is stated on the authority of an eye-witness that the Turks are invisible in this part of the war zone in the same way as the Germans are invisible in Flanders.

[227] *Civil and Military News* (Ludhiana), 20 March 1916

Although Great Britain has not as yet granted to the people of British India rights of equality with Englishmen, still lakhs of Indians have shed their blood for their Emperor and are even now sacrificing their lives. Indians regard the interests of England and India as being absolutely identical. The British should also repose implicit confidence in Indians and totally obliterate the inequality that exists between the two nations. Government should recruit Indians as volunteers and let them receive training in the use of arms.

[228] *Lamaat* (Lahore), 21 March 1916

Ultimate success [in the war] will depend upon the resources of the belligerents, but it is premature to say whether German resources are nearing the point of exhaustion. According to the *Times of India*, the enemy has given no indication of shortage of men on the western front, and on the eastern front he still holds all strategic points. There are, however, signs that the goal of the Allies is to destroy the power of the enemy and not merely to acquire territory. We should patiently wait for the winter and summer campaigns to favour the Allies.

[229] *Desh* (Lahore), 29 March 1916

Military experts are of the opinion that after costly movements and attacks extending over a period of a month the German forces in France are in exactly the same position as they were two months ago. These experts interpret the terrible German failure in the attempt to capture Verdun as a crushing defeat. The congratulations received by France from her allies on her valiant defence are significant, as indicating the defeat of the Germans. The failure of the Germans at Verdun has produced a very bad impression in Germany and has led to the outbreak of riots in Cologne and other cities. A neutral traveller who has lately arrived in Holland from Berlin states that the general opinion in Germany is that the fighting round Verdun is the last attempt to bring the war to an end. German military officers openly admit that Germany cannot continue the war for any length of time. In one month the total strength of the German forces has been decreased by three hundred thousand men. Weather conditions are now improving. The armies of the Allied Powers now stand ready, and as soon as the ground is sufficiently dried a general assault will be made from all sides, an assault which will be the beginning of Germany's final defeat and destruction.

[230] *Lamaat* (Lahore), 31 March 1916

The Turks are very anxious to save their Asiatic empire, and in consequence cannot take part in any attack which might be delivered on the Allies at Salonika. The Bulgarians also have no wish to fight against the English and the French. Travellers who have recently come from the Balkans say that [the] Germans [... are] on the horns of a dilemma, because none of her allies is prepared to put his fingers in the fire for her sake. Her allies are anxious only to save their own territories.

[231] *Tribune* (Lahore), 4 April 1916

The decision of the Government of India to form an Anglo-Indian regiment has given further strength to the question of allowing educated Indians to enlist in the army. For a concession made in favour of one community cannot be restricted to that particular community alone without arousing hopes among others. Whatever reasons apply to the one also apply to others to some extent; and a liberal view taken is respect of the former cannot be withheld from the latter. Evidently the Government of India have looked at the question from a new standpoint and are willing to recognise the new spirit of the people aroused by the war.

[232] *Tribune* (Lahore), 8 April 1916

The decision of the Government of India to permit the enlistment of Anglo-Indians in the army has already created hopes among the rest of British Indian subjects that they have an equal right to be enlisted in the army [... Once] the colour bar [has] removed in respect of one Indian community, it cannot be maintained for all others. France has already set the example of treating Indian recruits in the same way as those of European descent. The further extension of the privilege to

Indians cannot be long delayed, and we hope the proposed deputation by the Bengal leaders to His Excellency the Viceroy will elicit an important opinion from His Excellency as regards [to] the enlistment of Indians, if not to the regular army, then at least to the volunteer corps. It will be a reform with which Lord Chelmsford may well begin his sympathetic and progressive rule of India.

[233] *Paisa Akhbar* (Lahore), 8 April 1916

The Germans have lost heavily at Verdun, and the unexpected destruction of their brilliant hopes has naturally alarmed them; for their attack on Verdun was their last chance.

[234] *Desh* (Lahore), 12 April 1916

In the course of the present war the German Emperor has, merely out of selfish motives, resorted to various tricks to prove that Germany is a true friend and well-wisher of Islam. Most of his moves have been already exposed, but the report recently received from General Smuts has entirely disclosed the hollowness of German pretensions [. . .] If the Germans have acted in German East Africa against Muhammadans and the natives of the soil as is reported by General Smuts, there is nothing surprising in this. In view of the attempts which the Kaiser and his countrymen have made to entrap Muhammadans and the conspiracies that they have hatched in every part of the world to destroy civilisation and righteousness, it is difficult to believe that the Kaiser or his nation can be a friend of Muhammadans. They are the false friends of Muhammadans and declare themselves to be the well-wishers of Islam merely to gain their own ends.

[235] *Desh* (Lahore), 15 April 1916

The condition of Germany has become very critical. The German Government has seized and hoarded all the cocoa and tea in the country. The German Chancellor is very sorry to see that the speeches delivered by the British Ministers contain no reference to peace. This would imply that Germany was prepared to make peace as soon as the Allies showed any readiness for it. Germany has also lost her credit.

The sovereign, the British standard coin, has not fallen in value, but the mark, which is the German coin, has lost 25 or 30 per cent in value. It is evident from this that neutral countries believe that Germany will be ultimately defeated and ruined.

[236] *Panjabee* (Lahore), 26 April 1916

Germany cannot abandon the submarine war without forsaking what in reality is the last weapon, however ineffective, that is left to her on the sea. That means in plain English that she cannot comply with America's Note, and that a rupture is imminent. America herself anticipates this, for she is tentatively arranging to cope with a possible severance with Germany. All her representatives abroad have received necessary instructions. What precisely will be the effect upon the general situation of this impending rupture it is difficult to say. There is no reason to believe that it will be immediately followed by war between the two countries, though it is by no means improbable that war will follow at a later stage. And if war does not immediately follow, the mere break-up of diplomatic relations will not be an unmixed good to the Allies. It will deprive them of America's good offices in Germany and also in Belgium. At the same time its moral effect is bound to be great. It is easy for irresponsible German newspapers to sneer at American intervention. At least the responsible German Government cannot be indifferent to the good opinion of the last and most powerful among neutral nations. If they did not value American opinion they would not spend millions in a vain attempt to mislead it. Nor would they, at a time when they required the whole of their energies for the prosecution of the war, waste any part of them in stirring up a spirit of faction in America.

[237] *Vakil* (Amritsar), 29 April 1916

For the last two months the Germans have neglected all other fronts and are trying their utmost to take Verdun. The German[s] have attacked Verdun about fifty times and have always failed. The natural formation of both banks of the river Meuse saves the Allies from great losses; while the Germans, in spite of the sacrifice of a large number of soldiers, have not yet secured anything that can hold out for them the assured prospect of future success.

[238] *Desh* (Lahore), 29 April 1916

The European war and aeroplanes

Most of the aerial attacks delivered by the Germans on England aimed at the demoralisation of unprotected inhabitants by terrorising them. But the Germans have not achieved their object. Their attacks have, on the contrary, so exasperated the English that the latter have resolved to punish the murderous Germans for the injury to innocent women and children. It may be asked why the Germans behave as they are doing. The answer is that they are well aware of their own critical condition. Their forces are diminishing in numbers and they want to encourage their dispirited countrymen by resorting to such dreadful practices, hoping at the same time to discourage the British and create in England public opinion in favour of peace.

[239] *Tribune* (Lahore), 6 May 1916

The surrender of General Townshend with his heroic men at Kut has been severely criticized, but this is obviously unfair when we have no facts to judge the situation. It is apparent that everything possible under the circumstances was done to send up relief to General Townshend, but unforeseen and difficult obstructions presented themselves; and it appears to us absolutely unreasonable to blame the responsible authorities in the matter. Critics who want to win the war without a single reverse or without making a single mistake are preaching an idealism which exists nowhere. Of course, it is impossible to witness the great sacrifice of men without disappointment, regret and suffering. But these are the natural consequences of a world-wide war against a powerful and obstinate enemy. Though India suffers greatly in the Mesopotamian disaster, we are sure that the people will bear the loss and the sorrow it has caused with manly and loyal endurance in the satisfaction that we have done our duty and will continue to do it till we win.

[240] *Tribune* (Lahore), 6 May 1916

The Irish rebellion is an incident which is dramatic in the history of the war. It is apparent that those who organised it were the blind imitators of their mistaken brethren in India, some of whom fell victims to enemy machinations. It is impossible to attach any deep significance to the Irish disturbances, since they have no real support in the country and are denounced by the great bulk of the loyal population. The ringleaders have already surrendered and their followers have doubtless found out their mistake. There was absolutely no reason for enacting this stupid farce by the rebels since the Irish Home Rule Bill has received the King's assent and Ireland will be a self-governing unit of the Empire after the war. The Irish have no ground for discontent, especially at the present time. They were probably instigated to create trouble by German influences. The ease and quickness with which the disturbance was put down once again proves the strength of the Imperial Government and its great resources. It is unfortunate that this incident should have marred the otherwise unshaded picture of a calm and resolute empire engaged in the single object of vanquishing the enemy. But here again the value of self-control and preparedness for temporary and passing troubles will be admitted. India does not stand alone in containing isolated specimens of humanity who exhibit their political or economic discontent by disloyal efforts. Even so close to the seat of the Imperial Government as Ireland have such isolated but futile disturbances been occasioned, and we are sure they do not upset the minds of sound administrators and courageous statesmen, who do not require a series of repressive laws applicable to the bulk of the loyal population who are free from such tormentation.

[241] *Vakil* (Amritsar), 6 May 1916

Though no sensational news has been received from the Russian front in Asia Minor, still reports come daily of Russian and Turkish fighting on the road leading to Erzinjan. It is stated that the 9th Turkish Army Corps is stationed at Erzinjan, the strength of which must have been increased by the forces that have retreated from Erzeroum and been brought up to Angora by train [. . .] It is absurd to anticipate a cheap victory at Erzinjan similar to that which the Russian achieved at Erzeroum or Trebizond. The Turkish position at Erzinjan is strongly fortified, as the Turks have had time to strengthen their natural fortifications and bring up reinforcements, which they could not do at Erzeroum and Trebizond.

[242] *Bulletin* (Lahore), 10 May 1916

Our brave English and Indian soldiers are displaying unique valour in fighting against superior numbers in Mesopotamia. When a large Turkish army under German officers attacked a small force under the gallant General Townshend, the valiant British army did not step back but continued to fight for five months even after it had been besieged. Hunger and thirst did not dishearten the troops in the least and they fought with undiminished bravery, surrendering only at the command of their officers, who told them that Government wanted to avoid unnecessary bloodshed. This step was taken with great reluctance and extreme regret at the troops not having been allowed by their officers to die the death of martyrs. Although the defeat and surrender of General Townshend may produce an unfavourable impression on the minds of less intelligent and credulous persons, still in our opinion this failure against heavy odds is a matter of no consequence, and the temporary capture of 9,000 men is quite insignificant as compared with the hundreds of thousands of Turks and Germans who have been killed in the war. Moreover, our gallant troops are encamped at a distance of only fifteen miles from Kut, and we shall retake Kut in a day or two and soon release our men from captivity.

[243] *Parkash* (Lahore), 28 May 1916

The great difference [. . .] between the rulers of England and India [is striking]. In this country Anglo-Indian newspapers represent a trivial affair as an extremely dreadful event; but an organised rebellion in Ireland, backed up by Germany, has not upset the ministers and English newspapers are announcing that Ireland will shortly get Home Rule. A similar policy should be pursued in India, as owing to the peculiar circumstances of this country['s] misunderstandings can be easily created between the rulers and the ruled. A policy of confidence and sympathy is the need of the day. Lord Hardinge pursued such a policy, but he was abused by Anglo-Indian newspapers and incurred the displeasure of Anglo-Indian officers.

[244] *Kisan* (Lahore), 28 May 1916

High Government offices [. . .] depend on high education, which the agricultural classes find it difficult to acquire; while the preponderance of the non-agricultural element in the public service works as an obstacle in their way. This element makes it difficult for the *zamindar* (landowner) to enter service or prosper in it. The doors of military service alone are open to the *zamindars*. If they take up military service at the present moment, their condition will be greatly improved. They may be afraid of their lives, but they should remember that where there is no risk there is no gain. If we are convinced that no one can die before his allotted time, why should we then fear death? Are not many dying in India of plague, cholera and other epidemics? It is better to die a brave death, as such opportunities seldom come. If about a million *zamindars* now accept military service, the condition of the whole community will be vastly bettered. Decent pay is offered and rations and uniforms are supplied in addition. What is the condition of the *zamindars* in India? Their earnings are meagre and they are confronted with financial difficulties. In fact, there is no life in them, though they seem to be alive. Military service outside the country is much better than living in it. Our *zamindar* brethren should convene meetings in different villages and be ready to recruit. It is our duty at this juncture to extend a helping hand to our benign Government and assist it with soul and body in every way.

[245] *Akhbar-i-' Am* (Lahore), 7 June 1916

Shameful lying by the Kaiser of Germany

The paper learns from the *Mashir-i-Deccan* that the German Kaiser, to bolster up his prestige, is spreading false rumours in Africa, where all his possessions are being captured by our powerful armies.

One of these rumours is that the Kaiser has captured Lord Kitchener with ten thousand troops. Lord Kitchener was considered the best English General and was certainly the worst enemy of Muhammadan aborigines of Africa, who had captured a whole country from the Sultan. At a meeting of the Church Missionary Society in London, the Lord Bishop referred to the strange and dreadful rumours which the Kaiser had mischievously spread in Muhammadan countries, especially among ignorant Muhammadans who cannot distinguish between truth and falsehood. A report which has gained currency among these simple-minded persons is that the Kaiser himself went to Mecca and waited at the sacred shrine for three days and three nights to know the will of God, when a voice came from above saying: 'Rise, O Messenger of God and Protector of Islam; take the Divine sword in thy hand and slay thy enemies!' But the fact is that the Kaiser has not so far gone to Mecca at all. Another mischievous rumour similarly spread by the Germans ascribes to the English the intention of digging up the grave of the Prophet Muhammad and carrying his remains to the British Museum, an intention which the English are determined to carry out at all costs [. . .] A thousand curses on those [. . .] who invent such rumours; ten thousand on those who spread them, and a hundred thousand on those fools who believe them!

[246] *Panjabee* (Lahore), 8 June 1916

The victory [at Jutland], indeed, was not a decisive one. It could not be when the enemy had no intention of engaging in a prolonged action and took to flight as soon as they had the opportunity. But it was remarkable, and cannot fail to have a profound effect. From the point of view merely of the actual losses inflicted upon the enemy, the present is one of the most important naval actions recorded in present times [. . .] But the actual German losses, heavier [. . .] than the British losses both absolutely and relatively, are the least part of the matter. The prestige of the German fleet cannot fail to be materially affected by the last engagement. Already both in France and Russia the feeling prevails that Germany has sustained a great defeat. The leading French journal says that the German flag should be half-masted, while the Petrograd press is emphatic in the statement that the British have won a great victory. Even more important than the question of prestige is the question of self-confidence which, as the history of the growth of the British fleet indubitably shows, is not the least important factor in the creation of an invincible navy. The German fleet does not appear to have ever had any great confidence in itself [. . .] against the British. The latest action is likely to destroy even the [small] confidence it had.

[247] *Paisa Akhbar* (Lahore), 8 June 1916

Not only Persia, but Russia and England as well deserve to be congratulated on preserving peace in Central Asia. Fortunately there is no longer any fear of peace being broken in Asia. Japan seized German possessions in China long ago and German machinations have been stopped in Persia, which it [. . .] once seriously feared, would fall a victim to German intrigue. The attitude of Persia has proved that the responsible Persian authorities appreciate England's friendship. The German and Turkish forces that had taken advantage of Persia's weakness and entered the Shah's dominions have been now driven out. All this shows clearly that a strong Persia can prove of great help to her neighbours, and especially England. It is to be hoped that in [the] future British ministers will adopt the policy of strengthening the national Government of Persia and Russia and England will not occupy Persia, in spite of their power to do so.

[248] *Tribune* (Lahore), 9 June 1916

The sudden and tragic end of Lord Kitchener will be mourned throughout the great Empire as a national misfortune. By common consent he was the greatest authority on British military strategy and was acknowledged and obeyed as such throughout the Empire. When Lord Kitchener took up his stand, every other authority, however distinguished in other respects, instinctively deferred to him and rendered implicit obedience to his command. In the national controversy over conscription, both the great parties turned to him for guidance and advice, and when he at last gave his vote for compulsion the great differences that had till then divided the politicians were quickly made up, and the country, with a few exceptions, readily fell in with his suggestions.

[249] *Vakil* (Amritsar), 14 June 1916

The present war will be followed by a commercial war between the Allies and their enemies. Just as this war is being waged to inflict a crushing defeat on Germany, so will another war be undertaken to make entirely helpless. But the forthcoming conflict will be an economic and commercial struggle. As association has been already formed in Great Britain which aims at making the Allies accord preferential treatment to each other in trade matters. The projected scheme will no doubt injure the trade of Germany and Austria and greatly profit England. It was their commercial prosperity which enabled Germany and Austria to make their preparations for war; and when they lose their trade, they will suffer heavily. The consequences of this conflict will be far more ruinous to Germany and Austria than those of the present war.

[250] *Panjab Samachar* (Lahore), 24 June 1916

The impudence of General Carranza towards America [can be ascribed to] German machinations and [. . .] it has been amply proved that Germany has during the past eighteen months continually worked to bring about war between America and Mexico. In this Germany's real object is to divert the attention of America in another direction, so that America may not object to the violation of international laws by German submarines and be unable to supply ammunition to the Allies. To bring about a war between America and Mexico, Germany has been all along bribing Mexico.

[251] *Tribune* (Lahore), 24 June 1916

The inevitable has happened. The Arabs, who have always groaned under the oppression and rapacity of the Turks, have thrown off the yoke of the Turkish temporal power. The Grand Sheriff of

Mecca, who is in charge of the Holy of Holies of Islam, has, with the support of the Arab tribes, taken the field. Mecca, Jeddah and Taif have been captured and the Turkish garrisons have surrendered, with the exception of two small forts a the last named place. Medina, the resting place of the Prophet, is closely besieged and all communications with the Hedjaz are in the hands of the Sheriff. This action on the part of the representatives of Mecca separates the spiritual interests of the Muhammadan world from the temporal power of Turkey, and puts an end to the difficulties which Turkey has been putting in the way of comfort and convenience of pilgrims to the Hedjaz. For the present, however, it is rightly urged that the shortage of shipping, apart from the question of supplies and the necessarily unsettled conditions, makes it undesirable that any large number of persons should attempt to proceed on pilgrimage.

[252] *Paisa Akhbar* (Lahore), 27 June 1916

The fears of heavy Turkish losses owing to the imprudent participation of the Turks in the war are being realised. By linking their destinies with Germany, the Turks have acted in a suicidal manner. The holy cities in the Hedjaz, the possession of which was a source of pride and honour for Turkey and through the blessings of which she wielded spiritual influence all over the Muslim world, are now slipping out of her fingers. The Allied Powers had announced at the very outset that they would not attack the holy places of the Hedjaz. But it is quite a different thing if the Arabs themselves desire to throw off the Turkish yoke, and, as a matter of fact, they have under the leadership of the Sheriff of Mecca declared their independence. If the Sheriff succeeds in attaining his object, Turkey's spiritual influence will come to a permanent end.

[253] *Tribune* (Lahore), 28 June 1916

The British public were on the outbreak of the war struck by the loyalty and valour of Indian troops fighting against the enemy in France. That was the first great 'surprise' that the British people, usually indifferent to and ignorant of India, had for this great country. Most of them had very vague ideas of India, ideas that were derived from assiduous Anglo-Indians about the 'sepoy mutiny' of 1857, the tropical heat, the mosquito, the dark and ignorant 'masses' and the frontier tribes carrying depredatory excursions. Of the real India they knew precious little. Since there was no necessity they did not care to learn either. Naturally they were agreeably surprised when, on the outbreak of the war, they found a loyal and enthusiastic people, who, they once imagined, were only held by the British bayonet. They were pleased that the Indian soldiers fought bravely in defence of the British Empire. In the exciting period of the war they have no time to consider why the Indians are loyal and why before the war contrary opinions were circulated. They have also no time to consider whether the people here are fully contented and the administration is all that it should be. All these points will be considered after the war. For the present, however, it is enough to know that there is a change of opinion regarding India, and an awakened interest manifests itself in the future.

[254] *Desh* (Lahore), 28 June 1916

There is general rejoicing in Muslim circles over Arabian independence. Indeed, Muhammadans should realise that since the Young Turks have assumed the administration of Turkey, pilgrimage to the Hedjaz has become a dangerous enterprise and pilgrims have been plundered at the instance of the Turkish authorities at Mecca and Jeddah. It may be now expected that the Arabs will be able to protect the pilgrims properly with the help of the British. Many Muhammadans in India are rejoicing over the attempt of the Arabs to throw off the Turkish yoke.

[255] *Vakil* (Amritsar), 1 July 1916

The conduct of Anglo-Indian newspapers

While statesmen in England are acknowledging the invaluable services rendered by Indians in connection with the war, the [Anglo-

Indian newspapers] are engaged in belittling these services. They say that India has not taken her proper share in providing the sinews of war, but there is a world of difference between their and Indians' points of view. These papers expect us to make all kinds of sacrifices, but they are not prepared to give us our rights. They wish us to provide the largest number of men to fight, but they will never recommend that we should be appointed to higher posts in the army. They certainly desire that millions of Indians should go to the front, but they can never wish that we should be permitted to get ourselves enrolled as volunteers.

[256] *Paisa Akhbar* (Lahore), 5 July 1916

The present is the best opportunity for the Arabs to establish a permanent national government in their country. Turkey is engaged in a life and death struggle in Mesopotamia and Asia Minor, and the Arabs know full well that she can send no reinforcements to the Hedjaz just now. She could do so only by the Hedjaz railway, but the stations on that line to a distance of one hundred miles from Medina are reported to have been destroyed by the Sheriff. And even if the Turks manage to collect troops, they will find it difficult to bring them to Medina.

[257] *Desh* (Lahore), 7 July 1916

The British and the French armies, which have attacked and are fighting with the Germans, are distinguished by two characteristics. In the first place, it has been proved that the artillery of the Allies is superior to that of the Germans. In the second place, Great Britain and France [. . . now have] aeroplanes which are also superior to those of the Germans. This superiority in artillery and aircraft will prove a decisive factor in the war. Since the French and the British armies have taken the offensive they have continually advanced, gaining considerable success in capturing [a] country which is at present in German possession. It can be safely inferred that ultimate victory will assuredly rest with the British and the French armies. Their present offensive is the precursor of victory.

[258] *Al Asar* (Lahore), 9 July 1916

It appears from letters found in the possession of German prisoners that famine prevails in Germany. It is mentioned In the letter that there was a serious riot in the course of which people broke the glass windows of shops and carried away whatever they could lay their hands on. The letters in question also dwell on the difficulty of obtaining food.

[259] *Kisan* (Lahore), 10 July 1916

The offensive movement of the Allied army

A careful consideration of Reuters news will show that during the last three or four days the Allies have captured very important places. The time has now come for the Germans to try to reduce their boasts to practice. But the victorious British army has been stirred to its depths. It has already started on a victorious career. Its assaults do not constitute mere show and they are not periodic outbursts of rough and boisterous activity as were those by which Germany has hitherto tried to draw the attention of the world to herself. The action which the British army is now undertaking is a measured and carefully calculated action. Its movement is undoubtedly slow, but it is none the less sure. We are anxiously awaiting the time when the Union Jack will victoriously flutter on the palace at Potsdam.

[260] *Kisan* (Lahore), 11 July 1916

Though the condition of prisoners of war in Turkey may not be enviable, still the Turks are, according to their understanding and means, treating their prisoners well. All our soldiers who have fought with the Turks bear witness to the fact that the Turks fight like gentlemen. This is a remark which has never been made regarding the German soldiers. If on the strength of any agreement Turkey were to take over from Germany the charge of British prisoners of war, we are sure she would not let them die of starvation.

[261] *Desh* (Lahore), 20 July 1916

The view of some short-sighted people, who think that the proposal of granting Home Rule to Ireland is the result of the recent rebellion in that island, is wrong. It is a cardinal principle of British administration to grant rights which are deserved and the statesmen of Great Britain have always acted upon this principle. The idea that they can be coerced by rebellion is foolish madness. The fact is that Ireland has for long exerted herself to secure self-government; and the British Government which is based on justice and equity, has been ever anxious to grant Home Rule to Ireland. It has properly punished the Irish rebels and at the same time proved that it is a merciful and not a revengeful Government. The proposal to grant Home Rule to Ireland is viewed with joy and satisfaction by Indians, who entertain a confident hope that their justice and liberty-loving Government will bestow upon India also the blessings of Home Rule at an opportune moment after the termination of the war.

[262] *Watan* (Lahore), 21 July 1916

Relations between Turkey and Germany are [. . .] already rumoured to be strained. There can be no doubt that Germany has so far rendered ample help to Turkey, as in addition to the supply of war material she has provided officers for the Turkish army. Nevertheless, it must be admitted that Germany has gained more than Turkey and she has her own wellbeing in view in acting as she is acting. But now that Germany herself has been obliged to fall back on the defensive and her resources are diminishing daily, it is impossible to say what she will do. The answer to this question will be found in the cruel oppression she is practising in Belgium and Poland and the treatment she is according to prisoners of war. When Germany is reduced to such straits as will make it difficult for her to maintain her position, she will assuredly throw overboard those whom she had hitherto deceived. Turkey is, no doubt, running the risk of her connection with the Central Powers being cut off. In that case she will have to fight single-handed[ly] with the British in the Balkans and the Russians in Asia Minor. In Asia Minor she is already engaged in severe fighting. It is true that for some time the Russians have not been able to gain any great victory, but owing to their continuous activity the Turks have been obliged to maintain a large army, for if the Russians advance the Turks will be practically ruined. When the Russians occupy Erzanjan, they will be able to strike at the very heart of Anatolia.

[263] *Shanti* (Rawalpindi), 29 July 1916

Not a single Turk is to be found in Mecca now. God has so willed that no trace of the kingdom, which once ruled the holy city of Mecca, should be found to-day. Owing to the war several countries have undergone changes of fortune and many others, which could not even dream of freedom, have secured liberty. Our Muslim brethren regard the independence of Arabia with disfavour and have passed resolutions against the Arabs. But what can these avail? What was destined has come to pass. Independence is a natural instinct in man and it cannot be suppressed.

[264] *Desh* (Lahore), 29 July 1916

Mr. Bonar Law [stated in Parliament] that the British Government was adopting measures for taking military service from the people of Eastern, Western and Central Africa. This raises the question of military service of Indians. It is admitted on all hands that, if Great Britain had recruited a reasonable number of Indians in her army, she would have received substantial help in the war with Germany, which would have come to an end by this time. If, therefore, the British Government is going to recruit the residents of Africa, she should extend the same treatment to those of India.

[265] *Desh* (Lahore), 5 August 1916

Although two years have passed since the war broke out, still the Allies are in high spirits to-day. In the winter of 1914, Germany could not defeat the British army, which was small in numbers, the French army, which was short of ammunitions, and the Russian army, which was almost unarmed, though the Germans had been preparing for war for a quarter of a century. It is too much to suppose that they can now defeat the Allied armies which are [... expanding daily] and are equipped with every kind of war implements. Moreover, the Allies have defeated and driven off the seas the fleet which Germany had taken so long to build and of which she was very proud. The Allies having gained marked superiority over the enemy in numbers and war material, the door of their victory has been opened and is widening day by day.

[266] *Panjabee* (Lahore), 9 August 1916

[Referring to the decision of the Government of India to raise an infantry double company of Bengalis] In itself the decision does not mean much. A double company of infantry raised out of a population as large as that of Bengal, will not materially affect the fortunes either of the country or of the Empire. Its importance lies in the fact that it opens the opportunity of active service to a people who have been burning with the zeal and enthusiasm to do and dare, to serve their country and their King; and what is more it removes a disability which Bengal has always keenly resented as being both inconsistent with her loyalty and galling to her self-respect. Once the opportunity is opened and the disability removed, it will be impossible for the Government of India not to go very much farther than they have at the present decided to go. That the experiment will be a success, all who know the Bengalis will feel sure; and the success of the experiment will necessarily lead the Government to extend and develop it, until Bengalis are put on the same footing as those races from whom the Indian Army is at present recruited.

[267] *Al Asar* (Lahore), 13 August 1916

The Germans habitually send news of fictitious victories to deceive the Turks. As a result of this, the *Sabah*, a Turkish newspaper of Constantinople, recently published an article, headed 'The critical condition of Italy,' which speaks of the Austrian army as being about to reach Milan and conquer Rome in a month's time. It is added that the Turkish army will soon cross the Suez Canal and seize Egypt, after which it will reach North Africa. Another newspaper, the *Tanin*, says that French and British fleets have been destroyed by German submarines in the Mediterranean, that Verdun has been conquered and that the French Government has fled to England.

[268] *Desh* (Lahore), 20 August 1916

The events of the last two weeks have been favourable to us from several points of view. The Turks, for instance, who attacked the Suez Canal, have disappeared and have lost rather than gained by their attacks. The world has now come to realise that the British army in Egypt is far superior to the Turks, who dare not fight with the English for a considerable period. The success thus gained by the Allies in all fields of war clearly points to the exhaustion of the resources of the enemy.

[269] *Volunteer* (Lahore), 25 August 1916

In the Punjab even those men who used to do some work before have now gone to sleep. Did any Punjabi ever preside over a session of the Indian National Congress? Is not this due to want of a qualified man for the position? It is also a matter for pity that the brave Punjabi soldiers include very few educated men in their ranks. We have to admit with shame that, in spite of the fact that sanction was obtained before the outbreak of the war for the enlistment of educated Punjabi Khatris, sufficient young men have not been forthcoming for the purpose.

[270] *Paisa Akhbar* (Lahore), 30 August 1916

Roumania can bring into the field 600,000 troops who are equipped with arms of the latest design. She has also got guns of all sorts, which were manufactured in Krupp's factory. Roumania possesses so large a number of troops that she can well set the teeth of Austria on edge.

[271] *Kisan* (Lahore), 6 September 1916

The world has seen what heroic deeds the gallant sons of mother India can perform. The swords of the enemies have been blunted, their hands have become tired and their determinations wavered; but Indians who devoted their lives for the purpose did not betray the least sign of weakness. The war has now reached its final stage. The timely participation of Roumania in the war has strengthened the position of the Allies. The enemy is already out of breath and the irresistible blows of Roumania will further weaken him. The time has come for us to know what reward we shall get for our labours. Great Britain, whose ideal is 'live and let live,' is responsible for the protection of our lives. We have great hopes of her. We should have full control over our hands and feet and our lands, rivers, hills, houses and fields, so that we may enjoy the pleasures of life under the protection of British rule and the world may count us among living nations.

[272] *Vakil* (Amritsar), 6 September 1916

Someone has calculated that every great Power will spend four thousand million pounds sterling in the war. It is also believed that this amount would suffice for the establishment of 730 new universities with colleges and endowments or the construction of ten million excellent houses for the residence of families. In the height of their glory nations display the grossest madness and apply the term of war to it. This calculation shows that if the nations act wisely and, instead of spending such an enormous amount in testing the power of the talon of madness, they spent it in promoting the well-being of mankind, there would be every likelihood of the political affairs of the world reaching the highest water-mark of advancement. But in the present circumstances, when the world is swayed by sheer madness, who will lend ear to such wise counsels?

[273] *Jhang Sial* (Lahore), 11 September 1916

As an incentive to further loyal service [Indians] should have been extolled for their pains, but a European has thought fit to taunt them by saying that their services cannot bear comparison with those of the Colonies. One does not know why he has levelled this taunt at Indians when the fact is undeniable that the Colonies have rendered military service to England on the occasion only of the present war, but India pays every year hundreds of thousands of rupees for the military expenditure of the Empire.

[274] *Kisan* (Lahore), 17 September 1916

The opportunity which the present war has given Indians to show their loyalty is a providential one. Indeed, the services of Indians in the war have extorted the love and sympathy of British statesmen and even members of Parliament have been interested in the subject of Indian self-government. The question of Home Rule, which we are anxious to obtain but which we never expected to obtain for an indefinite period, has entered within the range of practical politics.

[275] *Desh* (Lahore), 24 September 1916

[The Honourable Dr. Tej Bahadur Sapru and the Honourable Mr. Sharma in the Imperial Legislative Council asked Government] if they had any scheme under consideration for promulgation after the war, and, in case they were considering any scheme, if they would consult public opinion before arriving at a final decision. The official reply was that Government had nothing to say in this connection. The reply was not satisfactory. The British Government is considering the question of the future administration of the British Empire and Indians are anxious to know what their futures after the war will be. If Government declares what its intentions are, Indians will get an opportunity to express their views.

[276] *Dodharakhanda* (Amritsar), September Edition 1916

A picture of the battlefield

War is nowadays waged in Europe,
The storm of Death has spread below the sky.
Hundreds of thousands of young men have fallen a prey to the arrow of Death,
As if life was a borrowed thing to be returned afterwards.

Germany is on one side and France on the other;
Fighting is the pastime of England also.
Aeroplanes and cruisers, which are in evidence,
Are moving on land, in air and on the sea.
Every youth is riddled with wounds.
It is thus that tomb is being raised on tomb.
Those soldiers who used to vaunt their prowess
Are receiving Dum Dum bullets on their breasts.
The brave soldiers are very glad,
For true pleasure lies in dying.
This is, however, not war;
It is merely the bridge over which the righteous will pass into paradise.
To say nothing of men, angels too are afraid.
Even Jesus Christ, who is in the fourth Heaven, is afraid,
Lest an aeroplane should appear there.

[277] *Desh* (Lahore), 26 September 1916

India is quite willing to contribute as much as she can towards the Imperial expenditure on the war. But those who want India to contribute to the expenditure should also promote the cause of India by seeking such changes in her administration as Indians desire and as would bring this country closer to self-government under British rule.

[278] *Kisan* (Lahore), 2 October 1916

This is an age of blessing for agriculturists. Every family which has three or four men capable of doing work should send at least one man for employment in the army. The salaries paid to the soldiers are reasonable and they receive other monetary help also. They will not be required to do service for a long time, and after the war they will return home and receive rewards and lands. If a man receives a square of land after a year or six months' service, he will practically get ten thousand rupees. Government has reserved a large area of land in the Montgomery District for the army. Let us see who are destined to receive it. It is difficult to see why people are afraid of death, especially when Government is ready to look after the children of those who die at the front. Those people are fortunate who die pleasing Government. Moreover, recruits will have to spend a considerable time in learning drill, etc., and before they become accomplished soldiers the war may come to an end. The present is, therefore, an excellent opportunity for young men to get themselves enrolled in the army. Those among them who want to enter the army through the *Kisan* should send their applications to its Manager. We shall try to do them good. If a lakh persons from Panjabi Zamindars come forward to join the army, they will receive at least forty lakhs of rupees per month.

[279] *Kisan* (Lahore), 5 October 1916

No doubt Bengal has offered the best of her sons for serving the British Government and has dedicated highly educated youths for sacrificing their lives in its defence. Can we, relying on the traditional justice of the British Government, be so bold as to ask it to grant the wish of the Bengalis, for which they are trying so much, that they should be given in the army an equal status with European soldiers? Bengal is the most educated Province in India and the acceptance of the demand would not be improper.

[280] *Desh* (Lahore), 12 October 1916

India and Egypt should be granted special representation on the Imperial Conference to be held on the termination of the war [...] India can be fully satisfied only when her status is raised to one of equality with the self-governing British Colonies.

[281] *Bulletin* (Lahore), 18 October 1916

People are generally anxious to know when the war will come to an end. War prophets have already made predictions regarding its termination. But the fact is that so long as Germany has money, men and ammunition, there is no prospect of the struggle coming to an end. The war will terminate only when German resources are wholly exhausted and Germany is absolutely ruined.

[282] *Jhang Sial* (Lahore), 30 October 1916

The war is, as usual, in full swing and there is no prospect of its intensity abating. Reuter lately sent the news that Germany and Austria no longer possessed sufficient troops and that sixty thousand soldiers were left to each country, the defeat of whom was expected in the near future. But the German Kaiser has not as yet given up the use of proud language, which necessarily raised doubts about Reuters report. The Kaiser asks his soldiers not to put the enemy to flight, but to kill him. He has also told them that one German soldier is equal to six soldiers of the enemy. Such boasts on the part of the Kaiser indicate that he is still obstinate and is not prepared to give in. It is, however, a matter of pleasure that the enemy is generally getting the worse of it and news of his victory is not received from anywhere. Of course, recently German submarines have shown activity, which has put the Allies on their guard and German submarines will now rarely get a chance of indulging in rapine. As a matter of fact, the present European war has brought ruin upon the whole world; but the masses in Germany and Austria cannot even get sufficient food to fill their stomachs. This gives rise to unrest. People demand that the war should be concluded, but Government does not listen.

[283] *Kisan* (Lahore), 30 October 1916

The condition of the city of Constantinople is pitiable. The widows of Turkish soldiers killed in the war are suffering starvation. All Turkish Departments are under German influence and the Turks view this with apprehension.

[284] *Kisan* (Lahore), 2 November 1916

Immediately after Roumania's declaration of war against the Central Powers, General Mackensen began to take the offensive against Dobruja and launched an attack on Tartikvai. The military correspondent of *Truth* writes to say that the Bulgarians captured at Tartikvai twenty-eight thousand soldiers, guns and a great quantity of war materials. Emboldened by this victory, General Mackensen advanced further and in a few days' time he occupied

Silistria and a part of Dobruja. The danger was increasing, but Russian reinforcements arrived in time, which at once changed the aspect of the war. Russian troops so harassed General Mackensen that he was compelled to beat a retreat at certain places.

[285] *Nau Ratan* (Amritsar), 15 November 1916

American newspapers have published the opinion of Italian experts that the war will last for another three years.

[286] *Reformer* (Lahore), 26 November 1916

The Germans are experimenting with submarines, so that when they are defeated and the Allies are hammering at the gates of Berlin, the Kaiser may escape to America and settle there. The story is not incredible. Since the blockade of Germany, the Kaiser has been very anxious for his life; and for some time past the question of the treatment of the Kaiser and his eldest son when they fall into the hands of the Allies has been under consideration and it has been discussed whether they should be treated like Napoleon. A crushing German defeat is inevitable; and when that event takes place, the Kaiser, who has brought so much misery on the world, will be surely dealt with as he deserves.

[287] *Punjab* (Lahore), 26 November 1916

The German ministers regard the new Austrian Emperor as being more friendly towards Germany than the deceased Emperor and think he will prove a more useful weapon in their hands. If this is so, we are sorry for the Austrian people, who have fallen into the clutches of a young lion after their release from the grip of an old bear.

[288] *Tribune* (Lahore), 28 November 1916

Human hideousness

A brainless brute is odious enough, but his brainlessness excuses him. But when brains and brutality are combined we have a human hideousness that might make the most degraded savages blush. It was this form of hideousness that was disclosed in the British official reports on the German treatment of war prisoners at Wittenberg, especially in connection with the typhus epidemic which raged there during the first six months of 1915. Of that story we have almost a complete replica in the report published [...] on the typhus epidemic at the German camp for prisoners at Gardelegen. It is the same calculated ruthless cruelty, the same appalling absence of chivalrous and humanitarian promptings that is revealed here. The desertion of her prisoners by Germany has been imputed to cowardice, but we do not believe it is merely that. It is worse than cowardice even – it is sheer brutal inhumanity, callous gloating over the sufferings of their enemies.

[289] *Punjab* (Lahore), 29 November 1916

It is desirable that the patriotic company, which is exhibiting the photos of those persons who have rendered help in the war, should also exhibit the photos of the Indian leaders who have been rendering political services in the war, so that the British public, influenced by the photos, may compel responsible authorities to give to Indians a share of the booty of the war.

[290] *Tribune* (Lahore), 16 December 1916

The re-organisation of Allied War Cabinets with a view to carry on the war with fresh and added vigour has synchronized with the enemy's dramatic announcement of peace proposals. The press opinions in England and other parts of the Empire are eloquent evidence of the manner in which the proposals have been received. They have met with the contempt they richly deserved not only from the British Empire but from the various Allied Empires. For Germany, the author of the war, with all its dastardly crimes and brutal barbarities, to pretend to shed crocodile tears at the havoc caused by the war, is to offer an insult to the commonsense and intelligence of the whole civilized world and to throw dust in the eyes of outraged humanity. The responsibility for breaking the peace of nations lies on the shoulders of Germany, which violated the neutrality of Belgium and compelled Britain to unsheathe her sword in defence of right and truth. Germany threw not only the rights of smaller nations to thee winds, but also violated the canons of international law. The sword drawn by England and her Allies can only be sheathed now when right and justice have triumphed and the liberty of smaller nations secured. That means that German militarism must wait until it is crushed once [and] for all.

[291] *Panjabee* (Lahore), 16 December 1916

For Germany to talk of 'guarantees' after having publicly declared that the most sacred of treaties was no better than a scrap of paper to her, is to make herself the laughing stock of the world. The only acceptable guarantee that she can give in the future is the guarantee afforded by her own emasculation.

[292] *Tribune* (Lahore), 20 December 1916

German *kultur* marches on from savagery to savagery. Readers may ask, 'why pile up the charges against a people already fully convicted of the worst outrages the human mind can conceive?' Because it is the duty of every citizen of civilised countries to follow the course of German degradation and to protest with all his might against each added brutality. And if ever it was the duty of civilisation to protest, it is so now that the horrors of the German occupation of Belgium are being revealed; and it is civilisation's duty not to protest, but to vow that never again will the German be admitted to the comity of nations.

[293] *Al-Asar* (Lahore), 23 December 1916

As peace is essential for civilisation, every civilised nation will undoubtedly appeal for the restoration of peace. At the same time, it will demand that the German Government should be called upon to make reparation for the blood which it has spilt and furnish guarantees for maintaining the peace in future. So far as we are concerned, we think that Turkey is also justified in demanding from Germany indemnity for the loss she has sustained in the present war.

CHAPTER 4

1917

Revolution in Russia and the American declaration of war against Germany were perhaps the two most monumental events of 1917. An especially cold winter left Russia's soldiers and civilians increasingly desperate for some manner of salvation. In January, strikes erupted in Petrograd. These carried into February, alongside calls for the Tsar's abdication. Finally, on 9 March, the Duma, Russia's parliament, formed a provisional government. Three days later, Tsar Nicholas II abdicated the throne, ending 300 years of Romanov rule. The provisional government vowed to continue fighting the war, however. In April, the Germans transported exiled Russian revolutionaries to Petrograd, including Vladimir Ilyich Ulianov, better known as Lenin, the leader of the Bolsheviks. Lenin announced his party's intention not to cooperate with the provisional government, and the Bolsheviks promised Russians 'bread, land and peace'. On 7 November, the Bolsheviks seized power in Petrograd, and Lenin's new government announced that it intended to end Russia's participation in the war. In March 1918, the Russians and Germans agreed to peace terms at Brest-Litovsk. Russia was out of the war. The collapse of Russia could not have been timelier from the perspective of the Germans. In February 1917, the German navy resumed unrestricted submarine warfare. This, combined with the intercepted Zimmerman telegram, a secret memo from the German government promising Mexico territories in the United States in exchange for Mexico's co-operation in waging war on the United States, forced America's hand. On 6 April, the United States Congress approved President Wilson's request for a declaration of war against Germany. The Americans, however, were not in a position immediately to send an expeditionary force to Europe. That would have to wait until 1918.

The war in the Middle East continued to occupy much of the attention of the Indian Army in 1917. In March, a newly resupplied and rejuvenated IEF D took and secured Baghdad. Fallujah followed shortly thereafter. In September, India raised the 17th Division. The 18th Division and the 11th Cavalry Brigade formed in October. In November, the Indian Army secured Tikrit. At this point, the War Cabinet learned that the Germans and Ottomans planned a joint offensive in Palestine, and so ordered IEF D on the defensive. The Indian 3rd and 7th Divisions – which had thus far fought in France, Belgium and Mesopotamia – transferred to Egypt. At the start of 1917, the Egyptian Expeditionary Force, the EEF, had been a 'directionless, demoralized' army, a mix of veterans dating back to the disastrous Gallipoli campaign, and replacements who had cut their teeth in the trenches of the Middle East.[1] Sir Edmund Allenby took command of this force in April and spent the summer months breaking the Turkish Gaza lines. At the start of December, the EEF reached the walls of Jerusalem, and on 11 December, walked ceremoniously into the city, marking the symbolic end of the British Army's 'most successful major campaign to date in the Great War.'[2] As the Indian Army experienced successes on the battlefield, the push for Indian Home Rule gained traction when Edwin Montagu, the new Secretary of State for India, articulated on 20 August that establishing 'Responsible Government' was the goal for India. Montagu had an 'unconcealed distaste' for the traditional Raj. He, and the new Prime Minister, David Lloyd George, believed that India 'could and would do more for the war effort "if her warm heart is touched".'[3]

Selections from the Indian newspapers published in the
Punjab, 1917

CONTENTS

[294] *Tribune* (Lahore), 7 January 1917

Without a doubt a peace signed at the present moment would be the
best thing that could possibly happen to Germany. The German tide
is at the full. Now is the appointed hour – for Germany. A peace now

would mean that she had won the war. She is in the position of the gambler who has had all the evening's luck and wants to leave off play, with a pile of gold in front of him, before the luck turns. Whatever be the cost in blood and treasure, it is a thousand times better to go on spending and suffering now to fight this struggle to a decisive conclusion than to let all the agony be endured in vain, the mere prelude to years of strain and anxiety and another war which would drench the world in blood.

[295] *Khalsa Samachar* (Amritsar), 11 January 1917

Educated Indians cannot obtain a better opportunity to display their loyalty to Government. Those enlisted [in the Punjabi Double Company] will be employed till the end of the war, after which they may remain in the army if they like. It is to be hoped that educated Punjabis will readily respond to the call and maintain the honour of their province.

[296] *Punjab* (Lahore), 12 January 1917

While the present war, which is the greatest war in the history of the world, is devastating the blooming garden of Europe, America is getting richer at an extraordinary pace. From the individual point of view, the present wealth of America is fifty times greater than the wealth of Great Britain before the outbreak of the war. President Wilson's peace note is very pleasant for the soul; but in view of the great benefits which America has derived from the war, its importance cannot be admitted by worldly-minded people.

[297] *Hindustan* (Lahore), 12 January 1917

A complete regiment should be raised in the Punjab, consisting of educated young men of every nation and sect in the country. These men should receive military training and thereafter display their heroism in any place where they may be sent. We do not think Government will hesitate to accept the proposal, for when we desire to serve the Empire there is no reason why the representation of Bengalis should be accepted and that of the Punjabis rejected. If we demand self-government, we should be prepared to sacrifice ourselves in defending the Empire.

[298] *Akhbar-i-Am* (Lahore), 13 January 1917

Educated Punjabis had been long waiting for this opportunity and they will now avail themselves of it with enthusiasm.

[299] *Reformer* (Lahore), 13 January 1917

Government will gain conspicuous success in its scheme of raising a Double Company of Punjabi graduates and undergraduates.

[300] *Al-Asar* (Lahore), 13 January 1917

It is a matter for rejoicing that the Punjab Government has afforded an opportunity to the young men of the Punjab to render military service. We hope that the gentlemen who were waiting for this opportunity will eagerly take part in the movement and the proposed single or double Company will be soon raised.

[301] *Al-Asar* (Lahore), 14 January 1917

Prima facie it appears that only those persons will be able to serve the country through this scheme who belong to high families and have independent means of livelihood. It would have been proper if Government had offered special salaries to raise a Company of graduates. Many people in the Punjab receive education merely to obtain the wherewithal to fill their stomachs. If, therefore, they are offered only the salary of an ordinary sepoy, the offer will not prove attractive. We would urge Government to fix special salaries for graduates and thereby enable the common people also to serve the country.

[302] *Siraj-ul-Akhbar* (Jhelum), 15 January 1917

The world is highly extolling the brilliant patience and perseverance which His Majesty the Amir of Kabul is displaying in the present war. The world imagined that the Amir would throw England overboard and join her enemies who have a Muhammadan country like Turkey on their side. But notwithstanding the numerous efforts and machinations of Germany, His Majesty has firmly stuck to the agreement which his august father made with England. The Amir having once agreed that he would be friendly to England, it is inconceivable that he would break his covenant and turn hostile. Moreover, now when the present world-wide war is about to end, His Majesty cannot take part in it.

[303] *Al-Munir* (Jhang), 16 January 1917

Young men belonging to the communities that have been hitherto refused admission to the army have got an excellent opportunity to show their military spirit and secure the removal of the restriction for the future. It is to be hoped that these communities will avail themselves of the opportunity and, regardless of financial considerations, keep in view those benefits which they can obtain through loyalty; as it is hoped that the time is not distant when the door of high military service will be thrown open to Indians.

[304] *Vakil* (Amritsar), 17 January 1917

While the whole of Europe is ablaze with war, Japan and America are quietly amassing great wealth. America is, at present, fifty times richer than Great Britain was before the outbreak of hostilities. Similarly, Japan is also collecting wealth. The condition of India is pitiable, for she is still where she was before the war.

[305] *Khalsa Samachar* (Amritsar), 18 January 1917

O educated Punjabis! Dally not.
O matriculates and graduates! Go to the front.
Show your bravery by raising a Double Company.
Kill the wicked Germans and reach Berlin.

[306] *Khalsa Advocate* (Amritsar), 20 January 1917

[After referring to the Bengali Double Company] But the case of the Punjab, the sword-hand of India, is quite different. This province is a veritable mine of soldiers, having already supplied one-half of the whole number so far enlisted in the Indian army. It is therefore quite an ordinary thing for it to give another 250 of its youths from the various communities inhabiting it. It has often been regretted and pointed out as a hindrance that the educated youths of the Province could not serve the Government like their uneducated brothers as combatants. And now that, thanks to the attention of Sir Michael O'Dwyer, an opportunity has been created, who is there who would not like to avail himself to it? It is therefore time for the gallant Sikhs, the martial Muslims, the courageous Khatris, the brave Rajputs, the soldierly Mohyals and all others to exhort the educated among them to come forward, and what to say of a mere Double Company the forming of which can do credit only to the Bengali *babus*, the Punjab should not rest till there is available a full regiment of matrics, under-graduates and graduates. In England educated young men as willingly take the sword as they use pen; so will the brave Punjab, of whose warlike spirit and traditions the whole of India is so rightly proud, fail to rise to the occasion now that a call has been made? No, we are sure they will not fail.

[307] *Paisa Akhbar* (Lahore), 24 January 1917

[We] hope that Indians will make a generous response to Mr. Lloyd George's appeal for pecuniary assistance and that India will not fail to bear the burden of war-expenses as an important part of the Empire. Evidently, the war can be brought to a successful close if adequate funds are placed at the disposal of the British Government.

[308] *Hindustan* (Lahore), 31 January 1917

We are anxious to see when, in due regard of the traditions of our families, we are appointed to commissioned ranks in the army and honoured as a respectable nation. If this is done, not only the Punjab but the whole of India will be ready to sacrifice herself. We belong to a nation which, if its national sentiments are duly respected, can successfully fight not only Germany but the whole world. Let commissions in the army be given to us and then see what India does.

[309] *Karnama-i-Punjab* (Rawalpindi), 1 February 1917

Sometimes the salaries of soldiers are compared to the wages of coolies and labourers. But the fact is ignored that military service is an honourable service and worthy of men of high social standing. Besides, it is a permanent service ending in pension. On the other hand, labourers will get the wages at these rates for a few months only.

[310] *Bulletin* (Lahore), 2 February 1917

Certain concessions [ought to be granted] to students enlisting in the Punjabi Double Company. Their scholarships should not be discontinued; none of them should be debarred from appearing in the University examinations on account of deficient lectures; their abilities might, in the case of professional examinations, be tested before the date of examination and special privileges should be granted to them for admission into the public service.

[311] *Paisa Akhbar* (Lahore), 7 February 1917

Finding that the Allies have contemptuously rejected her peace proposals and refused to accede to her request before crushing her military power, Germany is now threatening neutral States with her destructive submarines to force them to interfere. In consequence of this, America, which was hitherto trying to bring about peace, has been obliged by German excesses to enter the arena of conflict.

[312] *Al-Asar* (Lahore), 8 February 1917

German submarine activity is not apprehended to do as much harm to Great Britain as to the neutral Powers. It is also sure to do one good in that another instance of German tyranny, unprecedented in the civilised world, will be established. But we should rest assured that the European war will certainly end in the annihilation of the power of Austria and Germany. It is a matter of pleasure that America has now realised her responsibility.

[313] *Punjab* (Lahore), 9 February 1917

There can be no denying the fact that after two-and-a-half years' fighting on all fronts, Germany is still strong enough to make a stand against the Allies everywhere, but the recent announcement of the Kaiser cannot have originated from any pride of military strength. Either the old tradition is true that the Kaiser is liable to fits of madness or, like the morning lamp, Germany is about to be extinguished after the last flicker. It is a foregone conclusion that Germany can never gain her end by fighting against the whole world. Whatever other people may think, we are glad that the new announcement of Germany has brought the end near.

[314] *Punjab* (Lahore), 11 February 1917

It is established by facts that in her present condition India has not failed to render her best help to the British Empire and that she will not hesitate to help Government to the best of her power in future. Hardly a day passes when we do not hear of some Raja or Taluqadar has made an offer for the war. India is not negligent in offering recruits also. It will be deplorably unjust to accuse Indians if the rate at which recruits are enrolled is not commensurate with the total population of India. The martial spirit of the people, barring that of a few tribes, has been killed by the Arms Act, while Indians do not receive the salary of even ordinary white soldiers.

[315] *Tribune* (Lahore), 14 February 1917

The people of India have been hitherto admitted to the army very sparingly. What are called the fighting classes or castes have been, to some extent, recruited to the Indian army as sepoys and the more intelligent of them are sparingly appointed as Jamadars and Subedars. As a nation, Indians, therefore, have not been encouraged to feel that they are very much wanted in any scheme of the defence of the country. The fact that the people are prohibited from using arms, even for personal defence against the depredations of wild beasts and dacoits, except under very stringent and special conditions, shows that for generations the Indians, as a race, have lost all instinct for military service and they have taken little or no interest in military questions and in the defence of the country. His Excellency the Viceroy, in the course of his opening speech at the Imperial Legislative Council, gave us a hint that Indians would be admitted into the new Indian Defence Force. We have as yet no details of the present scheme and the most essential point is whether there would be any invidious distinctions made in the pay and conditions of service between European and Indian subjects of similar class and position. Much depends on the new spirit of justice and equality which will be recognised now as a result of the new angle of vision; and it is sincerely hoped that during the *régime* of the present Viceroy the inequalities long-complained of will be swept away once [and] for all. We hope that His Excellency will also take into consideration what it is exactly that Indians want when they desire to serve in the army. It is necessary to fully understand the question from the Indian point of view before definite schemes are announced and estimates are made. In the first place it is the natural privilege of every citizen to defend his country against its enemies; and what Indians want is that this privilege should be granted to them now and in future both in the Indian Army of all ranks and in volunteering. Secondly, such inequalities of treatment between man and man that exist at present must be removed. It is hoped that these objects will be kept in view when the scheme is hammered into shape and that the authorities will not ignore the main contentions of the people when they express their desire to serve in the army. It is evident that recruitment will be purely voluntary and hence its success will largely depend upon the extent to which the real demands of the people are conceded.

[316] *Paisa Akhbar* (Lahore), 15 February 1917

The United States of America will have to go to war with Germany sooner or later, as Germany is determined to pursue a policy of ruthless submarining, regardless of consequences. Let us see what the result of Mr. Wilson's hesitation will be.

[317] *Panjabee* (Lahore), 25 February 1917

The people of India will welcome with genuine enthusiasm the statement made in the House of Commons by Mr. Chamberlain that the Viceroy had informed him that Indians would be eligible for Commissions under the Indian Army Act in the Indian units of the new Indian force, as soon as they were qualified for them. A more important or more statesmanlike declaration has not been made for many years, so far as the people of India are concerned. This, as our readers are aware, is precisely the reform which public opinion has been urging in connection with the Indian units of the Defence force, and now that the concession has been made, we are convinced that the experiment will prove an unqualified success. We trust that the present step will lead, and that in no distant future, to the final eradication at once of the policy of distrust in matters military that has hitherto been believed to exist and of the barriers of inequality that have in some essential respects divided the people of India from other classes of the King's subjects.

[318] *Panjabee* (Lahore), 3 March 1917

It was a strikingly democratic speech which President Wilson delivered at a recent meeting of the Senate about the conditions of peace which would terminate the present war and so establish the reign of peace in this world that the diverse nations could pursue their even tenor without fighting with each other. What gives a peculiar point to his deliverance is the profound sympathy which it breathes out for the struggling nationalities in their efforts towards freedom and the realisation of their particular destiny. 'I am proposing,' said President Wilson, 'as it were, that the nations should, with one accord, adopt the doctrine of President Monroe as the doctrine of the world, that no nation should seek to extend its polity over any other nation or people, but that every people should be left free to determine its own polity, its own way of development, unhindered, unthreatened, unafraid, the little along with the great and powerful.' We are sure that all sane and sensible men will fully share President Wilson's sentiments, for it is only by the practice of the principles of justice, freedom and equality in the civilised world that humanity can progress towards the high goal of the parliament of men and the federation of the world.

[319] *Siraj-ul-Akhbar* (Jhelum), 5 March 1917

People who lose the opportunity of enlisting in the army will repent afterwards. Signs of famine are visible in the country and it is necessary that young men should gain honour and fame by joining the army and, instead of ruining their ancestral property by borrowing on interest, should earn money for the maintenance of their families by enlistment in the army and sacrificing their lives in killing the enemy of the British Government.

[320] *Siraj-ul-Akhbar* (Jhelum), 12 March 1917

A rumour is current in the streets of Calcutta that the Germans have invented a flying submarine. We agree with our contemporary [the *Englishman*] in asking how such rumours are set afloat.

[321] *Panjabee* (Lahore), 14 March 1917

No more gratifying news has been received for a long time from any of the theatres of war than that of the capture of Baghdad.

[322] *Paisa Akhbar* (Lahore), 15 March 1917

Baghdad, which after many vicissitudes fell into the hands of the Turks, has again fallen a victim to the vicissitudes of the day. It is difficult to say what more incidents like this will be witnessed by us owing to the misdeeds of the Young Turks.

[323] *Vakil* (Amritsar), 17 March 1917

The fall of Baghdad is a great blow to the Ottoman Empire and a blessing to the Allies. British statesmen regard the capture of Baghdad as the most important event of the present war. According to *Reuters* the Turks are consoling themselves by saying that they retreated for military reasons.

[324] *Al-Asar* (Lahore), 17 March 1917

The capture of Baghdad [has washed] away the stain which General Townshend's surrender had cast on British arms. Wherever the British flag waves, the news of the capture will be hailed with great rejoicing. It was expected that after their retreat from Kut the Turks would make a brilliant stand at Baghdad, but the present news shows that the Turks offered no resistance. This is probably due to their having failed to obtain reinforcements. The importance of the capture would have been doubly great, if Baghdad had been occupied after stubborn resistance.

[325] *Al-Asar* (Lahore), 17 March 1917

Truly speaking, the capture of Baghdad has totally effaced the stain, if any, of the failure of the British expedition in Mesopotamia. The event is highly painful and affords an exhibition of military prowess. Its moral effect is extremely injurious to the Turks and most beneficial to the English. The capture of Baghdad by England is an incident which will be certainly viewed with anxiety by the Turks and the effect of it Turkey will not forget for a long time. The losses which Turkey has sustained in the war through the kindness of Germany may have strained their relations. But it will not be improper to say that this incident will so widen the gulf of estrangement that their mutual relations will be severed. Anxiety will now naturally be created in Turkey for, while Turkish soldiers are giving their lives for the defence of Germany and Austria, their own possessions are gradually passing into the hands of the Allies.

[326] *Al-Asar* (Lahore), 18, 19 March 1917

If during the present war Great Britain had, like the mighty Roman Empire, devoted her whole attention to the defence of England and severed her connection with India, this country would have fallen a prey to disorder and lawlessness as England did thousands of years ago. But it is a matter for thankfulness that Great Britain did not commit such a mistake. In view of the religious connection of the

Indian Muhammadans with Turkey, they did not wish the Turks to go to war against a power to whom they were indebted. Now while the fall of Baghdad has given satisfaction to Muhammadans, because victories like these prove the superiority of the British, and have put an end to German activities in Central Asia, the event has also renewed their past regrets at Turkey's participation in the war. Anyhow, Muhammadans can see that Baghdad has been wrested from the possession not of an Islamic kingdom but Germany which is an enemy of Islam. It is none the less deplorable that the Islamic kingdom of Turkey is acting like a puppet in German hands.

[327] *Al-Asar* (Lahore), 23 March 1917

Political revolutions, political agitation, sedition and rebellion are generally believed to be the special products of the European soil. It cannot also be denied that absolute monarchy does not prosper in Europe. The Czar of Russia has now been compelled to taste the cup of bitter experience which was some time ago tasted by *ex*–Sultan of Turkey. Though possessed of many personal virtues and qualifications, the deposed Czar lacked that strength of will which was essential for a ruler of such a vast territory. The revolution in Russia aimed at the improvement of the administration of the country and the elimination of the foreign element. But the revolution started by the Young Turks resulted in the spread of discontent in Turkey and eventually led to the participation of Turkey in the war on the side of Germany.

[328] *Desh* (Lahore), 24 March 1917

One of the greatest empires in the world, which was the chosen home of despotic rule, has thrown off the rotten chains and secured the exalted blessing of *Swarajiya*. Humanity is justified in expressing pleasure and satisfaction at the brilliant success of the principles of freedom and justice. The shackles of the nations have begun to be cut down even before the termination of the war. The world is not fruitlessly bearing the calamities of the war nor shedding in vain streams of its blood nor wasting the money in its treasuries. A new chapter is beginning in human history, and that sacred day is approaching when all the men in the world will enjoy equal rights and will consider each other as brothers.

[329] *Desh* (Lahore), 25 March 1917

There can be no doubt that the Nihilists' movement had been long in existence in Russia and that the anarchists were bent upon murdering the Russian Emperor and thus putting an end to the despotic form of government. But this object has now been gained without any special struggle. As compared with former revolutions very little blood was shed in the capital during the present revolution and the loss of life would have been still less if the police had not in accordance with their disreputable traditions thoughtlessly showered bullets on the troops, who had joined the revolutionists. But as the days of the Russian police were over, none cared for their empty threats and they had to eat humble pie.

[330] *Panjabee* (Lahore), 25 March 1917

It is one of the greatest glories of England that never has a foreign people in any part of the world risen in revolt against tyranny, oppression or absolutism without its receiving the blessings from that land of freedom, the august mother of free nations, as she is justly called. She sympathised with France in the early days of her revolution. She sympathised with Italy in her successful endeavour to emancipate herself from the yoke of Austria. She sympathised with Greece and other minor nationalities in their struggles for freedom. She was the first to sympathise with Russia when the Duma was established. And now that Russia has finally cut herself off from the bondage of ages she is also the first to sympathise with her. The House of Commons has adopted a resolution sending the Duma its fraternal greetings and tendering to the Russian people its heart-felt congratulations upon the establishment among them of free institutions. The adoption of the resolution as well as the language of the mover and his supporters is a significant commentary upon the shallowness of those who ask us to believe that England can have any feeling but sympathy for those members of the British Empire itself who have not yet attained to self-government in their efforts to win constitutional freedom.

[331] *Bulletin* (Lahore), 4 April 1917

The revolution in Russia is an incident which cannot but produce a conspicuous effect on the other parts of the world. It will make the relation between the rulers and the ruled friendlier than before and those Governments, which believe that their power is best displayed by suppressing the legitimate demands of their subjects, will now consider their policy dangerous and will (hasten) to give it up. They will now grant greater liberty to their subjects.

[332] *Tribune* (Lahore), 17 April 1917

People of India welcome this great speech of the British Premier [Lloyd George, on the value of democracy]. We are sure he was expressing not only a general principle of national justice and progress in Europe but also a principle that is applicable to Asia and other parts of the world. The next question is that after the war this principle of freedom should be extended beyond Europe to Asia and Africa. These nationalities have come under the influence of the European pioneers of freedom and democracy. Will these pioneers, after the war, say that freedom and democracy is good for themselves and not good for Asiatics and Africans – and give some excuse, such as their backwardness, poverty, want of education and organization, to back their refusal? Will they say that sugar tastes sweet in European mouths but will cause dyspepsia to Asiatics? We are sure that Lord Curzon and Sydenham and scores of others have stood up as apostles of autocracy in the East before the war, but what will be inevitable prejudices when the time comes to apply the principle evolved from the great war – *viz.,* democracy and freedom – to Indian and other nationalities in Asia and Africa. Let it not be said that a sound principle applicable to all humanity during the war does not apply to certain nationalities after the war.

[333] *Paisa Akhbar* (Lahore), 22 April 1917

Germany and Islam: Startling disclosures

To win over the sympathies of Muhammadan Powers, the Germans did not hesitate even to give out that they were the supporters of Islam. But this was done simply to deceive Muhammadans, for in their heart of hearts the Germans are the bitter enemies of Islam. They professed to be the friends of the Turks and their object was to derive certain political and economical advantages from Turkey.

[334] *Tribune* (Lahore), 25 April 1917

It will give great satisfaction to people in India to find that a resolution has been passed at the Imperial War Conference to secure full representation to India at future Imperial Conferences. We do not derive pleasure by merely being admitted to sit and talk with high Imperial representatives unless this representation brings to us, people in India, the same advantages and rights which people in the Dominions enjoy. Otherwise we will have a mere symbol without the substance. It is evident that at present the fact of Sir S.P. Sinha and the Maharaja of Bikaner sitting at the Imperial Conference could not prevent the Gandhi incident at Champaran, Behar, which could not be dreamt of in the colonies. So let us not be blind worshippers of mere formalities, but make sure of the fact that the representation of India is as real and conveys as much meaning as the representation of the other parts of the Empire. The war has undoubtedly served the purpose of altering the colonial outlook. Their hearts have softened enough to admit Indian representatives to the Imperial Conference. But imperial co-operation, to be genuine and efficient, should be co-operation among equals – but not among independents and dependents or among masters with powers to control and servants with the privilege of being controlled by others. It is impossible for India to receive this gratifying announcement with perfect satisfaction as it is unaccompanied with any Imperial assurance about Indian self-government. We cannot think of a perfect Imperial Conference with Indian representatives sitting there as members of a dependency making themselves heard with any pretence to pride and effectiveness among free self-governing nations.

[335] *Paisa Akhbar* (Lahore), 26 April 1917

[We are glad] to learn that the Imperial War Conference has passed a resolution, suggesting that India should be also given the right of full representation on the Imperial Conferences to be held in future in England. The right thus conceded will be undoubtedly a valuable one and will raise the position of this country.

[336] *Panjabee* (Lahore), 9 May 1917

It will have been seen from the statement issued by the Colonial Secretary respecting the work of the Imperial War Conference that the Conference has expressed the opinion that the re-adjustment of constitutional relations between the component parts of the Empire is too important and intricate a subject to deal with during the war and that it should be discussed by a special Imperial Conference immediately after the war. There is every reason to believe that preparations for holding this Conference will commence immediately and our countrymen will be making a grave blunder if they will not make up their minds to tell the authorities without any unnecessary delay what their views are regarding the proposed Conference. Our own views we have already stated. The position, so far as India is concerned, may, indeed, be summed up in a few words. In the first place the special Imperial Conference, or by whatever other name the Conference to be held immediately after the war may be called, must have nothing to do with India's domestic problem, its only concern, in the case of India and of other parts of the Empire, being inter-imperial and foreign relations. Secondly it is essential that before this Conference is held, British statesmanship shall have come to a definite decision regarding India's domestic problem. Thirdly whatever instalment of self-government may be conferred on India before the special Conference is held, India must be represented in it not merely by nominees of the Government but by an equal number of such nominees and of elected representatives of the people. It is no use concealing the fact that the three delegates sent by the Government of India, however valuable may be the work they have rendered as members of the Imperial Conference, have, judging from their public pronouncements, made no serious effort to place the central Indian problem before the British public. They have not done the one thing which the educated community in India regard as more needful than anything else. They have not voiced the Indian aspiration for self-government, its volume, its strength, its intensity, though two of them have occasionally referred to it in a more or less academic manner.

[337] *Parkash* (Lahore), 13 May 1917

News was received that the Allies had agreed in 1915 to hand over Constantinople to Russia on the victorious termination of the war. It now appears that on the abdication of the Tzar the point of view of Russia has changed. A Russian Socialist Minister, who is a strong personality, has declared that he and his friends of the Labour party do not desire Constantinople.

[338] *Desh* (Lahore), 15 May 1917

Mr. Lloyd George, in discussing the question of Irish Home Rule, observed in Parliament that the grant of freedom signifies that freedom should be granted to all parts of the Empire and not to any particular part. If these words are true, India also can entertain many hopes, as what is to-day true of Ireland can to-morrow prove true of India also. We believe the heartfelt desire of Indians will be realised on the termination of the war.

[339] *As-Sabah* (Lahore), 15 May 1917

Six hundred thousand English women have been granted the right to vote at the next Parliamentary elections. This shows that England has changed her angle of vision. Those whose rights were not recognised some time back are being granted the rights they demanded. This will have an agreeable effect on India also.

[340] *Vakil* (Amritsar), 16 May 1917

English women and Indian men

English women have, by giving solid proof of self-sacrifice and rendering meritorious services during the war, succeeded in securing the right to vote at Parliamentary elections. Indians too have not been backward in rendering valuable services to Government. Can it be hoped that consistently with the above the legitimate demands of Indian men too will be fulfilled?

[341] *Hindustan* (Lahore), 16 May 1917

One cannot learn swimming so long as one does not enter water. Similarly, fitness for self-government will come of itself after self-government has been granted.

[342] *Arya Gazette* (Lahore), 17 May 1917

In his speech at London His Highness the Maharaja of Bikaner observed that India was unfit for self-government. Admitting this, will the Maharaja take the trouble of telling us who sent him to England as a representative of Indians? Did he on departure from India consult Indians on the subject? Sensible Indian newspapers have not viewed with approval this unnecessary interference of the Maharaja in matters of British Indian interest.

[343] *Panjabee* (Lahore), 17 May 1917

At a recent function General Smuts made a notable speech describing graphically the efforts of the different parts of the Empire in the war, and demanding 'the maximum of freedom and liberty, the maximum of self-development for the young nations of the Empire, and machinery that will keep all these nations together in the years which are before them.' In the course of his speech the General made an eloquent reference to the intrepidity and soldierly qualities of Indian troops. 'I can say, as one who has commanded thousands of Indian troops in one of our campaigns,' he said, 'that I never wish to command more loyal, brave and better troops. The Indian troops who are now breaking up the Turkish Empire in Mesopotamia are making a contribution to the war which should never be forgotten.' But though Indians are inferior to none in loyalty, courage and initiative – a fact which numerous persons who are in a position to speak with authority on the subject have borne eloquent testimony – they are not treated with equality in the matter of pay, prospects and other matters. Is it too much to hope that these invidious distinctions should now go to the way of all indefensible things?

[344] *Parkash* (Lahore), 20 May 1917

From the conditions in Russia [it can be inferred] that a party is in existence in that country, which is in favour of separate peace with Germany, though it is not an influential party. Germany has long worked for separate peace with Russia, and since the abdication of the Czar her efforts have assumed special activity. The socialists have succeeded in forming a party which has espoused the cause of peace and which is organizing and parading peace processions. We do not know why the Russian Government does not take action to suppress the party. If, however, Russia makes a separate peace with Germany, the situation will become very unpleasant.

[345] *Paisa Akhbar* (Lahore), 20 May 1917

When peace comes the Allied Powers will gain possession of vast territory outside Europe. But it may be asked whether the annexation of this territory will be useful for the Allies and whether the possession of Mesopotamia and the German colonies in Africa by England will not create feelings of envy and jealousy in the minds of other Powers. The spirit of land-grabbing and the mania for extension of the sphere of influence have always resulted in war. Anyhow, England should carefully consider if the inordinate expansion of her empire will be helpful in good administration.

[346] *Virat* (Lahore), 21 May 1917

No journalist, so long as he lives in India, can publish a correct account of the war. But from the news received from the seat of the war, we can form an estimate of the terrible aspect which the war is assuming day by day. German submarines have had such an unpleasant effect on the movement of ships that even the overland mail steamer will now come to India fortnightly, instead of weekly. They have also forced British statesmen to adopt measures for economising the consumption of foodstuffs in England. Still England has not lost courage and the speeches recently delivered by her Ministers in the House of Commons show that they have made every possible arrangement for overcoming the danger of German submarines. The Kaiser cannot now gain the object he had in view in undertaking the present submarine campaign. America and France are also considering the question. It has been stated in different papers that America has discovered means of combating the German submarine campaign. Nevertheless, the danger of German submarines cannot be denied. The campaign presents a problem which is worthy of special consideration and on which the eyes of the whole world are fixed.

[347] *Hindustan* (Lahore), 23 May 1917

The greatest blessing which the war has bestowed on Europe is the improvement of its morality. India has also benefited and all the clouds of suspicion with which her people were regarded in England have been dispelled. Moreover, the idea is gradually gaining strength all over the world that all nations should live in freedom. Even the colonists, who used to regard Indians as coolies, are now realising that India is inhabited by intelligent men like Sir S.P. Sinha and the Maharaja of Bikaner. The war will remove the false feelings of nationality, to which the narrow-mindedness, enmity and jealousy of the world are attributable. Making is ruled by social laws, intended to help and not injure each other. The founders of religion gave the same advice, but the world repeatedly forgot it. Nature has this time, however, taught the lesson in a rather rough manner and we hope the world will not forget it for a long time to come.

[348] *Virat* (Lahore), 28 May 1917

Germany is determined to deal rigorously with the ships of foreign countries to prevent their sailing from the seaports. Hitherto the lives of those who were in the ships were saved; but Germany is now resolved to destroy them outright. America and Great Britain are taking steps to put an end to this mischief and it is to be hoped that it will be soon stopped.

[349] *Panjabee* (Lahore), 2 June 1917

If there is one country rather than another where there has been too much talk about the war and too little readiness to learn the lesson which the war impressively teaches, that country is India. The great lesson of the war is the lesson that, as against all forms of organised unscrupulousness, hooliganism and brutality, the one thing that avails is national efficiency, efficiency in government, in social institutions, in industries, and above all in education which is at the root of all other things. And in none of these respects has India, especially official India, shown any excessive desire to move with the times. As regards the first, while both in Europe and in America people have recognised the present war to be a war of democracy against militarism, while both the President of the United States and the British Premier have declared that what is at stake in the present war is nothing less than the future of democracy, in India it has been found impossible to make any attempt to democratise the Government and the political institutions of the country without bringing down upon the devoted heads of those who make the attempt the wrath of official extremists. In the sphere of industries we stand exactly where we did before the war, and even the belated Commission on Industries has been compelled, owing to the exigencies of war, to suspend work at least until the next cold weather, and probably for a longer period. In the sphere of education all that we have been hearing since the war began is that the Government is unable, owing to the existence of war conditions, to continue its campaign against illiteracy with the vigour of the period immediately following the royal visit.

[350] *Sadiq-ul-Akhbar* (Bahawalpur), 7 June 1917

The daily growing loss of ships by means of torpedoes and the inability of the wounded to return to England are facts really signifying that the control of the sea is passing out of our hands. The difficulties of the Admiralty have assuredly increased, but before the outbreak of the war no one thought of the importance of submarines. This is the reason why our big dreadnoughts are proving useless. Since Lord Fisher has severed his connection with the Admiralty, the British fleet has taken no offensive. If this has been done under compulsion, the Admiralty should be reorganised and young officers appointed to responsible posts.

[351] *Al-Asar* (Lahore), 15 June 1917

In these days no war news is received from the eastern front and various rumours, calculated to create commotion and anxiety, are being circulated. The *Bombay Chronicle* has laid stress on the desirability of a clearly-worded announcement about the situation on the eastern front being made by the Military Department to put an end to the circulation of such rumours.

[352] *Al-Asar* (Lahore), 27 June 1917

Jesus Christ preached to his followers: 'And unto him that smiteth thee on one cheek offer also the other.' None of the Christian Powers which are now at war is following the above principle. In England, however, there are a few persons who are still preaching to this effect. A few days ago, when some British politicians suggested that England should take revenge on Germany for her atrocities, the Archbishop of Canterbury protested against the suggestion. The spirit displayed by the Archbishop may be commendable from the moral standpoint, but truly speaking it is an act of injustice to refrain from punishing a tyrant. If the Archbishop thinks that Englishmen should not make air-raids on Germany by adopting the policy of retaliation, why does he not advocate the argument in respect of ordinary fighting?

[353] *Vakil* (Amritsar), 11 July 1917

Neither the Government of India nor Lord Hardinge is responsible for the failure of the Mesopotamia expedition. It is the British War Office which is responsible. If India had been an independent colony, it would have refused to undertake the responsibility for the expedition. But since it is not independent, it had to bow before higher authorities.

[354] *Panjabee* (Lahore), 14 July 1917

It is gratifying to find that strong resentment is being expressed in all parts of the country at the censure passed upon Lord Hardinge by the Mesopotamian Commission. The occasion undoubtedly calls for a strong and united expression of India's continued confidence in Lord Hardinge, whose courage and statesmanship, as a Bombay telegram points out, made possible the great achievements of India in this war. Indeed, if the Commission had a better appreciation of the services rendered by Lord Hardinge to the Empire at what was perhaps the gravest crisis in its history, they would have voted him a crown of gold, instead of censuring him. But that is their [out-look]. Our concern is to see that no doubt may remain in the minds of the people of England as to our own attitude in regard to one who has been universally acclaimed as the greatest Viceroy since Lord Ripon. To this end the suggestion of the *Bombay Chronicle* that a motion voting India's confidence in Lord Hardinge should be brought before the Joint Conference of the All-India Congress Committee and the Council of the Muslim League will, we feel sure, command universal sympathy and support.

[355] *Al-Munir* (Jhang), 1 August 1917

The world-wide war and England

England is in a position of advantage in every respect. He who thinks that this statement is based on flattery or exaggeration can test its veracity by reviewing the facts bearing on the question.

[356] *Jat Gazette* (Rohtak), 7 August 1917

Taking into full consideration all the circumstances, it can be confidently affirmed that the war will last another year at least. How many more recruits will be required is the question. In our opinion it is necessary to supply the Government a larger number of recruits than have been hitherto supplied. Newspaper readers know that the old administration of Russia has been changed. When once the administration of a country is changed, everything shows signs of slackness and weakness, while an abnormal change in the Government of a country during a great war terribly weakens its military strength. Such is the case with Russia, where a civil war is proceeding on a small scale. England alone can help Russia at this crisis, and the deficiency in the fighting troops can be easily supplied by India in a short time. If we wish to bring the war to a successful termination within a year, we should be prepared to make further sacrifices. Moreover, owing to the relaxation of the Russian pressure on the Russian front the Turks and the Germans are likely to exert themselves to their utmost in Mesopotamia and on the eastern front. India is, in particular, responsible for not only maintaining, but also extending, the conquests made by our armies in Mesopotamia. Indians are well aware that the future advancement of their country is bound up with the stability of the British *raj*, although in their opinion many reforms are needed in the administration.

[357] *Municipal Gazette* (Lahore), 12 August 1917

Speaking at the durbar at Kasur, His Honour the Lieutenant-Governor expressed his displeasure with Lahore, because with the exception of the Sikhs no community in the Lahore District had contributed a satisfactory number of recruits. His Honour also stated that if this state of affairs continued, he would by way of punishment transfer the capital from Lahore to Amritsar. The people of the Lahore District should learn a lesson from this and make a zealous effort to secure recruits. It is to be hoped that all influential persons will consider His Honour's orders and the Lahore District will supply sufficient recruits to afford no opportunity to His Honour to feel displeased with it.

[358] *Paisa Akhbar* (Lahore), 16 August 1917

His Honour remarked that if Lahore did not make sufficient reparation in giving recruits, some successor of his might shift the capital to Amritsar, which has shown a highly loyal spirit. It is not out of place to expect better recruitment in Lahore, which has excelled other cities of the Province in contributing to the War Loan. But it is surprising to see that the threat of changing the seat of Government is due to a comparatively smaller number of recruits. People did not know that Government wanted to select for its capital a city the population of which is distinguished for its martial spirit. Generally the case is the reverse. Calcutta was not chosen for its martial spirit and Delhi also has not been preferred for this reason. Moreover, the Government will have to spend large sums of money in building a Government House, offices and other public buildings at Amritsar if it shifts its capital there. And if Amritsar displeases any Lieutenant-Governor, the capital will go on rolling indefinitely.

[359] *Jat Gazette* (Rohtak), 21 August 1917

It is the opinion of military experts that the war will not come to an end in 1917. Its result will be similar to the war of the Mahabharata. Europe will take long to recover her former glory and her map may be changed a little, while the political principles of Europe will also undergo a transformation. The condition of Russia has not yet improved. There has been a great disturbance in Kronstadt on account of the efforts of a student. It was hoped that the participation of Italy in the war would produce extraordinary results; but Italy is as slow as a tortoise. Italy has attacked Austria several times, but Austria has not yet received any fatal blow. Turkey is silent. Either she is at her death-bed or is awaiting reinforcements. Russia is in possession of Turkish territory. It is stated that the Turks are collecting forces in Mesopotamia.

[360] *Tribune* (Lahore), 22 August 1917

We must welcome the announcement made by the Secretary of State in the House of Commons of the grant of King's Commissions to

9 Indian soldiers who have served in the field. Obviously this is the first practical Army reform adopted by the Government of India of the many that have been ceaselessly urged by the Congress during the last 30 years. It is also announced that a regular scheme of granting similar Commissions to Indians and of training them in a military college is under consideration. We hope that in adopting this reform the Government will not make any differentiation or create differences in pay rank, status &c., of Indians, but will grant Commissions to Indian youths of required fitness on equal terms with those of non-Indian subjects of the King-Emperor. Any attempt to differentiate will be inconsistent with the Proclamation of 1858.

[361] *Kashmiri Magazine* (Lahore), 28 August 1917

The Pope's peace proposals [...] make absolutely no mention of unfortunate Turkey. Perhaps this Empire is not of sufficient importance to justify even a mention of its name.

[362] *Virat* (Lahore), 17 September 1917

Since the passing of the Compulsion Bill in England, people have invented strange crimes to avoid enlistment in the army. It is stated that many of those who are summoned for recruitment are found to be unfit for military service. But when these persons are closely examined surprising revelations are made. Many of them use medicines which render them weak. These men assume all sorts of disguises and endanger their health. Several doctors and clerks are also a party to the deception. Even bribery is often resorted to. It is a pity to see what these men do to save their mortal bodies.

[363] *Desh* (Lahore), 22 September 1917

An article published in a German newspaper [...] says that the Germans would have prohibited Indians from drinking, or bathing in, the unclean water of the Ganges, if they had been in possession of India. Thus it can be imagined how cruelly the Germans would have wounded the religious feelings of the people had they been the rulers of India.

[364] *Parkash* (Lahore), 18 November 1917

The eyes of the whole world are now fixed on Italy. The Austro-German forces seem to have gained a complete success. We do not know how much loss Italy suffered, but it is heavy; and the enemy is still advancing and the Italian army still retreating. This unpleasant state of affairs has been caused by the carelessness of the Italian military officers and German propaganda.

[365] *Bulletin* (Lahore), 21 November 1917

A German Lieutenant-Commander boasts of having sunk 198 ships by means of his submarine. The fact came to light in this way. A friend of his recently telegraphed to congratulate him on having sunk 100 ships, whereupon he replied that either the telegram was seven months old or the sender should have waited until he had made the number up to 200 by sinking two more ships.

[366] *Desh* (Lahore), 28 November 1917

It is high time that the patriots of Russia took the reins of administrative matters into their own hands by suppressing the party of rebels. If strenuous efforts are made at the present moment to save Russia from its imminent danger, we have every reason to believe that Russia will gain double strength and preserve the honour of her brave people.

[367] *Kshatri* (Gujranwala), 30 November 1917

The need for a new civilisation

The civilised nations of Europe and America are so fond of luxury, wine, beauty, love-making, fashion and innovation that they cannot leave blandishments and eating and drinking even in the conflagration of the present war.

[368] *Jat Gazette* (Rohtak), 4 December 1917

An American soldier draws 250 rupees per mensem in addition to food and clothing. In India no military officer, except a Subedar-Major gets as much. The American Government will also have the lives of its soldiers insured, so that they may not be tempted to save their lives and so that the surviving members of their families may pass their days in comfort.

[369] *Panjabee* (Lahore), 14 December 1917

Ever since the retrieval of the Kut disaster, the British troops have been literally marching from victory to victory in Mesopotamia and Palestine. Those who watched the course of events in Palestine were almost hourly expecting the fall of Jerusalem. The renowned city redolent with the memories of early Christianity had been in the past the scene of many bloody conflicts between Christians and the Muslims. Round its walls the tide of crusades beat and here the Cross and the Crescent contended for mastery till the holiest place of Christianity, just as holy as the sacred Kashi to the Hindus and Mecca to the Mussalmans, passed into the hands of the followers of the Arabian Prophet. Now once more after so many centuries a Christian nation is in possession of a Christian city.

[370] *Khalsa Akhbar* (Lahore), 14 December 1917

It has been officially announced that a German fleet of airships made a terrible attack on England on the morning of the 6th instant. The estimate of loss has been made very low. Mr. Bonar Law, speaking on the subject in the House of Commons, observed that by this attack 7 persons have been killed and 22 wounded. The inhabitants show no sign of consternation.

[371] *Paisa Akhbar* (Lahore), 19 December 1917

Since [Jerusalem] is a sacred city of Islam, as the first *Ka'aba*, it is to be hoped that the pledges about the protection of sacred buildings will not be lost sight of at the time of final settlement.

[372] *Sikhs and Sikhism* (Lahore), 19 December 1917

That the brave and perseverant armies of the British have captured Jerusalem, and with that *wrested Bethulam*, the Holiest of Holies of

Christians from the clutches of Turks, has the greatest historical significance from the Christian point of view. The Holy Sepulchre has for many centuries been in the Turkish possession and all efforts hitherto made to rid it of the Non-Christian sway failed most dismally. The Turks too have lost nothing in respect of religion. [Bethlehem] is a Christian shrine, having religiously no connection whatever with the Moslem rulers who possessed it, and that a Christian power has taken it back from the Turks means the recovery of what has been due to the former from the latter for centuries past. The conscientious British respect the sacred places of other religions. It is but natural therefore that we people of religions other than Christianity should reciprocate by an expression of pleasure at their recovering a place which belongs to Christianity.

[373] *Hindustan* (Lahore), 21 December 1917

The conquest of Jerusalem is the greatest event in the history of the world. Now at last Jerusalem has been won by a Christian power. The event seems to have disturbed certain Muhammadan newspapers which say that the administration of the country should be made over to Muhammadans in the same way as the administration of Mecca and Medina. We consider this demand most unreasonable. In the present war many Governments in Europe have been overturned. Many Kings and Emperors who once reigned over crores of people are now in prison or aimlessly loitering about here and there. But none of these incidents is so important as the conquest of Jerusalem.

[374] *Bulletin* (Lahore), 24 December 1917

A well known French journalist writes in the course of an article: 'Our British Ally hesitates to bring all his forces in France under the command of our Commander-in-Chief, General Joffre. Let us curse traditions and national pride at such a time! If we wish to gain victory we must follow the example of the Germans and appoint like them a Commander-in-Chief of all our forces.'

CHAPTER 5

1918

On 21 March 1918, 44 divisions of the German army attacked beleaguered British soldiers of the Fifth Army as part of a massive offensive operation code-named Michael. Storm-troop tactics, rehearsed the previous year in Italy and Russia, paid dividends. In the first two weeks, the German army advanced 50 miles. By early April, the British had lost 170,000 men, 1,000 heavy guns, and the entire Somme river area for which they had paid such a high price two years prior. But the Germans failed to break the British and French armies, and their successes cost them 239,000 casualties, many from Germany's elite units. The Germans launched another offensive against the British in Flanders on 9 April, and a third against the French in the Chemin des Dames in late May. The timely arrival of the American Expeditionary Force on the Western Front in June halted any significant further advance by the now exhausted German forces. With the threat to Paris gone, the Allies – now counting among them 786,489 fresh Americans as of 1 August – commenced their own massive counter-offensive on 24 July. All along the Western Front, British, French and American armies began steadily recapturing all of that spring and summer's lost territory. German soldiers and commanders, sensing that the war was indeed lost, began seeking a way out. On 8 August, in one day at Amiens, the Germans lost 28,000 men. The majority of these men surrendered rather than fought. Their commander, Erich Ludendorff, called it the 'black day' of the German army. In early October, combined Australian and American forces broke the Hindenburg Line, an imposing network of trenches, bunkers, barbed-wire and machine guns Ludendorff hoped might delay the Allies through the winter. The Germans began sending out peace-feelers, hoping for a diplomatic solution based on American President Woodrow Wilson's Fourteen Points. Meanwhile, the collapse of Germany's allies began in earnest. The Italians finally broke through the Austrian lines at the close of October. The Austro-Hungarian Empire came unstuck. Hungary declared independence. So did Czechoslovakia, Slovenia, Bosnia and Croatia. Bulgaria capitulated to the Allies on 29 October. The Ottomans surrendered the following day. On 10 November, the German Kaiser abdicated. On 11 November, 1,597 days since the murder of Archduke Franz Ferdinand in Sarajevo, the armies on the Western Front agreed to an Armistice.

Events on the Western Front commanded the attention of the Punjabi press throughout 1918. On 9 April, Prime Minister David Lloyd George said in the House of Commons of the German offensives then-underway, 'We have entered the most critical phase of this terrible war.' 'The fate of the Empire,' he added, 'the fate of Europe, and the fate of liberty throughout the world, may depend on the success with which the very last of these attacks is resisted and countered.' Later, in the same session, the Prime Minister reminded the House of Commons, 'There is a menace to our Eastern Empire through Persia, because through Persia you approach Afghanistan, and through Afghanistan you menace the whole of India.' This comment caused a flurry in the Punjabi press. India's educated middle classes wanted to know when they might have the opportunity to enlist in the Indian Army. A special war conference in Delhi summoned by the Viceroy in April pledged 500,000 more recruits. The Punjab was asked to furnish 200,000. A public meeting in Lahore in May, presided over by Lieutenant Governor O'Dwyer and 600 representatives of the Province and of the Native States, unanimously decided to supply the quota. It is not altogether clear that authorities in India would have been able to meet this demand. 'Fortunately,' O'Dwyer wrote, 'within six months the problem was solved by the Armistice.'[1] The system of quotas on which the Punjabi state and Indian Army relied to furnish recruits resulted in numerous cases of abuse, notwithstanding whatever denials the Lieutenant Governor later offered. As Dennis Showalter has observed, 'The men who stood in the ranks of the Indian Army infantry in 1918 were by no means all "true volunteers," motivated by the prospect of advantage and a willingness to fight, on which that army had historically depended.'[2]

Selections from the Indian newspapers published in the Punjab, 1918

CONTENTS

[375] *Tribune* (Lahore), 13 January 1918

One significant omission in President Wilson's speech will strike every one. Mr. Lloyd George, as our readers are aware, laid considerable emphasis on Germany making the necessary reparation for the wrongs she has done as a condition precedent to peace. One misses any reference to this important subject in the President's statement of the concrete conditions of peace. Even in the case of Belgium all that the President seems to want is that her independence and integrity should be restored and safeguarded. We do not know if the omission is deliberate or merely an oversight. We prefer to think that it is the last, for it goes without saying that unless Germany is compelled to make reparation for the effects of her aggressive and wanton folly there will be nothing to prevent her from repeating it whenever she likes or finds it congenial to her purpose.

[376] *Bulletin* (Lahore), 15 January 1918

It is now universally admitted that it was the Indian soldiers who saved the situation in a critical stage of the war, and a large number of them are still fighting in France and Flanders. But for reasons which cannot be easily divined Reuters is the last quarter to look to for any reference to their doings, far less anything beyond a bare mention if the said doings are of an extraordinary nature. This fact cannot but compel attention in India, especially in the striking contrast it offers to the enthusiasm felt in the very same quarter for Anzacs and Canadians.

[377] *Panjabee* (Lahore), 27 January 1918

As a specimen of flamboyant oratory which is a characteristic of the German War Lord, it is difficult to beat the following passage from the Kaiser's speech delivered at the private gathering of German business men and taken from a pamphlet unearthed by an American newspaper and published in our yesterday's issue. Said the Kaiser, 'We shall not merely occupy India. We shall conquer it and the vast resources which the British allow to be taken by the Indian Princes will, after our conquest, flow in a golden stream into the Fatherland.' How the Kaiser's dream came from the gate of ivory and what part the Indian troops played in arresting his designs is a matter of recent history.

[378] *Tribune* (Lahore), 29 January 1918

It is characteristic of German diplomacy that the Chancellor, while readily accepting all the general and more or less abstract terms of President Wilson, regarding which there will be ample room hereafter for any amount of evasion, rejects all the concrete terms. As long as Germany is in this mood to talk of peace between her and the Allies is to waste one's breath. The hope of an early peace has entirely vanished, and the Allies have to recognise that they must, in the language of the President of the Labour Conference, fight on and fight to a finish.

[379] *Panjabee* (Lahore), 29 January 1918

The German Chancellor introduces new conditions whose insistence further complicates the situation and makes the chances of a settlement a remoter contingency than had hitherto been considered to be the case. If peace were concluded under the terms now dictated by Germany, it would mean a success for Germany after she had committed the greatest crime a nation could commit. It is to be hoped that such a catastrophe will never befall the world.

[380] *Panjabee* (Lahore), 31 January 1918

Nothing is more tragic in the history of the world than the fate of the Jews who, though the chosen race of God according to the Old

Testament, have suffered untold miseries. The war, it appears, promises to prove a blessing in disguise to this afflicted race. Mr. Balfour, writing to Lord Rothschild, states that the British Government view with favour the establishment in Palestine of the national home for the Jewish people and would use their best endeavours to facilitate the attainment of that object.

[381] *Tribune* (Lahore), 3 February 1918

The strikes in Germany, which, according to the latest message, continue to spread, are one of those signs of the times of which Germany, if she has any part of her sanity still left, cannot possibly fail to take note. It may be quite easy to suppress newspapers, as the German Government have just suppressed such influential news-papers as the *Vorwaerts* and the *Tageblatt*, but it is not equally easy to suppress popular discontent and the rising tide of democratic fury. There is one and but one way of meeting the demand of the situation. If the Kaiser and his advisors do not want to be swept away as the Tsar recently was, as autocrats in all ages have been at such epochs, they will adopt this way.

[382] *Panjabee* (Lahore), 14 February 1918

The death of Abdul Hamid, Ex-Sultan of Turkey, removes one of the greatest despots and weakest monarchs that the world has ever seen. His reign in Turkey has been one of continued oppression and misrule and resulted in the Young Turk party coming to power and in his eventual removal from the Ottoman throne. The Armenian massacres which agitated Europe from one end to the other and drew out in England men like Carlyle and Ruskin from their scholastic retreats to publicly condemn the gruesome tragedy were, as our readers are aware, connected with the name of Abdul Hamid, who came to be nicknamed by Mr. Gladstone as 'the sick man of Europe.'

[383] *Paisa Akhbar* (Lahore), 28 February 1918

As England has always been a friend and supporter of the Turks on most critical occasions and as she is a first class Muslim Power owing to her having the largest Muslim population under her rule, it is to be hoped that in consideration of the feelings of the large number of her Muhammadan subjects who are the co-religionists of the Turks she will pay due consideration to the pressing circumstances of the Turks in the present war and will see that severe injury is not done to Turkey.

[384] *Visvkarma* (Amritsar), February Edition 1918

Great activity is being shown in Germany in connection with the war and a new fleet of airships, large and unique in length and strength, is being prepared with great rapidity. The Germans are also constructing an airship of some metal, which will fly at a short distance from the earth and help the army, being a kind of walking 'Tank.' The Government of America has received information that Germany is building cruisers which are so light that they can dive deep into the sea and move about unobstructed.

[385] *Khalsa Akhbar* (Lahore), 1 March 1918

The present war has led to extraordinary proposals in Europe concerning virgin marriages. Such is the condition to which those have been reduced who regarded with contempt Asiatics and Africans for indulging in polygamy. It is true that the freedom and greatness of Europe do not depend upon virtue but upon guns and cannon balls [. . .] Labour will soon turn the whole of Europe topsy-turvy. Recently the Labour party of England passed a resolution in favour of Home Rule for India. It is possible that at the end of the war the Labour party may gain power in Parliament, with the result that India may get Home Rule at once. As for Mr. Montagu, when the proclamation of a sympathetic queen like Victoria, Lord Ripon's days of freedom, the reforms of Lord Morley and the sincerity of Lord Hardinge failed to reassure the Indians, he will be a strange magician if his reforms succeed in removing anxiety from their minds.

[386] *Jat Gazette* (Rohtak), 12 March 1918

The day dreams of a German professor

Professor M. Charahun has written a pamphlet and divulged the secret reason for the promises of the Germans not to ask for an indemnity or territorial annexation. The writer says that during the three years of the war, the area of the German Empire has expanded to 3,600,000 kilometres from 540,000 and its population to 280,000,000 from 68,000,000 men. The Professor also says that Germany has gained great wealth in this war. For instance, the Belgian railways are considered to be worth 13 crores. Besides, Germany is getting work out of two lakhs of war prisoners and 2 crore and 60 lakhs of men in the conquered territories for her own advantage. This is why Germany has considered it proper not to demand a war indemnity or an annexation of territory.

[387] *Sitara-i-Subah* (Lahore), 23 March 1918

On the Western Front the Germans are using star-shells in heavy long range rungs. These shells have two advantages. When ejected from a gun they burst upon reaching a certain height and illumine the whole place; and when they fall down they destroy many things. Great Britain has also recently used such shells on the Western Front. The Germans have lately invented a new shell filled with poisonous gas, which on bursting spreads poisonous gases all round and stops breathing.

[388] *Paisa Akhbar* (Lahore), 24 March 1918

The British Government [should keep ...] Jerusalem and Mesopotamia in Muhammadan hands. It should not allow itself to be imposed upon by the Jewish capitalists and journalists of Europe and America. The desire to which expression was given by Professor Mipsgey before the Royal Institute can be fulfilled only by entrusting the administration of Mesopotamia, especially of Jerusalem, to the Turks again, who for centuries past have looked after its sacred places and never interfered with the monuments and religious ceremonies of the non-Turks. Moreover, the majority of the population is Muslim.

[389] *Desh* (Lahore), 25 March 1918

In 1917 German submarines sunk 2,930 ships, or more than 50 a week. This is incredible and the figures should be taken to include all the Allied and neutral ships, [. . . and] also fishing boats.

[390] *Sitara-i-Subah* (Lahore), 28 March 1918

The Allied Powers have undoubtedly bigger armies than the Central Powers. But they do not give evidence of that power of co-ordination which the Central Powers have shown in the present war. The military control of Germany, Austria, Turkey and Bulgaria is in the hands of Hindenburg and Ludendorff. They move their combined armies wherever and whenever they like. But the Allies cannot do this. It is impossible for the French army to work in subordination to a British General and for the Italian army to move to another front and work under a French or English general. It is owing to this selfishness that the Allied Powers have failed to gain the desired success in their great efforts. When Japan joined the Allies people thought that the end of Germany was near, believing that the powerful navy and veteran army of Japan would not only destroy German influence in Asia but also inflict a deadly blow on her in Europe. But apart from the capture of Tsingtao, the whole of which is so close to Japan and where Germany could send no relief or help, Japan has gained no practical distinction in the war worth mentioning. What Japan has done is this. When the submarine warfare rendered the sea highways of Europe dangerous to a large extent and commerce could not be carried on as usual from Europe to India, Japan showed extraordinary activity and zeal in the commercial arena and began to collect immense amounts of money by exporting her manufactured goods to India. We have been hearing of the zeal and activity of America for a year or more, but America has hitherto failed to complete her preparations. If all the

Allied Powers had placed their armies and navies under the absolute control of British statesmen, the end of Russia would not have been so deplorable and Belgium, Servia, Roumania, etc., would never have been confronted with the misfortunes they have undergone. If the Allies afford proof of their alliance in the true significance of the term they can even now very easily make the Central Powers lose heart.

[391] *Paisa Akhbar* (Lahore), 29 March 1918

German tactics in transferring fresh troops from the eastern to the western front will not succeed for any length of time. Righteousness will triumph in the end.

[392] *Tribune* (Lahore), 30 March 1918

The war has reached its most critical, perhaps its decisive phase. Germany recognises that this is her last chance and is likely to do her worst. She is doing it. But the Allies are not daunted and have no reason to be. Their ultimate victory has never been in doubt and is no more in doubt to-day than it was some months ago when Germany had sustained a succession of reverses on the western front.

[393] *Bulletin* (Lahore), 2 April 1918

On the Western Front the situation is clearer than since the beginning of the offensive in the north of Somme. Ground has been gained at certain places and in spite of the force of the attack of the enemy it did not make any considerable impression on our battle positions. In fact, it has resulted in a severe enemy defeat.

[394] *Paisa Akhbar* (Lahore), 2 April 1918

The war has now reached [an] acute stage and Germany desires to make a final effort. But there is no cause for anxiety for the Allied Powers, because they will triumph in the end. Nevertheless, in order to strengthen this hope and to gain this end promptly, the Allies and their subjects should [... still make] more united efforts.

[395] *Paisa Akhbar* (Lahore), 2 April 1918

The revolution in Russia has changed the whole aspect of affairs and thrown open the path of intrigue to Turkey. What better neighbour can we have for India than republican Russia and what better compensation can there be for the ancient rivalry between England and Russia in Asia? But if Russia is divided into small states, the position will be full of anxiety. The management of some of these states will be in the hands of Turkey and the Turkish dream appears to be entering the region of possibility. But the final issue depends on Russia, because the experiment which she is engaged in making will affect the fate of the world. If she succeeds in establishing a republican government and in giving freedom and unity to her subjects, she will succeed in solving a difficult problem, indeed.

[396] *Paisa Akhbar* (Lahore), 4 April 1918

England and France have a larger number of guns than the enemy. The Allies can also turn out more guns. Moreover, it will be interesting to ascertain the reason of the shells falling on Paris and to unravel the mystery. If it be true that a gun has become manufactured which is capable of throwing shells from so long a distance, this will effect a revolution in artillery warfare.

[397] *Desh* (Lahore), 4 April 1918

The King-Emperor's visit to the western front has created fresh aspirations in the minds of the army and steeled our soldiers with increased perseverance. As General May observed, the enemy will soon spend his power in the offensive and become weak, when the Allies will be able to overpower him.

[398] *Desh* (Lahore), 5 April 1918

The advance of the enemy has been fully checked on the whole front. The lull shows that the Germans are as usual engaged in making fresh preparations. Still the present cessation of the attack has a special importance for the Allies, as it will enable them to strengthen their position. The public already had great faith in the Allied forces and their recent magnificent achievements have inspired increased confidence in England and France. All are now fully confident that the enemy will have to suffer humiliation in this battle as he did in previous engagements.

[399] *Desh* (Lahore), 5 April 1918

The present lull suggests the idea that the enemy's object has been frustrated. His objective is obviously Paris in the belief that if he can reach Paris he will bring the war to a decisive stage. But there can be no doubting the fact that he has been greatly weakened and has gained a bitter experience by discovering that it is not easy to oppose the Allies, who are fixed to their moorings like a rock.

[400] *Kapurthala Akhbar* (Kapurthala), 6 April 1918

During the past week the greatest battle of the war has been fought on the western front, in which the enemy has made some advance at a very heavy price. But the British forces have resisted the enemy so bravely that the latter has admitted their bravery and his advance has been checked. Hindenberg boasted that he would reach Paris by the 1st of April. His army has been smashed in striking its heads against an iron wall and the Germans are still as far away from Paris as they were last year. The war situation is satisfactory on all fronts.

[401] *Sanatan Dharm Parcharak* (Amritsar), 8 April 1918

The war has reached a critical stage. Germans look upon the English as their greatest enemies, but victory and defeat lie on the lap of the gods alone and no one can foretell the result of the war. Nevertheless, all humanity hopes that God will take the side of truth and justice. A thousand German guns were being fired at three British Divisions only and the German nation utilised its whole strength in the attack. The result of this 'storm' was the retreat of the British. The area of conflict is spreading, but the Allied forces of Great Britain and France have had to retreat further at various places in face of the enemy's large forces.

[402] *Bulletin* (Lahore), 8 April 1918

Magical guns of 24 centimetres are firing shells on Paris. These shells, it is said, reach a distance of 70 miles and go flying to a height of 22 miles. Military experts are of [the] opinion that acceleration is created in the velocity of the shells by means of electricity, a new thing altogether.

[403] *Desh* (Lahore), 10 April 1918

Though the Germans attacked the Allies from various sides with large armies, still they have not been able to gain any advantage and have wasted enormous numbers of men. The Allies are fighting for truth and according to the law of nature truth is sure to come out triumphant in the end.

[404] *Sitara-i-Subah* (Lahore), 10 April 1918

Mr. Wilson is not showing as much zeal and activity in the war as are necessary at present. American troops do not appear to have completed their preparations. No strong American force has been sent to France, with the exception of a small American army which is fighting in Alsace Lorraine. Turkish and Bulgarian Ambassadors are still moving about freely in America. Mr. Wilson is acting very slowly. The war has reached its last stage and America should help the Allies promptly in every possible way.

[405] *Tribune* (Lahore), 10 April 1918

The telegrams that have just passed between the Premier and His Excellency the Viceroy, though in the highest degree significant, cannot be said to be altogether unexpected. The situation they reveal is the direct outcome of the elimination of Russia as a fighting unit and of the partial check which Germany has met with on the western front. Germany realises that this is her last chance, and that she must strike wherever she can hope to strike with effect. Naturally Germany looks in other directions for speedier successes that may be both of immediate and ultimate advantage to her. That is the clear meaning of the new move. We know nothing about this move yet. The Premier's message is the first authentic intimation of it, and it must be said that it is somewhat meagre in the information it gives. Our suggestion to the Government is that the Viceroy should immediately convene two conferences, one of the representatives of the Princes and the other of the representatives of the People, to decide upon the plan of action, should take them fully into his confidence, throw upon them the responsibility of doing all that is necessary at the present time, and express the readiness of the Government to fully co-operate with them and to accept their own co-operation to the fullest extent. We are particularly anxious that the executive bodies of the Congress and the League should meet in a joint session at a central place. Under ordinary circumstances the two main bodies were to have met after the constitutional reforms had been announced. The new situation that seems to have arisen does call for a deviation from the normal course. We have persistently refused to separate the war and the reforms. We do refuse to separate them even now. But just because we refuse to separate them, and for the very reason for which we refuse to separate them, we realise to the full that a time has now come when a very great part of our energies and our attention should be devoted to the question of 'safeguarding the soil of the motherland.'

[406] *Panjabee* (Lahore), 11 April 1918

The people of India [. . .] realise the gravity of the situation as nothing else [. . .] before. Indian leaders had repeatedly urged the Government to be prepared for such an emergency. There were many who feared that the war would not end quickly. There were some who thought that India might be directly involved in this terrible catastrophe. It was such an apprehension that prompted Indian leaders to suggest to the Government that all possible means should be adopted to train Indians for military duties. The first thing that the authorities should do is to take the people into their confidence. They should confer with the Princes and Indian leaders and devise means for preventing 'the German menace from spreading to the East.' Indians will rise like one man to defend their country and to save the East from the aggression of Germany.

[407] *Khalsa Advocate* (Amritsar), 13 April 1918

It may be feared that some danger in the East also may be ahead, although the telegrams do not explicitly locate the direction from which the menace comes. As for the Sikhs we beg to submit that we endorse every word of the Viceroy and assure the Prime Minister that of all the sections of the Indian nation Sikhs in particular will see that their response to his trumpet call beats all previous records of human devotion and sacrifice. Here we would like to sound a note of warning to the Sikh democracy. It is not time that we should weep over spilt milk or dilate upon our grievances still remaining unredressed. We must forget them all for the time being and devote ourselves, heart and soul, to bringing all the forces at work to one common point.

[408] *Kapurthala Akhbar* (Kapurthala), 13 April 1918

The recent German attack will also fail. The enemy used a powerful army in attacking the British front but was repulsed with a heavy loss. The French also repulsed all his attacks and even recaptured one or two places.

[409] *Sitara-i-Subah* (Lahore), 14 April 1918

A short while ago [this paper] observed that the American President was moving very slowly in prosecuting the war. But repeated telegrams from Reuter show that America is giving sufficient help to the Allies in military and naval forces and that the Allies have full confidence in America, which has been making military preparations for the last two years-and-a-half. The world will be astonished when the American army soon reaches the western theatre with complete equipment to help the Allies.

[410] *Bulletin* (Lahore), 17 April 1918

In the violence of the enemy's present effort lies not only the indication that she is in desperate straits, but also the germ of her own exhaustion. The situation, critical as it is, is not discouraging to the cause of the Allies. The cohesion of the British troops is not only not destroyed but, judging by the results of the recent onslaughts, is not likely to be very materially affected before enemy exhaustion sets in. The object of the renewed attack in the south is to retain the French forces there.

[411] *Paisa Akhbar* (Lahore), 19 April 1918

It is difficult to say anything definite [about Turkish atrocities in Armenia] in the absence of detailed particulars. That the Turks should adopt such an attitude towards the Armenians without rhyme or reason is surprising.

[412] *Khalsa Advocate* (Amritsar), 20 April 1918

We Sikhs are proud that in our district we have given the largest number of men to the army. Our present struggle demands all the resources of the Empire to be thrown in the balance to win a lasting and an honourable peace. The duty of India to the Empire in this world-struggle is clear.

[413] *Paisa Akhbar* (Lahore), 21 April 1918

The Germans are trying to gain their object speedily by means of a decisive battle. It should be the duty of General Foch not only to frustrate the enemy's object but also to inflict a crushing defeat on him. The Allies will be able to take the offensive when the German failure becomes certain. The success of the Allies is guaranteed by the huge army which they have raised for the purpose.

[414] *Paisa Akhbar* (Lahore), 23 April 1918

It is necessary for every section of the community to concentrate its attention on devising means to carry the war to a successful issue and avoid controversial matters and mischievous discussions. It is extremely improper to think of using the present occasion to make a bargain and demand political concessions in return for India's help in the war. For those who are crying for the moon to take advantage of the difficulties of the Government to force it to accept premature demands is anything but loyalty.

[415] *Paisa Akhbar* (Lahore), 25 April 1918

The Germans have not succeeded in breaking through the English and French lines and have suffered a heavy loss of life. They will not be able to stand the strain of this wastage much longer.

[416] *Paisa Akhbar* (Lahore), 26 April 1918

The frontiers of India are absolutely safe. German soldiers are not birds that they can reach this country by flying with war materials over thousands of miles.

[417] *Shanti* (Rawalpindi), 27 April 1918

The Prime Minister's message and the Viceroy's appeal show that if the military power of Germany is not crushed, there is every possibility of Asia and, for that matter of India, being confronted with serious danger. Finding that he can gain no success in France, the enemy desires to turn his face towards the East and to deluge Asia with blood and devastation. Every Indian should consider it his duty to gird up his loins to save the countries of Asia generally and India particularly from the impending danger.

[418] *Akhbar-i-' Am* (Lahore), 27 April 1918

The unparalleled bravery with which British soldiers are frustrating the designs of the enemy cannot be too highly praised. Such instances of valour, devotion and self-sacrifice cannot be found in the history of the world [. . .] The Allies will be victorious. The advance of the enemy on the western line has been brought to a standstill. The Allies army will shortly attack the enemy and administer a crushing defeat to him.

[419] *Sitara-i-Subah* (Lahore), 27 April 1918

When the Germans found that the moving tanks of Great Britain caused them heavy injury, they began manufacturing similar tanks themselves. For some time all German attempts failed, but in the end they were successful and we now learn for the first time that the Germans have brought into action not one but several kinds of tanks and land cruisers. The world has come to know that like Great Britain the Germans have moving iron tanks and Krupp's factory has not lagged behind English factories in their manufacture. The Germans might well take pride in their achievement. After the collapse of Russia the Germans hoped to defeat the Allies by one supreme effort. But their effort have, after a great sacrifice, succeeded merely in pushing back the Allies a little, and they have failed to break the front line and to separate the English and the French armies.

[420] *Akhbar-i-' Am* (Lahore), 27 April 1918

Indians [must] open their eyes and see the importance of the present times. They should show self-sacrifice and enthusiastically render military aid to Great Britain. The people of this country should enlist in large numbers.

[421] *Sitara-i-Subah* (Lahore), 28 April 1918

While Mr. Lloyd George's appeal has been enthusiastically welcomed by all communities in India, it has at the same time filled the minds of illiterate and ignorant men with perplexing thoughts, as they fear that India is about to become the victim of war conditions, the position of the Prime Minister and his responsibility lending a definite colour to the view. The Lieutenant-Governors of the United Provinces and the Punjab have, however, contradicted the various rumours afloat. On the face of it, the enemy can threaten India from three sides; firstly, from the side of Persia, which is contiguous to the frontiers of an ally of Germany. But England has a large and efficient army in Mesopotamia. Secondly, the enemy might begin operations from the Caucasus and after entering Turkistan, where independent rule has been established, threaten Afghanistan. But the Caucasians have not welcomed Germany or Turkey and there are very few chances of a successful invasion of India from that side. Thirdly, the enemy might come through Siberia and after traversing Turkistan appear on the frontier of Kashmir. But even this imaginary programme is not feasible, as China will never tolerate the German attempt to create a disturbance in the country of her neighbour and ally. All these three possibilities are thus impossible of realisation and India has no reason to fear any danger. The measures which the Government of India want to adopt are only precautionary measures; so that if the enemy ever invades India he may be received with a shower of bullets.

[422] *Tahzib-i-Niswan* (Lahore), 29 April 1918

Some wicked persons are spreading [a] false rumour that the Germans are going to invade the country. The rumour is absolutely baseless.

[423] *Sitarah-i-Subah* (Lahore), 2 May 1918

Owing to their heavy losses the German armies have lost their heart. Moreover, the resources of Germany as compared to the Allies are small and limited. The success that Germany has so far gained is largely due to the fact that universal military service is compulsory in that country, so that the whole German nation in a way constitutes an army. British statesmen, on the other hand, never paid much attention to the question of increasing their armies. In the present war, however, England has enlisted nearly 75,000,000 soldiers and her resources are so extensive that if the war continues for four years more, this will make no difference in her military strength and resources.

[424] *Brahman Samachar* (Lahore), 3 May 1918

The problem which needs the greatest attention at the present moment is the supply of an adequate number of young men from every class of people for military service. The best way for India to serve itself and His Majesty the King-Emperor lies in providing military recruits in large numbers. We have previously said that it is possible to secure millions of recruits from India for the defence of the country. Somewhat similar views have been expressed by Pandit Tilak.

[425] *Tribune* (Lahore), 3 May 1918

The madness of the idea of conscription at present in India in general and in the Punjab in particular is happily only too well-known to the authorities, and we are perfectly certain that if conscription in any shape or form were proposed the Punjab Government would be the first to object to it.

[426] *Tribune* (Lahore), 4 May 1918

We only hope that in making the provisional allotment the authorities will bear in mind that the Punjab has already been drawn upon far more largely than any other Province, and that fairness demands that the rest of the country should, as far as possible, make up the lee-way.

[427] *Tribune* (Lahore), 5 May 1918

We cordially and whole-heartedly associate ourselves with the strong and emphatic desire which found expression at the public meeting held in the University Hall that the proud record of the Punjab in the matter of war contributions should be fully maintained during the current year, and that our people of all communities should continue to do their duty to their utmost capacity in the great crisis through which the Empire is passing [...] Justice demands that in determining what a particular area should do in the future we should take into account what it has already done both absolutely and relatively. The Punjab is proud of being constantly described as the 'sword hand of India,' but equality of sacrifice, especially in so vital a matter as national defence, is an accepted principle at the present time, and the Punjabi, while continuing to do his duty to his king and country, has a right to expect that the burden laid on him will be equitable.

[428] *Bulletin* (Lahore), 5 May 1918

We think it would be unjust to draw so heavily on the province which has been bled white already. We hope other provinces will be made to play their part more vigorously before ours is tapped on a still more extensive scale. The King's Commision is put off for some time, but we do hope that the stigma of unfitness for the said Commission will soon be removed from the Indians, who have fought shoulder to shoulder with their European colleagues and have won many an honour.

[429] *Tribune* (Lahore), 5 May 1918

We are strongly opposed to conscription in present circumstances, and in any case without the consent of the people obtained through their chosen representatives [...] And as regards [to] the war loan, while we are anxious that it should be as great a success as it can be in the circumstances of the case, we will venture to remind His Honour that it was only about a week ago that he said in the Council Chamber that it was almost too much to hope that the Punjab would repeat the magnificent achievement of last year. Between that expression of opinion and the present determination to eclipse last year's achievement there is something more than a verbal difference.

[430] *Loyal Gazette* (Lahore), 5 May 1918

So far as the Sikhs are concerned conscription and voluntary recruitment mean the same thing because the flower of the Sikh community is already serving in the army. But why should not all other communities be forced to supply men for the defence of the country, so that all communities may equally bear the burden of the war? Conscription is necessary in some districts to keep the balance even.

[431] *Tribune* (Lahore), 8 May 1918

Circumstances may arise when conscription will be necessary. If instead of the half-million troops which the Government require now, they will ever require ten or twenty times half-million, which

Heaven forbid, then there will be no choice but to resort to conscription. The actual and paramount necessities of the State must be the supreme law for the individual. But before conscription is resorted to even in these circumstances, those at the head of the State will have to take steps to make it clear to the individual that the State is his own higher self, and that in being called upon to defend the State he is really being called upon to defend his own vital interest. In other words the State will have to be transformed and remodeled on a modern democratic basis.

[432] *Paisa Akhbar* (Lahore), 10 May 1918

The demand of 200,000 recruits from the Punjab out of a total of 500,000 men for the whole country [is] excessive, seeing that most martial races of the Province have already joined the army. All the same, it will not be improper to hope that the Punjab, which is the sword-hand of India, will display the spirit and enthusiasm which it has hitherto shown.

[433] *Khalsa Advocate* (Amritsar), 11 May 1918

Large though the demand [for recruits] is, it is confidently hoped that the unswerving loyalty and the unique patriotism of the sons of the Punjab will ensure its easy supply and we further trust that for such tremendous sacrifices as are demanded by the grave exigencies of the situation no monetary consideration will weigh in the minds of the people to adequately meet the demands. Heavy as already the sacrifices of the Punjab have been, we still believe that the Province will prove that her sacrifices are voluntary and that no threatened resort will ever be had by the Government to 'such measures as may be necessary to produce the requisite number of recruits.' At any rate in our Province, we trust, there will be no necessity for it.

[434] *Sitara-i-Subah* (Lahore), 13 May 1918

The present lull on the western front [is attributed] to the absolute discomfiture of Germany and her prostrate condition. It appears that

Germany wants to be very careful before re-assuming the offensive. The question now is why the Allies do not attack Germany without waiting for the latter's attack at this hour when Germany is eager to avoid battle. The reader should patiently await developments. General Foche is engaged in making mighty and important preparations. The British General is also collecting more army and armaments. When these preparations are complete, the Allies will assume the offensive. There is no wonder if, in the meantime, lakhs of American soldiers come to their aid, in which case the condition of the western front will be entirely changed.

[435] *Panjabee* (Lahore), 15 May 1918

The most important question of the day is how to prepare India against the threatened German aggression. His Excellency the Viceroy in his speech at the Delhi Conference, while stating that Germany had already thrown into Central Asia her pioneers and agents of disintegration, gave the assurance that she had yet made no military move in the direction of India. The *Times*, moreover, in a manner contradicts the statement of the Viceroy. In any case, so far as the people's leaders are concerned, they have been fully alive to the danger and have called upon the Government to take necessary steps, and [. . . to] immediately to equip India against any foreign invasion. In order that this might be done in the most effective way, what was required was that the Government should give up the policy that they have hitherto pursued and go in for a whole-hearted measure of organising the whole country from a military point of view and removing once and for all the invidious and galling distinctions that are still allowed to exist.

[436] *Tribune* (Lahore), 16 May 1918

Let us show both to the Government and the world that we at least are alive to our duty, that, while we are unremitting in our effort to induce the Government to do that which statesmanship demands and the situation calls for, we are equally unremitting in our effort to make the country realise both the nature of the German menace and the absolute necessity of averting that menace in the best and most effective way we can. Perhaps there are difficulties in the way of opening an actual recruiting campaign. But there should be no difficulty in proceeding with the part of the work without which the recruiting campaign can never be the success that it should be, the work of educating the country to cheerfully accept the sacrifices imposed by the war so far as those sacrifices are both necessary and just.

[437] *Paisa Akhbar* (Lahore), 16 May 1918

It is our national, moral and religious duty to crush tyrannical Germany. We should collect together under the flag of our just Government.

[438] *Panjabee* (Lahore), 17 May 1918

Some critics complain that, instead of wholeheartedly helping the Government in winning the war, Indian leaders are bargaining for political privileges. But did not the Prime Minister declare that England and her Allies were fighting not a war of conquest but a war of liberation? Regret is no doubt felt throughout the country that [the] Viceroy should have uttered words at the Delhi conference which mean that India must wait for her freedom until after other parts of the world have secured theirs. But in spite of their disappointment, Indians of all shades of opinion are united in their determination to do their duty to their country and Empire to their utmost capacity. The Presidents of the Provincial Conferences recently held at Bombay, etc., gave expression to this feeling in no uncertain terms. Will anybody have the hardihood to say that the pronouncements were made in a spirit of bargaining?

[439] *Punjabi Bhain* (Ferozepore), 19 May 1918

Indian women [should] help the Government in the defence of the country. They could urge their relations to go to the front and induce large numbers of men to come forward as recruits.

[440] *Paisa Akhbar* (Lahore), 24 May 1918

While the speeches of Mr. Tilak, Mrs. Annie Besant, Pandit Malaviya and Mahatma Gandhi, who are said to be very influential leaders, have failed to bring in recruits, not a few people in the Punjab are, without the aid of eloquent speeches, supplying large numbers of recruits by making use of personal and local influence.

[441] *Panjabee* (Lahore), 25 May 1918

Now that the fallen monarch is going to be tried by a Bolshevik Commission, there seems to be very little chance of his being shown any mercy by them. He would perhaps share the cruel fate that has been the lot of many a despot unless Germany intervenes for some motive of her own.

[442] *Desh* (Lahore), 25 May 1918

To arms

Young men of India! Get armed and add to the ancient splendour of India. Having armed yourselves, protect the chastity and honour of your wives, sisters and daughters and then obtain perpetual freedom for yourselves and your descendants. Let it not be recorded in history that India stood aloof, witnessing the scene on a critical occasion, that it allowed the freedom of the world to be trampled in fire and blood and that it itself fell a victim to oppression and high-handedness, thereby adding a shameful chapter to its brilliant history.

[443] *Vakil* (Amritsar), 29 May 1918

As a result of the present great war the Russian provinces are gradually becoming independent. When a nation practices undue oppression on others, it is sure to be visited by the wrath of God. Who can say that the fall of Russia is not the result of her own misdeeds? [. . .] Now that Germany has been found to have ulterior objects in view of Poland, it will not be wrong to say that all the newly constituted republican states, which have been set up as the result of the collapse of Russia, will be again brought under the yoke of the oppressor.

[444] *Vakil* (Amritsar), 1 June 1918

The number of American troops now in France far exceeds that of the German soldiers sent to the Western Front since the collapse of Russia. American forces will shortly reach the Italian front also. It is believed that the enemy will be unable to withstand the Allies in the end.

[445] *Jat Gazette* (Rohtak), 4 June 1918

The entire burden of defeating the enemy will fall on the soldiers of India. Her sons should rise to the occasion and avert the threatened danger.

[446] *Bulletin* (Lahore), 8 June 1918

The Government of India should issue special instructions to recruitment boards to keep a strict eye on recruiting officers and warn the latter not to treat the people in a manner likely to give rise to dissatisfaction.

[447] *Jat Gazette* (Rohtak), 11 June 1918

The war services rendered by British India – with the exception of the Punjab and the north-west districts of the United Provinces – are not such as may be an object of pride for an Indian endowed with a sense of shame. The non-martial races, particularly the trading classes, have done absolutely nothing. They knowingly shirked their duty, asking why they should risk their lives when their purpose can be served without their making any sacrifice. If the urban population and non-martial classes do not make up for past remission Government has every right to introduce conscription in the country.

[448] *Panjabee* (Lahore), 14 June 1918

Great Britain and her Allies are passing through one of the most critical periods of the war at the present moment. The German offensive is being repeatedly renewed, of course to be ultimately checked. Germany is fighting with almost superhuman energy. She is carrying on her struggle with unprecedented persistence and is hoping against hope to bring the civilised world under her feet. But equally stern is the determination of purpose, and no less invincible is the spirit, of the great nations of the world who are arrayed against the Central Powers. The speeches and pronouncements that have been made during the last few days by some of the foremost statesmen and political leaders of the Allied nations demonstrate that they are as hopeful and confident as ever that victory is certain to them in the end. On the other hand, it appears that the faith of Germany in her ultimate triumph is on the wane.

[449] *Kapurthala Akhbar* (Kapurthala), 29 June 1918

The fire [. . .] has assumed such proportions that no human power can now put it down. The only thing that can now be done is to add fuel to it, so that one of the contending (*lit.* conflicting) elements may destroy the other and leave it no power of resistance. This is the duty which devolves on all who are in a position to render bodily or monetary help (in connection with the war) [. . .] It is our foremost and most sacred duty to help the Government in bringing [. . . the] war to a happy end. It is also incumbent on wealthy Indians to end the troubles from which their poor fellow-countrymen are suffering. They should put forth their best efforts to promote indigenous industries and see that their country is relieved of dependence on foreigners. Woe to India! Neither peace nor strife has so far had the effect of waking her (sons to this necessity). If the lakhs of rupees spent on starting 'national educational institutions' were used for imparting industrial education much of the prevailing unrest and suffering would be banished from [this] country.

[450] *Aftab* (Lahore), 6 July 1918

The arrival of over ten lakh Americans in France proves that the German submarine campaign has failed and the Allies are supreme on the sea. The Allies' military preparations are now complete and they are about to deal a crushing blow to Germany.

[451] *Paisa Akhbar* (Lahore), 18 July 1918

The Allies are firmly determined to continue the war till they have cut the claws of Germany. On the contrary, if Germany continues to exhibit her present spirit she will be certain to reduce her neighbours to the position of slaves, both politically and economically.

[452] *Panjabee* (Lahore), 24 July 1918

The present victory of the Allied army is extremely significant not only as a strategic move but also [. . .] of great moral value. This is the first time after many months of weary defence that the Allies have been able to take the offensive and this is sure to greatly improve the *morale* of their army. The fifth anniversary of the war is drawing nigh. Let us hope that the anniversary will be celebrated this year by a greater victory of the Allied arms.

[453] *Aftab* (Lahore), 24 July 1918

The German retreat is the first example of General Foch's military tactics, which have utterly confounded the martial Germans. And now that the spirits of the Allied troops have been raised and their minds have been fired with hopes of victory, it will not be surprising if General Foch deals a crushing blow to the Germans and leaves them no alternative but to accept the Allies' peace terms. The question, however, is whether the reverse sustained by them has made it impossible for the German forces to rally and engage in 'any military operations.' The whole German Empire consists of warriors and it is difficult for it to keep quiet so long as it does not suffer a series of such serious reverses. Nevertheless, the able and experienced Allied statesmen have perfected their plan for crushing the military strength of Germany.

[454] *Tribune* (Lahore), 25 July 1918

No words are adequate praise for the gallantry and skill of the French army in turning an enemy offensive, the greatest of its kind, into an enemy rout in a few days. The Allies' victory will cause universal rejoicing.

[455] *Bulletin* (Lahore), 27 July 1918

The shadow of the first battle of the Marne, the glory of which belongs to the Indian troops, has never been off the subsequent efforts of Germany. The second battle of the Marne has deepened it into positive darkness for her, for the time being at any rate. She will yet fight, and fight desperately, but the balance of power is no longer on her side.

[456] *Panjabee* (Lahore), 31 July 1918

The retreat of the Germans on the Western Front is the most momentous and significant incident in the present year of the war. It undoubtedly establishes the superiority of American soldiers and French generalship. The German order of retirement is nothing but an acknowledgement of the Allied superiority. This would, we believe, finally shatter the belief of the German people in the invincibility of their War Lords [... To the] Allied army the moral effect of this victory would be tremendous. It would put new strength in their arms and steal their determination to win the war. The news of this German defeat would, we have not the least doubt, be received all over the Allied world with great joy.

[457] *Tribune* (Lahore), 1 August 1918

It is yet uncertain where precisely they (the Germans) will take their new stand, but it is certain the enemy has been badly beaten and the Allies have gained important strategical points.

[458] *Tribune* (Lahore), 4 August 1918

No one can say with absolute assurance what the future may have in store, but if human calculations go for anything, the present turn in the tide is decisive, and before many months are over Germany will have no choice but to sue for peace.

[459] *Panjabee* (Lahore), 4 August 1918

The victory might not yet be near, but there is not a shadow of doubt that the ultimate victory is not with the Germans, but with the Allies and [the] Allies alone.

[460] *Paisa Akhbar* (Lahore), 4 August 1918

The end of the war is now in sight. It is true that Germany's back has not been broken yet, still her complete humiliation is to be the end. While the Allies' strength and resources are daily increasing those of Germany are steadily on the decrease.

[461] *Zulfiqar* (Lahore), 7 August 1918

The people of Mesopotamia are having a most happy and peaceful time of it under British rule. All classes are performing their religious duties without hindrance. Such blessed and benign rule never fell to the lot of their forefathers.

[462] *Urdu Bulletin* (Lahore), 15 August 1918

Recent reports from the Western Front are very gratifying and encouraging. One reason for the reduction of Germany's strength in the west [...] is that she has had to send a large number of her troops to Russia, where the people are turning against her. It is believed that Austrian soldiers will now be sent to the Western Front, but they are already exhausted and can produce no marked effect on the war.

[463] *Aftab* (Lahore), 29 August 1918

The recent Allies' successes have been such that the Germans have nowhere been able to drive back the British, French or American forces. The present state of Germany [...] is really very disappointing for her and has plunged the Germans into alarm and anxiety. The question, however, is whether Germany will remain in her present condition and will not utilize her few remaining resources for checking the advance of the Allies. It is an admitted fact that the Germans are a warlike nation by nature and will fight to the last in order to preserve their existence, sparing no efforts to terminate the war according to their wishes. And if they still fail to improve the situation, they will have to throw themselves at the mercy of the Allies and the war will come to an end. Signs and circumstances show that in the end the Allies will emerge safe and sound from the life-and-death struggle in which they are engaged.

[464] *Kashmiri Magazine* (Lahore), 7 September 1918

A semi-official German newspaper, while trying to wipe out the blot of the recent German reverses, writes that the Germans are luring their enemies towards the desolate places on the river Somme. This [...] may be perhaps sufficient to satisfy the unintelligent, but if the German public possesses even a little sense it can understand that this is a mere fabrication intended to conceal the reverses sustained by Germany.

[465] *Panjabee* (Lahore), 18 September 1918

Ever since the arrival of the American troops in France and the speedy pressure that the Allies brought to bear on the enemy the Germans have begun to talk of peace. Austria has long been anxious for peace and would have by this time concluded, perhaps, a separate peace if her German master had only allowed [...] But the recent turning of the tables on the Western Front appears to have opened the eyes of the German leaders that the chance of victory of which they talked so loud is gone forever. This consciousness has brought them to a reasonable frame of mind and hence the repeated talk about peace terms. Moreover, the internal situation both in Germany and Austria is becoming increasingly difficult.

[466] *Vakil* (Amritsar), 25 September 1918

The steady and continuous advance of the Allies has disheartened the enemy and led to his expressing his readiness to conclude peace.

[467] *Victoria Paper* (Sialkot), 24 September 1918

The Punjab supplied 19,700 recruits during August last. This beats the previous records of the province, nor has any other part of the country ever furnished so many recruits in a single month.

[468] *Tribune* (Lahore), 2 October 1918

It is the literal truth that ever since she embarked upon the war America has grudged neither men nor money, and no power has contributed more to the present brilliant successes of the Allies than the great western republic.

[469] *Panjabee* (Lahore), 3 October 1918

The latest reports from the various fronts are very encouraging. If the progress be maintained at this rate, the success of the Allies would be sooner than people expected.

[470] *Desh* (Lahore), 3 October 1918

Bulgaria has had to lay down arms owing to the superior military strength of the Allies. The day is not far distant when the enemy's forces in the west will share the fate of the Bulgars.

[471] *Panjabee* (Lahore), 4 October 1918

The news of the surrender of Bulgaria has been received throughout the country with great rejoicings. The fall of Bulgaria is undoubtedly a signal triumph of the Allies. Deserted by Bulgaria, driven out of Rumania, frustrated in Russia, pressed back in France and Belgium, Germany stands bewildered. The death-knell of militarism has been rung.

[472] *Tribune* (Lahore), 5 October 1918

There is universal rejoicing all over the Allied world at the rapid succession of victories on every war front. The far-reaching possibilities of these victories cannot be better realised than by a reference to what is happening in Germany. The Kaiser, who never before now indulged in any language except that of bluster, has now adopted a peculiarly subdued tone. In a message to the Fatherland party he appeals to the whole German people 'in these most earnest times to gather round me and give me your blood and wealth until the last breath for the defence of the Fatherland.' When the Kaiser drops for the moment his bombastic braggadocio and begins to talk of 'the last breath' we know we are nearing the beginning of the end, though the end itself may not be quite in sight.

[473] *Aftab* (Lahore), 12 October 1918

If, like Bulgaria, Turkey also withdraws from the war Germany may, in order to save herself, evacuate France and Belgium and accept all the terms offered by the Allies. The latter, however, who are now intoxicated with their victories, will probably not accept some of the conditions which have been proposed by President Wilson and which Germany wishes to make the basis for a peace.

[474] *Panjabee* (Lahore), 16 October 1918

The reply of the German Government [to President Wilson on the subject of peace] may be taken as a complete surrender. An immediate cessation of hostilities may under the circumstances be very reasonably expected now.

[475] *Paisa Akhbar* (Lahore), 20 October 1918

Although by accepting Mr. Wilson's conditions Germany has acknowledged her weakness, still it is a question whether the Allies will forego their opportunity of inflicting a crushing defeat on her. This being so, peace cannot be said to be near at hand; indeed, a military expert is of the opinion that further conquests are necessary for unconditional surrender on the enemy's part.

[476] *Paigham-i-Sulah* (Lahore), 20 October 1918

The iron grip of the Allies and their successive conquests have forced Germany to accept President Wilson's conditions. This

means a very heavy loss to the Fatherland and is synonymous
with a complete defeat. It is to be regretted that Turkey also by
joining in the war, should have worked harm to herself. We find
that the restoration of conquered Turkish territory has not been
provided for in Mr. Wilson's terms of peace. Again, these terms
include the condition that the Dardanelles should be permanently
kept open under an international guarantee. In other words, Turkey
will lose one great source of protection after peace has been
concluded. All this, however, is the result of her having chosen the
wrong path.

[477] *Panjabee* (Lahore), 20 October 1918

One of fourteen points of President Wilson's peace programme,
to which Germany has already signified her assent, is a general
association of nations to be formed under specific covenants for
the purpose of affording mutual guarantees of political independence
and territorial integrity for great and small states alike [. . .] But the
main difficulty of the problem lies in the fact that so long as
the democratic form of government is not established all over the
world and governmental power is concentrated, as is now the case in
respect to most of the States, in the hands of a few politicians and
statesmen, the soil can never be deemed to be ready for the fruition of
the idea of a league such as that advocated by President Wilson
and others. The first condition of success of a league of nations
which would enforce peace is certainly the universal establishment
of democratic government.

[478] *Parkash* (Lahore), 20 October 1918

The world unanimously desires the termination of the war, which
has entailed severe sufferings on God's creatures. All necessaries
of life had already grown very dear and a new calamity in the shape
of influenza has now befallen India [. . .] The disease is working
[havoc] in all parts of the country [. . .] The Government should not
continue the war even for a single minute after the objects in view
have been gained.

[479] *Khalsa Advocate* (Amritsar), 22 October 1918

The bursting of the German bubble:
The death-rattle of Germany

The German bubble like the South Sea Bubble is also about to burst [...] The sledgehammer of the Allies is hitting the Germans hard in the most vital parts and the Germans are unable to parry off the blow or counter-attack [...] It is not only in the West that the Germans have suffered serious reverses. In all theatres of the War the news have been equally heart-rending to the Germans [...] But the most important news which overshadows all other news is the unconditional surrender of Bulgaria. In the collapse of Bulgaria the German bubble has been effectively pricked [...] These defeats have caused extreme pessimism in Germany. The Pan-Germans and the Military Party of Germany who until recently croaked hoarse for annexations in Russia and in Flanders have disappeared [...] Austria is already pushing out peace tentacles [...] It is clear that the Allies are on the sure road to victory.

[480] *Vakil* (Amritsar), 23 October 1918

It appears that Turkey is withdrawing herself from the war and has even sued for peace to America. Again, the internal dissensions of Austria-Hungary have rendered that country also incapable of continuing the struggle, while Bulgaria has already surrendered to the Allies. Is it then possible that Germany can carry on the war any longer, especially when her designs in the Near East have been completely frustrated? She can have no alternative but to submit to the Allies, no matter how strong her military position may be.

[481] *Rajput Gazette* (Lahore), 26 October 1918

Thousands of Rajput children have been orphaned and countless Rajput women have become widows through the death of the latter's husbands in the war. There is now no comfort for them, and it is therefore the duty of both Government and the Rajputs to make proper arrangements for their livelihood. Government has no doubt granted pensions to the survivors of the soldiers who have died on the battlefield, but these are insufficient in these days of dearness, especially in cases in which a widow and some children are left behind [. . .] Rajputs [are urged] to go to the rescue of the widows [. . .] thousands of the latter suffer the pains of hunger within the four walls of their houses, but, keeping in view the honour of their families, do not open their lips in complaint.

[482] *Paigham-i-Sulah* (Lahore), 27 October 1918

Being afraid of the Allies [gaining further] successes the Germans are striving hard to conclude peace.

[483] *Hindustan* (Lahore), 1 November 1918

Evidently the war is now approaching its end and peace will be concluded on the principles announced by President Wilson. The question, however, arises whether India, who has sacrificed lakhs of her sons and spent crores of rupees in the war, will also receive a share of freedom. Will the question of the grant of responsible government to her be considered at the peace conference at which complete freedom is to be granted to petty states like Belgium and Servia? In our opinion so long as a strenuous struggle is not carried on by Indian leaders in this connection India will not even be mentioned at the conference, let alone her getting responsible government. And even if, to suppose an impossibility, her name is mentioned, the Secretary of State or some other officer will say that Indians have already been granted constitutional reforms in the Montagu-Chelmsford scheme. The matter will end here. We hope that before the conference meets the National Congress and the [Muslim] League deputations will go to England and America and spare no pains in expressing their real demands and desires to the public there. The foremost duty of Indian leaders at the present juncture consists in obtaining permission from Government for these deputations to proceed to England and America. We feel confident that the British Government, which has already proclaimed its intention of granting Home Rule to Indians, will not hesitate to issue passports for the deputations.

[484] *Panjabee* (Lahore), 3 November 1918

The news of the unconditional surrender of Turkey closely following upon the capitulation of Bulgaria will be received all over the Allied world with the utmost satisfaction. The intrigues of the Young Turks which led Turkey to join this war are at last at an end. The influence that the two leaders of that party, Enver Pasha and Talaat Pasha, had so long *exercised* over the affairs of Turkey had only contributed to her ruin and misery.

[485] *Jiwan Tat* (Lahore), 4 November 1918

There is now no alternative for Germany but to make a speedy surrender and conclude peace with the Allies.

[486] *Panjabee* (Lahore), 7 November 1918

The news of Austria signing an armistice received here [the] day before yesterday has been hailed with great joy all over the country. Now that Austria and Turkey, two of Germany's principal allies, are out of the war and Bulgaria has also surrendered unconditionally, Germany will not find it easy to continue the war and will be forced ere long to bow to the inevitable.

[487] *Panjabee* (Lahore), 12 November 1918

So the Kaiser has at last decided to renounce his throne [. . .] Gone are now all the boasts of the power and mission of Germany, all the blasphemous talk of Almighty as the Ally of the Kaiser, of the Imperial sword as the sword of God. To-day in the world there is no name which is held more in contempt, and which is more cursed than that of William II. Such has been the fate of autocrats since the beginning of history and such will it be till the world sees the last of them.

[488] *Tribune* (Lahore), 13 November 1918

We must be thankful for the successful end of the war to the brilliant feats of arms of the Allied powers and the unity and singleness of aim with which they pursued the war to the very last [. . .] It is impossible not to recall the heroism, the fortitude and the endurance which the armies of the Allied nations showed during the whole course of the war until full and complete victory was gained. The reward for all the pains and sufferings endured by the world through this relentless and protracted war must be commensurate to the price paid for it, and it is to be found in the establishment of the war aims of the Allied powers. These aims [...] are not based either on aggrandizement and greed – not on conquest and annexation of territories, but on the security of liberty and justice for all and the prevention of future wars. It is no small gratification to us Indians that we have taken a substantial share in bringing about the present victory and in the first stage of the war as well as in the last, it is the Indian valour and the Indian blood that produced momentous results in France and in Turkey. India's rejoicings on the present occasion will, therefore, be no less than those of England or France or America.

[489] *Paisa Akhbar* (Lahore), 13 November 1918

The sanguinary universal war which owed its origin to Germany's greed for world-wide dominion and which was a conflict between humanity and barbarism, between civilisation and cruelty, and between right and usurpation, has at last ended in the victory of the British Government and its Allies. This is so conspicuous a triumph of truth over falsehood as to be without a parallel in the history of the world. There will now be established a peace which will bring manifold blessings in its train and will cause the moon of civilisation, which had been eclipsed by barbarity, oppression and cruelty, to shine in all its splendid glory. The right of the weaker nations to promote their progress and prosperity will be safeguarded and the barbarous German principle of 'might is right' will be banished from the world.

[490] *Tribune* (Lahore), 14 November 1918

India has [...] proved her loyalty and devotion to the cause of the Empire by the most exacting test that could be laid down, the ordeal of a gigantic and mighty conflict. She has, therefore, by her deeds and sacrifices made good her claim to an equality within the Empire [. . .] India confidently looks to the statesmen at the helm of the Empire to admit her to an equal partnership with the other self-governing members of the great British Empire.

[491] *Vakil* (Amritsar), 16 November 1918

India has fully realised its duty in connection with the war. She has displayed courage and made efforts beyond her means in order to maintain the honour of Great Britain. Muhammadans have taken no mean share in the services rendered by this country. They have probably supplied nearly half the soldiers in the Indian Army. Nor have they hesitated to make monetary sacrifices also [. . .] The help given by Muhammadans in this war is of special significance. On one side there was among the enemies one [the Sultan] who is a Muhammadan and is united to Muhammadans by a permanent religious bond; while, on the other, there was the British Government which, in view of the number of its Muslim subjects, is the greatest Islamic Power in the world and to which the Prophet's followers in India are admittedly loyal. In these circumstances, it is desirable that the feelings of ten crore Indian Mussalmans should not be ignored at the coming peace conference.

APPENDIX

LIST OF NEWSPAPERS AND PERIODICALS EXAMINED BY THE SPECIAL BRANCH, AUGUST 1914

Where there are gaps in the table, the information was missing from the original document

No.	Name	Locality	Name of Editor	Circulation
	ENGLISH			
	DAILY			
1.	*Tribune*	Lahore	S. Aiyangar	2,000 copies
	TRI-WEEKLY			
2.	*Panjabee*	Lahore	K.N. Roy	2,400 copies
	BI-WEEKLY			
3.	*Observer*	Lahore	Barkat Ali, M.A.	1,200 copies
4.	*Punjab Times and Frontier News*	Rawalpindi	Harnam Singh	380 copies
	WEEKLY			
5.	*Arya Patrika*	Lahore	R.P. Chatterji	300 copies
6.	*Harbinger*	Lahore	Durga Parshad	250 copies
7.	*Khalsa Advocate*	Amritsar		850 copies
	FORTNIGHTLY			
8.	*Bjnasu*	Lahore	Bhagat Ishar Das	500 copies
	MONTHLY			
9.	*D.A.V. College Magazine*	Lahore	Ram Rattan, B.A.	500 copies
10.	*Durbar*	Amritsar	R.G. Wright, M.A.	300 copies
11.	*Forman Christian College Notes*	Lahore	Rev. L. Wilson Ross	300 copies

Continued

No.	Name	Locality	Name of Editor	Circulation
12.	*Punjab Educational Journal*	Lahore	E. Tydeman	500 copies
13.	*Punjab Mission News*	Lahore	H.E. Clark	400 copies
14.	*Ravi*	Lahore	F.R. Tomlinson, B.A.	500 copies
15.	*Review of Religions*	Qadian	Sher Ali, B.A.	800 copies
16.	*Science Grounded Religion*	Lahore	Har Narain	500 copies
17.	*Teacher*	Dinga Gujrat	Kalyan Singh	600 copies
18.	*Union*	Lahore	P.J. Richards, B.A.	400 copies
19.	*Vedic Magazine*	Lahore	Ram Dev, B.A.	500 copies

URDU

No.	Name	Locality	Name of Editor	Circulation
	DAILY			
20.	*Akbbar-i-' Am*	Lahore	Bal Kishen	1,000 copies
21.	*Amrit*	Lahore	Bishen Sabai Asad	2,000 copies
22.	*Azadi*	Lahore	Maulana Farrukh and Bashambar Dial	2,000 copies
23.	*Desb*	Lahore	Dina Nath	3,000 copies
24.	*Dipak*	Lahore	Ram Rachpal Singh	3,000 copies
25.	*Hindu*	Lahore	Hari Lal, Sharma	Between 3,000 and 4,000 copies
26.	*Jhang Sial*	Lahore	Prabh Dial	1,500 copies
27.	*Paisa Akbbar*	Lahore	Mahbub Alam	3,000 copies
28.	*Shanti*	Rawalpindi	Kishen Chand	3,000 copies

29.	*Watan*	Lahore	Insha Ullah	3,000 copies
30.	*Zamindar*	Lahore	Zafar Ali	15,000 copies
	TRI-WEEKLY			
31.	*Paigham-i-Sulah*	Lahore	Ahmad Hussain	2,000 copies
32.	*Fazal*	Qadian	Marza Mahmud Ahmad	630 copies
	BI-WEEKLY			
33.	*Vakil*	Amritsar	Moulvi Abdulla	3,000 copies
	WEEKLY			
34.	*Afghan*	Peshawar	S. Abdulla Shah	964 copies
35.	*Aftab-i-Hind*	Jullundur	Muhammad Hussain	700 copies
36.	*Ahl-i-Hadis*	Jullundur	M. Sana-ulla	1,200 copies
37.	*Ahluwalia Gazette*	Jullundur	Lehna Singh	500 copies
38.	*Akhbar-i-Am*	Lahore	Bal Kishen	2,000 copies
39.	*Arjuna*	Lahore	Raj Narain Arman	1,000 copies
40.	*Arorbans Gazette*	Amritsar	Narain Das	800 copies
41.	*Arya Gazette*	Lahore	Khushal Chand	2,300 copies
42.	*Azzia*	Lahore	Abdul Karim	
43.	*Bharat*	Jullundur	Sham Lal	500 copies
44.	*Brahman*	Lahore	Pt. Charanjit Lal	1,000 copies
45.	*Civil and Military News*	Ludhiana	Mishba-ul-Haq, B.A.	900 copies
46.	*Desh Upkarak*	Lahore	Thakar Dat, Sharma	1,200 copies

Continued

No.	Name	Locality	Name of Editor	Circulation
47.	*Falah*	Lahore	Abdul Rahman	1,000 copies
48.	*Ganga*	Lahore	Hai Lal, Sharma	800 copies
49.	*Hakam*	Qadian	Yaqub Ali	600 copies
50.	*Haq Pasand*	Amritsar	Ram Nath	
51.	*Himala*	Lahore	Dina Nath	
52.	*Hindustan*	Lahore	Ram Rachpal Singh	15,000 copies
53.	*Jhang Sial*	Lahore	Prabh Dyal	1,770 copies
54.	*Jiwan Tat*	Lahore	Amar Singh	400 copies
55.	*Kapurthala Akhbar*	Kapurthala	M. Hamid Hussain	150 copies
56.	*Kashmiri Magazine*	Lahore	Muhammad Din, Fauq	1,650 copies
57.	*Khalsa Akhbar*	Lyallpur	Lal Singh, B.Sc.	
58.	*Loyal Gazette*	Lahore	Amar Singh	3,000 copies
59.	*Millat*	Lahore	M. Shuja Ullah	1,000 copies
60.	*Mukhbir*	Amritsar	Lakhmi Das	300 copies
61.	*Municipal Gazette*	Lahore	Din Muhammad	700 copies
62.	*Munir*	Jhang	M. Ghulam Hussain	1,325 copies
63.	*Musalman*	Amritsar	Ilm Din	500 copies
64.	*Nazim-i-Hind*	Rawalpindi	Qalandar Khan	400 copies
65.	*Nur*	Qadian	Muhammad Yusaf	800 copies
66.	*Nur Afshan*	Ludhiana	Rev. Dr. E.M. Wherry	450 copies
67.	*Paisa Akhbar*	Lahore	Mahbub Alam	9,000 copies

No.	Name	Place	Person	Copies
68.	*Parkash*	Lahore	Radha Kishen, B.A.	3,500 copies
69.	*Philosopher*	Lahore	Sham Lal	500 copies
70.	*Punjab*	Lahore	Kishen Chand	
71.	*Punjab Samachar*	Lahore	Kahn Chand	1,700 copies
72.	*Rajput Gazette*	Lahore	Thakur Sukhram Das	3,300 copies
73.	*Rishi*	Lahore		
74.	*Sadiq-ul-Akbbar*	Bahawalpur	M. Ata Ullah	435 copies
75.	*Sadiq-ul-Akbbar*	Rewari	S. Maqbul Hussain	350 copies
76.	*Sanatan Dharm Parcharak*	Amritsar	P. Ralia Ram	750 copies
77.	*Shanti*	Rawalpindi	Kishan Chand, Mohan	1,300 copies
78.	*Sharif Bibi*	Lahore	Fatima	300 copies
79.	*Sialkot Paper*	Sialkot	Todar Mal	200 copies
80.	*Siraj-ul-Akbbar*	Jhelum	Maulvi Fakir Muhammad	700 copies
81.	*Tabrib-ul-Niswan*	Lahore	Sayed Mumtan Ali's daughter	2,000 copies
82.	*Ucb-Jiwan*	Lahore	Dev Rattan	1,000 copies
83.	*Victoria Paper*	Rialkot	Brij Lal	700 copies
84.	*Watan*	Lahore	Muhammad Insha Ullah	6,200 copies
85.	*Zamindar*	Lahore	Zafar Ali, B.A.	4,000 copies

FORTNIGHTLY

No.	Name	Place	Person	Copies
86.	*Brahman Gazette*	Rawalpindi	Vidya Rattan Praksher	600 copies
87.	*Khukhrain Samachar*	Rawalpindi	Prithmin Chand	
88.	*Mister Gazette*	Rawalpindi	Ali Bakhsh	100 copies
89.	*Mabryal Gazette*	Jhelum	Mehta Sham Das	225 copies

Continued

No.	Name	Locality	Name of Editor	Circulation
90.	*Mohyal Mittar*	Lahore	Mehta Dhera Mal	250 copies
91.	*Nihang*	Amritsar	Bawa Ram Jaitli	700 copies
92.	*Rahnuma*	Lahore	Bhagat Ram	
93.	*Suraj Parkash*	Amritsar	Fateh Chand	600 copies
	MONTHLY			
94.	*Adab*	Lahore	Mustafa Khan, B.A.	400 copies
95.	*Ahmwalia Magazine*	Lahore	Labh Singh	
96.	*Al Aziz*	Gurdaapur	Ghulam Mohiy-ud-Din	250 copies
97.	*Al Burhan*	Lahore	S. Mohd. Sibtain	300 copies
98.	*Al Muslim*	Ludhiana	Ghari Mahmud Dharmpal, B.A.	
99.	*Anwar-ul-Safa*	Lahore	Hafiz Zafar Ali	1,000 copies
100.	*Arya Musafir*	Jullundur	P. Vishnu Datt	450 copies
101.	*Bhatia Sewak*	Lahore	Mukand Lal	500 copies
102.	*Brahman Rai Patrika*	Lahore	Shivram Das	300 copies
103.	*Dharam Bir*	Lahore	Sant Ram	
104.	*Fanna-i-Khial*	Pathankot	Abdul Majid Khan	
105.	*Ikhlaqi Gazette Mehra*	Amritsar	Sher Singh	250 copies
106.	*Insan*	Amritsar	Ghulam Qadir	
107.	*Iqbal*	Ludhiana	Muhammad Sabiz	
108.	*Jain Udbey*	Amritsar	Fattu Ram	
109.	*Jauhar*	Amritsar	Dr Chiraq Din, Jauhar	400 copies

	Title	Place	Name	Copies
110.	*Makhzan*	Lahore	Abdul Qadir, B.A.	1,000 copies
111.	*Martand*	Lahore	Kanhya Lal	200 copies
112.	*Mastana Jogi*	Ferozepore	Sufi Lachhman Parshad	500 copies
113.	*Mifta-ul-Isrdz*	Jullundur	Muhammad Bux	
114.	*Prem*	Lahore	Baba Brij Balab Singh	
115.	*Prem Bilas*	Gujranwala	Ram Mittar	400 copies
116.	*Ragbbir Patrika*	Lahore	Bhagwan Das	500 copies
117.	*Safir*	Lahore		
118.	*Sanatan Dharam Parkasb*	Ferozepore		
119.	*Sat Sang*	Amritsar	Gobind Ram	750 copies
120.	*Shauq*	Lahore		
121.	*Shiv Shambhu*	Lahore	Gauri Shankar Lal	
122.	*Sufi*	Gujrat	Muhammad Din, Awan	5,000 copies
123.	*Tabzib-ul-Ikblsq*	Amritsar	M. Abdullah	400 copies
124.	*Tashbiz-ul-Azban*	Gurdaspur	Muhd. Ahmad	1,000 copies
125.	*Temperance Guide*	Amritsar	Mir Kiramat Ullah	2,000 copies
126.	*Temperance Magazine*	Amritsar	Sant Singh	
127.	*Zarif*	Lahore	Abdul Rashid	500 copies

GURMUKHI

	Title	Place	Name	Copies
		Amritsar	Lakhbir Singh	1,000 copies

DAILY

128.	*Bir*	Amritsar		
129.	*Panjab Darpan*	Amritsar		

Continued

No.	Name	Locality	Name of Editor	Circulation
	TRI-WEEKLY			
130.	*Khalsa Sewak*	Amritsar	Jiwan Singh	
	WEEKLY			
131.	*Bir*	Amritsar	Lakhbir Singh	500 copies
132.	*Khalsa Samachar*	Amritsar	Vir Singh	3,000 copies
133.	*Khalsa Sewak*	Amritsar	Jiwan Singh	1,000 copies
134.	*Nauratan*	Amritsar	Teja Singh	1,000 copies
135.	*Patiala Gazette*	Patiala	Gurbakhsh Singh	3,5000 copies
	MONTHLY			
136.	*Punjabi Surma*	Lahore	P. Munshi Ram	
137.	*Temperance Magazine*	Amritsar	Sant Singh	
138.	*Namdev Pattar*	Lahore	Khazan Singh	
	HINDI			
	WEEKLY			
139.	*Parabhat*	Lahore	Yagya Dat	
	MONTHLY			
140.	*Usba*	Lahore	Sant Ram, B.A.	

NOTES

Introduction

1. India Office Records [hereafter IOR] /L/R/5/195: 1914, Punjab Newspaper Reports.
2. See Santanu Das, Gerhard Hirschfeld, Heather Jones, Jennifer Keene, Boris Kolonitskii, Jay Winter, 'Global Perspectives on World War I. A Roundtable Discussion,' *Zeithistorische Forschungen/Studies in Contemporary History*, Online. 11 (2014), H.1. http://www.zeithistorische-forschungen.de/1-2014/id=5009.
3. Ibid.
4. See Hew Strachan, *The First World War in Africa* (Oxford, 2004), *The First World War* (New York, 2003), *The First World War: Volume 1: To Arms* (Oxford, 2001); John H. Morrow, Jr, *The Great War: An Imperial History* (New York, 2004); Michael S. Neiberg, *Fighting the Great War: A Global History* (Cambridge, 2006); William Kelleher Storey 2010; Lawrence Sondhaus, *World War One: The Global Revolution* (Cambridge, 2011).
5. See Andrew Tait Jarboe and Richard S. Fogarty (eds), *Empires in World War I: Shifting Frontiers and Imperial Dynamics in a Global Conflict* (London and New York, 2014); Rober Gerwarth and Erez Manela (eds), *Empires at War 1911–1923* (Oxford, 2014).
6. Richard Fogarty, *Race and War in France: Colonial Subjects in the French Army, 1914–1918* (Baltimore, 2008); Santanu Das (ed.), *Race, Empire and First World War Writing* (Cambridge, 2011); Heike Liebau, Katrin Bromber, Katharina Lange, Dyala Hamzah and Ravi Ahuja (eds), *The World in World Wars: Experiences, Perceptions and Perspectives from Africa and Asia* (Leiden and Boston, 2010).
7. Das, *Race, Empire and First World War Writing*, p. 4.
8. Erez Manela, *The Wilsonian Moment: Self-determination and the International Origins of Anticolonial Nationalism* (Oxford, 2007).

9. These newspaper reports are housed at the British Library. See IOR/L/R/5/ 195–200, Punjab Newspaper Reports.

10. See Kaushik Roy (ed.), *War and Society in Colonial India* (Oxford, 2006); Rajit K. Mazumder, *The Indian Army and the Making of the Punjab* (Delhi, 2003); Tan Tai Yong, *The Garrison State: The Military, Government and Society in Colonial Punjab, 1849–1947* (New Delhi, Thousand Oaks, and London, 2005).

11. IOR/L/MIL/17/5/2383, *India's Contribution to the Great War* 1923, p. 79.

12. The War Office, *Statistics of the Military Effort of the British Empire during the Great War* 1920, p. 777.

13. Robert Holland, 'The British Empire and the Great War, 1914–1918,' in Judith M. Brown and W.M. Roger Louis (eds), *The Oxford History of the British Empire, Volume IV: The Twentieth Century* (Oxford and New York, 1999), p. 122.

14. *The Times*, 21 November 1914; 10 November 1914; 5 November 1914.

15. Bhupendranath Basu, *Why India is Heart and Soul with Great Britain* (London, 1914).

16. 'Les Indiens et les Ecossais,' *Le Siècle*, 14 November 1914.

17. Niall Ferguson, *The Pity of War: Explaining World War I* (New York, 1999), p. 219–20.

18. Troy Paddock, *World War I and Propaganda* (Leiden and Boston, 2014).

19. See David Omissi, *Indian Voices of the Great War: Soldiers' Letters, 1914–18* (New York, 1999); Franziska Roy, Heike Liebau, and Ravi Ahuja (eds), *When the War Began we Heard of Several Kings: South Asian Prisoners in World War I Germany* (New Delhi, 2011); Gajendra Singh, *The Testimonies of Indian Soldiers and the Two World Wars: Between Self and Sepoy* (London, 2014); Rozina Visram, *Asians in Britain: 400 Years of History* (London and Sterling, 2002).

20. Tan Tai Yong, 'An Imperial Home-Front: Punjab and the First World War,' *Journal of Military History* 64.2 (2000), p. 374.

21. Ibid., p. 374.

22. Rajit K. Mazumder, *The Indian Army and the Making of the Punjab*, p. 465.

23. Michael O'Dwyer, *India as I Knew It, 1885–1925* (London, 1926), p. 223.

24. Mazumder, *The Indian Army and the Making of the Punjab*, p.11.

25. David Omissi, *The Sepoy and the Raj: The Indian Army 1860–1940* (London, 1994), p.12.

26. Tai Yong, *The Garrison State: The Military, Government and Society in Colonial Punjab*, pp. 70–1.

27. George MacMunn, *The Armies of India* (Bristol, 1984), p. 2.

28. Ibid., pp. 129–30.

29. Omissi, *The Sepoy and the Raj*, p. 19.

30. Tai Yong, 'An Imperial Home-Front: Punjab and the First World War,' p. 374.

31. Stephen P. Cohen 'The Military enters Indian thought,' in Kaushik Roy (ed.), *War and Society in Colonial India*, 2nd edn (Oxford, 2006), p. 173.

32. O'Dwyer, *India as I Knew It* (London, 1926), p. 226.

33. Ibid., pp. 216–17, 225.

34. IOR/L/R/5/200: 1918.

35. Ibid.195: 1914.
36. Ibid.198: 1916.
37. Ibid.
38. Ibid.197: 1916.
39. O'Dwyer, *India as I Knew It* (London, 1926), p. 174.
40. IOR/L/R/5/197: 1916.
41. See reports scattered through file, IOR/L/R/5/199: 1917.
42. Maia Ramnath, *Haj to Utopia: How the Ghadar Movement Charted Global Radicalism and Attempted to Overthrow the British Empire* (Berkeley, 2011).
43. IOR/L/R/5/199: 1917.
44. Ibid.
45. Ibid.
46. Ibid.
47. Ibid.200: 1918.

1914

1. Brigadier-General F.J. Moberly, *History of the Great War: The Campaign in Mesopotamia, 1914–1918. Volumes I and II* (London, 1924).
2. Michael O'Dwyer, *India as I Knew It, 1885–1925* (London, 1926).

1915

1. Ross Anderson 'Logistics of the Indian Expeditionary Force D in Mesopotamia: 1914–18,' in Kaushik Roy (ed.), *The Indian Army in the Two World Wars* (Leiden and Boston, 2012), p. 114.
2. The War Office, *Statistics of the Military Effort of the British Empire during the Great War* (London, 1920), p. 778.
3. Michael O'Dwyer, *India as I Knew It, 1885–1925* (London, 1926), p. 207.
4. Ibid., p. 176.

1916

1. Michael O'Dwyer, *India as I Knew It, 1885–1925* (London, 1926), p. 217.

1917

1. Dennis Showalter, 'The Indianization of the Egyptian Expeditionary Force, 1917–18: An Imperial Turning Point,' Kaushik Roy (ed.), *The Indian Army in the Two World Wars* (Leiden and Boston, 2012), p. 145.

2. Ibid.
3. Robert Holland, 'The British Empire and the Great War 1914–1918,' in Judith M. Brown and W.M. Roger Louis (eds), *The Oxford History of the British Empire, Volume IV: The Twentieth Century* (Oxford and New York, 1999), pp. 123–4.

1918

1. Michael O'Dwyer, *India as I Knew It, 1885–1925* (London, 1926), p. 225.
2. Dennis Showalter, 'The Indianization of the Egyptian Expeditionary Force, 1917–18: An Imperial Turning Point,' in Kaushik Roy (ed.), *The Indian Army in the Two World Wars* (Leiden and Boston, 2012), p. 150.

BIBLIOGRAPHY

Anderson, Ross, 'Logistics of the Indian Expeditionary Force D in Mesopotamia: 1914–18,' in Kaushik Roy (ed.), *The Indian Army in the Two World Wars* (Leiden and Boston, 2012).

Cohen, Stephen P., 'The Military enters Indian thought,' in Kaushik Roy (ed.), *War and Society in Colonial India*, 2nd edn (Oxford, 2006).

Das, Santanu (ed.), *Race, Empire and First World War Writing* (Cambridge, 2011).

Das, Santanu, Gerhard Hirschfeld, Heather Jones, Jennifer Keene, Boris Kolonitskii, and Jay Winter, 'Global Perspectives on World War I: A Roundtable Discussion,' *Zeithistorische Forschungen/Studies in Contemporary History*, Online. 11 (2014), H.1. http://www.zeithistorische-forschungen.de/1-2014/id=5009.

Fogarty, Richard, *Race and War in France: Colonial Subjects in the French Army, 1914–1918* (Baltimore, 2008).

Gerwarth, Robert and Erez Manela (eds), *Empires at War 1911–1923* (Oxford, 2014).

Government of India, *India's Contribution to the Great War* (Calcutta, 1923).

Holland, Robert, 'The British Empire and the Great War, 1914–1918,' in Judith M. Brown and W.M. Roger Louis (eds), *The Oxford History of the British Empire, Volume IV: The Twentieth Century* (Oxford and New York, 1999).

Jarboe, Andrew Tait and Richard S. Fogarty (eds), *Empires in World War I: Shifting Frontiers and Imperial Dynamics in a Global Conflict* (London and New York, 2014).

Liebau, Heike, Katrin Bromber, Katharina Lange, Dyala Hamzah and Ravi Ahuja (eds), *The World in World Wars: Experiences, Perceptions and Perspectives from Africa and Asia* (Leiden and Boston, 2010).

MacMunn, George, *The Armies of India* (Bristol, 1984).

Manela, Erez, *The Wilsonian Moment: Self-determination and the International Origins of Anticolonial Nationalism* (Oxford, 2007).

Mazumder, Rajit K., *The Indian Army and the Making of the Punjab* (Delhi, 2003).

Morrow, Jr, John H., *The Great War: An Imperial History* (New York, 2004).

Neiberg, Michael S., *Fighting the Great War: A Global History* (Cambridge, 2006).

O'Dwyer, Michael, *India as I Knew it, 1885–1925* (London, 1926).

Omissi, David, *The Sepoy and the Raj: The Indian Army 1860–1940* (London, 1994).

_____ *Indian Voices of the Great War: Soldiers' Letters, 1914–18* (New York, 1999).

Ramnath, Maia, *Haj to Utopia: How the Ghadar Movement Charter Global Radicalism and Attempted to Overthrow the British Empire* (Berkeley, 2011).

Roy, Franziska, Heike Liebau, and Ravi Ahuja (eds), *When the War Began we Heard of Several Kings: South Asian Prisoners in World War I Germany* (New Delhi, 2011).

Roy, Kaushik (ed.), *War and Society in Colonial India* (Oxford, 2006).

_____ (ed.), *The Indian Army in the Two World Wars* (Leiden and Boston, 2012).

Showalter, Dennis, 'The Indianization of the Egyptian Expeditionary Force, 1917–18: An Imperial Turning Point,' in Kaushik Roy (ed.), *The Indian Army in the Two World Wars* (Leiden and Boston, 2012).

Singh, Gajendra, *The Testimonies of Indian Soldiers and the Two World Wars: Between Self and Sepoy* (2014).

Sondhaus, Lawrence, *World War One: The Global Revolution* (Cambridge, 2011).

Storey, William Kelleher, *The First World War: A Concise Global History* (New York, 2010).

Strachan, Hew, *The First World War: Volume 1: To Arms* (Oxford, 2001).

_____ *The First World War* (New York, 2003).

_____ *The First World War in Africa* (Oxford, 2004).

Visram, Rozina, *Asians in Britain: 400 Years of History* (London and Sterling, 2002).

War Office, *Statistics of the Military Effort of the British Empire during the Great War 1914–1920* (London, 1920).

Yong, Tan Tai, *The Garrison State: The Military, Government and Society in Colonial Punjab, 1849–1947* (New Delhi, Thousand Oaks, and London, 2005).

_____ 'An Imperial Home-Front: Punjab and the First World War,' *Journal of Military History* 64.2 (2000).

INDEX